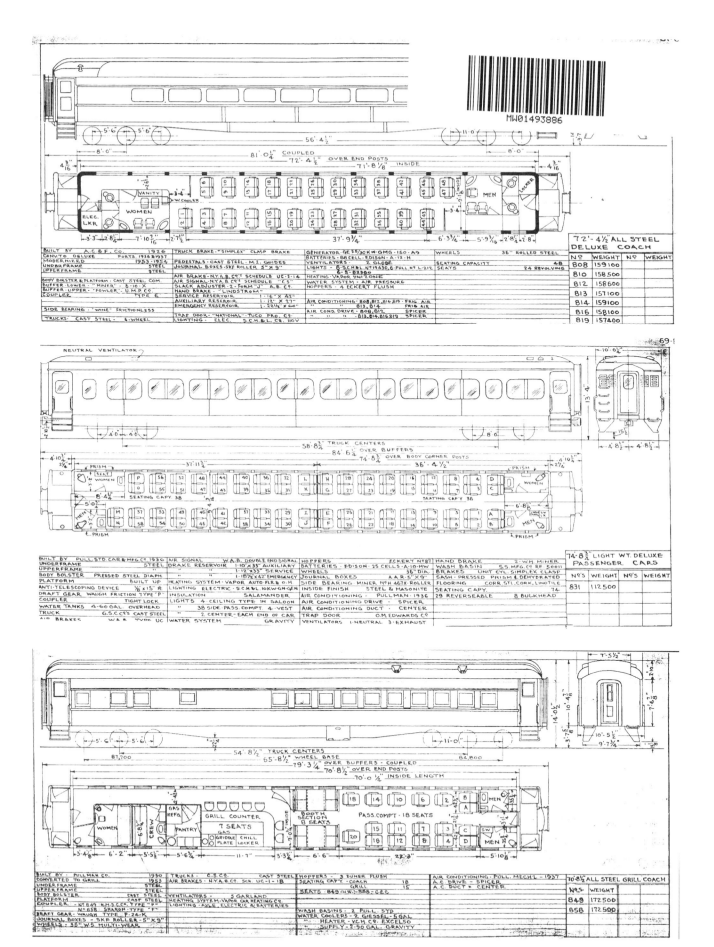

Seaboard Air Line Railroad Passenger Service
The Streamlined Era
Larry Goolsby

Published 2011 by
TLC Publishing Inc.
18292 Forest Rd.
Forest, Virginia 24551
434-385-4076
www.tlcrailroadbooks.com

Dedication

This book is dedicated to the men and women of Seaboard's passenger service – the ones who made it "The Route of Courteous Service."

About the author

Larry Goolsby is a southeastern railroad historian and author who has published two previous books, *Atlantic Coast Line Passenger Service – The Postwar Years* (TLC, 1999), and *Atlanta, Birmingham & Coast* (ACL & SAL Historical Society, 2000). He is a board member of the ACL & SAL Historical Society and edits the Society's quarterly magazine, *Lines South*. A native of Woodland, Ga., where he grew up on the ACL, he has continued to travel extensively throughout the southeast researching the ACL, Seaboard, and SCL. He currently lives in the Washington, D.C., area and works as legislative director for the American Public Human Services Association.

Published by TLC Publishing, Inc.
No part of this book may be reproduced without written permission of the publisher, except for brief excerpts used in reviews, etc.

ISBN 9780939487981
Library of Congress Control Number: 2010943475

Layout and Design by
Karen Parker

Printed in the U.S.A. by
Walsworth Printing Company, Marceline, Mo.

Cover: *Two Seaboard streamliners pass each other near West Palm Beach, Florida, along the railroad's busy east coast mainline in this late-1940s scene. Leading the southbound Silver Star at left is EMD E4 3001, built in 1938 for the fabled Orange Blossom Special and attired in Seaboard's famous "citrus" colors. Northbound at the right, the equally famous Silver Meteor is punctuated by the train's boat-tail observation car – a Seaboard symbol that remained on the train through 1971. (Painting by Robert West)*

Title Page: *Seaboard's Silver Comet was a member of the railroad's "Silver Fleet" that symbolized the streamliner era. This dramatic view shows the southbound (by timetable) Comet nearing Birmingham at Weems, on the city's eastern outskirts, on the morning of August 1, 1948. The train was scheduled to arrive at Birmingham at 10:45 a.m. and leave at 2:00 p.m. (Central Time), requiring rapid servicing and turning. Lightweight sleepers have not yet arrived, and three heavyweight Pullmans are up front in SAL's two-tone gray scheme behind E7 3040 and a second E unit. Weems was a popular railfanning location since the Seaboard main crossed over those of the Southern and Central of Georgia. (David W. Salter photo)*

Opposite: *All-stops local No. 4 crosses Seaboard's viaduct on the railroad's southern approach to Columbia, S.C., on April 26, 1942. The long steel structure carried the SAL across several other railroads and, here, Blossom Street. M2 4-8-2 No. 268 is in charge of a five-car train bracketed by express cars front and rear, with a baggage-RPO, combine, and coach in between. (George Votava photo)*

Table of Contents

Foreword

Before the coming of Amtrak in 1971, the Seaboard Air Line Railroad was long recognized as having some of the best long-distance passenger trains in the country, particularly its premier New York-Florida runs. Billing itself as "The Route of Courteous Service," Seaboard took great pride in running trains that the public would like the first time and would want to ride again and again. Seaboard fielded the first real streamliner in the South, the *Silver Meteor* of 1939, and kept coming up with fresh attractions to keep passengers loyal. After Seaboard's 1967 merger with the Atlantic Coast Line, SAL's passenger traditions remained prominent in successor Seaboard Coast Line's operations. Today, the main cities that Seaboard's New York-Florida trains connected are still served by Amtrak, and Amtrak continues two famous SAL train names, the *Silver Meteor* and the *Silver Star*.

Seaboard had many motivations to excel in the passenger business, but certainly one of the main ones was its well-heeled and determined competitor, the Atlantic Coast Line. The ACL enjoyed several advantages over the Seaboard including deep corporate pockets, a straighter and flatter profile, a mostly double-tracked mainline, and a direct Jacksonville-Miami route via connecting partner Florida East Coast Railway. Nevertheless, Seaboard always held its own against the Coast Line, with comparable passenger loadings and passenger mile figures over the two lines' major routes. Seaboard was particularly skilled in matching ACL's New York-Florida timings despite the SAL's largely single-main route; a hilly, curvy profile through the Carolinas; and Richmond-Miami mileage of 1,046 compared to the combined ACL-FEC route length of 1,025.

Seaboard also never stopped bringing out innovations that would draw passengers and help the railroad stay ahead of the competition. During its receivership from 1930 to 1945, Seaboard had particularly strong incentives to increase its business and put the railroad back on a sustainable footing. The line's receivers were taken with the idea of streamlined trains as early as 1934 and scored "firsts" in the South in air conditioning, passenger diesel locomotives, and full-length lightweight, stainless steel trains. In the postwar years, Seaboard promoted its onboard nurses and such innovations as the famous glass-roofed Sun Lounges of 1956.

The quality and extent of these passenger service distinctions, coupled with a corporate attitude that embraced prominent advertising, colorful paint schemes, and round-end observation cars properly placed on the end of the train, naturally created a loyal following among riders, shippers, and fans. The result was a railroad and a passenger train tradition that has long been celebrated and fondly remembered through books, models, and even popular song. I hope the material and photographs presented here will be fresh reminders of why Seaboard's passenger trains and service have been so highly regarded.

This book focuses on the last decades of Seaboard's existence. The late 1930s through the late 1950s in particular witnessed many dramatic changes – the replacement of steam with diesels, the ascendancy of lightweight trains, and the last hurrah of the once-familiar local passenger train. This is generally a chronological account, although I have given separate treatment to Seaboard's lightweight trains, other named trains, and locals. In reality, there was no strict separation between the streamliners, the named conventional trains, and SAL's "passenger, mail and express" (PM&E) runs. For example, the *Palmland* and *Sunland* essentially became locals on the southern portions of their runs, and the *Sunland* and *Tidewater* depended on the *Silver Comet* for their through cars. And then there were the trains that moved from one category to another; the *Cotton Blossom* dropped its name in 1955 in favor of the anonymous PM&E label, and Portsmouth line Nos. 17-18 were nameless until becoming the *Tidewater* in 1953. Still other trains were not quite fish or fowl; with the *Tidewater's* advent, Seaboard's winter-only Jacksonville-Hamlet night mail train was transformed into the *Tidewater's* shadowy southern extension – but northbound only, mind you.

These and other anomalies made understanding Seaboard's timetables and operating practices a challenging but highly interesting adventure. I am not the first to wonder whether Seaboard's ticket agents had to patiently tutor passengers on some of these trains' more unusual connections, changes of identity, and seasonal variations. Seaboard's penchant for using the same train numbers for different trains on different divisions added yet more spice to the stew. This all made for many hours of fascinating research, and I trust my explanations here are reasonably clear.

Acknowledgements

Nearly every railroad history effort is the product of many contributors, and this book perhaps illustrates the point more than most. I grew up on the Atlantic Coast Line and became a serious follower of the Seaboard only when their merger moved toward reality in the early 1960s; because of that late start, I have never had quite as much information and first-hand knowledge about the Seaboard as for the ACL. I have therefore had to be unusually reliant on the help of others and on previously published information.

Fortunately, the Seaboard's popularity has resulted in a number of fine books over the years – although most are now out of print – and much of the material here is drawn from them or is an expansion of points they first noted. Many magazine articles, and more recently web sites, have provided additional SAL passenger information. I hope the value of this book will lie in distilling material from these disparate and frequently unavailable sources, and in presenting the new details and photos that have not seen print before.

The major books I have used start with Richard E. Prince's 1969 history of Seaboard steam power, which for nearly 20 years was the only readily available book with detailed SAL information. Two excellent 1988 books broke the drought: *Seaboard Motive Power* by Warren Calloway and Paul Withers, and *Seaboard Air Line Railway Album* by Al Langley, Forrest Beckum, and Ronnie Tidwell. Both offered a rich trove of photographs, data, and passenger train information. Two other landmark books soon followed, led by Joe Welsh's 1994 *By Streamliner: New York to Florida*, a pioneering work that provided in-depth information and analysis on ACL and Seaboard trains, equipment, and passenger service philosophy along the east coast corridor. It was followed the next year by Robert Wayne Johnson's *Through the Heart of the South*, a thorough account of Seaboard's corporate history and system growth.

Other valuable books have appeared more recently, including William E. Griffin Jr.'s *All Lines North of Raleigh* and *Seaboard – The Route of Courteous Service*; Ted Shrady's *Orange Blossom Special* (co-authored with the late Arthur M. Waldrop); and Paul Faulk's two all-color Seaboard volumes from Morning Sun. I also made good use of the great amount of Seaboard passenger information published in various periodicals, particularly *Lines South*, the quarterly magazine of the ACL & SAL Historical Society.

My greatest debt is to the many friends, fellow historians, and correspondents who generously helped along the way. First on that list is David Salter, who to my great sorrow passed away unexpectedly in January 2010. David loaned enough excellent photographs to fill several volumes (together with his meticulously prepared captions) and provided a vast amount of other assistance including personal recollections, data from his collection, and valuable comments on

the manuscript. Many of the other photographs used here were from David's collection, especially those by Sam Appleby, Hugh Comer, and Frank Ardrey. David grew up across the street from Seaboard's Pitts, Ga., depot, and was one of the railroad's greatest fans. I think he enjoyed helping me put this book together as much as I did, and I regret so much that he did not live to see it.

Many others helped in major ways. "Professor" Michael Savchak, one of the country's leading experts on passenger equipment and operating practices, unfailingly responded in rich detail to my endless questions, and saved me from many embarrassing errors and omissions through his early reviews of the manuscript. His many in-depth articles for *Lines South* provided excellent information and first-hand accounts of riding Seaboard's trains. Particular credit also goes to Seaboard diesel expert and author Warren Calloway; Seaboard historian and author Bill Griffin; southeastern rail historian and author Robert H. Hanson; Seaboard photographer and retired employee Joe Oates; Pullman car and *Orange Blossom Special* expert Ted Shrady; and streamliner era expert and author Joe Welsh. Special thanks are due also to Buck Dean, Bill Griffin, Bill Howes, Joe Oates, and Ted Shrady, who also reviewed the manuscript and made many important suggestions and corrections. And of course, Tom Dixon of TLC provided information, photographs, and above all infinitely patient support as I took far longer to complete the book than anticipated.

Also in the "special thanks" category are those who have shared large numbers of photos they took or have collected, including Ron Dettmer, Harvey George, Bill Griffin, Bill Ingram, Oscar W. Kimsey Jr., Bob Liljestrand, Ken Marsh, Ed Mims, and the late George Votava.

Help and encouragement have come from many others as well, including the ACL & SAL Historical Society, Chris Allen, Frank E. Ardrey Jr., Milt Bell, Harry Bundy, Stan Burnette, Charlie Castner, J. David Ingles, Marvin Clemons, Paul Coe, Bill Cogswell, Jim Curtin, Bill Delmar, Larry Denton, the late Ed DeRouin, the late Francis M. "Happy" Egerton, Paul Faulk, John Golden, Danny Harmon, Anthony von Hornstein, Stanley Jackowski, Wally Johnson, Lyle Key, Parker Lamb, Dave Lambert, Al Langley, Frank Moore, Rick Morrison, Mike Palmieri, Ron Paul, Kevin Pytlak, Gary Riccio, Robert Richardson, Doug Riddell, the late Howard Robins, Leonard Robins, Karl Spence, Carey Stevens, Richard Stewart, Ted Strickland, Russell Tedder, the late Curt Tillotson Jr., Bill Todd, Emory F. Waldrop Jr., Jim Walker, and Randy

Young. Other photograph contributors are credited in the book's captions. I am grateful to them all, and sincerely hope I have not accidentally omitted anyone.

Finally, I appreciate again the indulgence and support of my family during the many long periods when this project completely took over my nights and weekends.

Larry Goolsby
Kensington, Maryland
December 2010

The following abbreviations are used for sleeping car accommodations:
Cpt – Compartment
DB – Double Bedroom
DR – Drawing Room
Rmt – Roomette
SB – Single Bedroom
Sec – Section

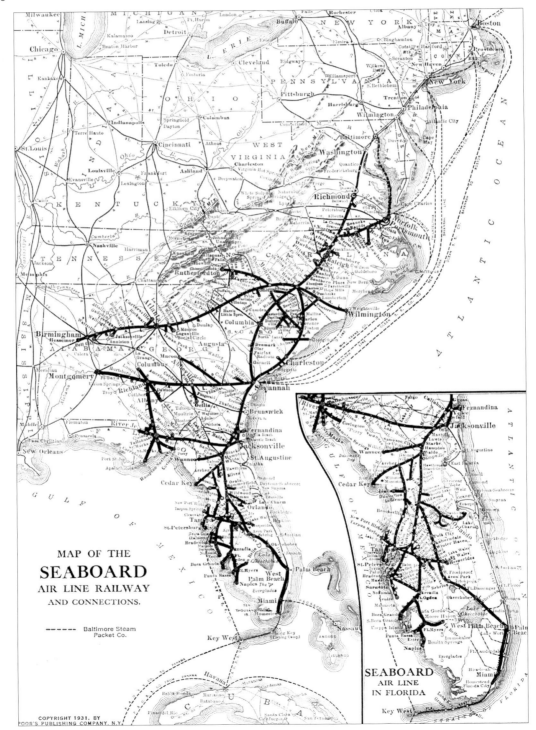

MAP OF THE
SEABOARD
AIR LINE RAILWAY
AND CONNECTIONS.

------- Baltimore Steam
Packet Co.

SEABOARD
AIR LINE
IN FLORIDA

COPYRIGHT 1931, BY
POOR'S PUBLISHING COMPANY, N.Y.

The Seaboard Air Line Railway formally came into being on July 1, 1900. The company's predecessor lines had been under common control for decades and had used the Seaboard Air Line label as early as 1871. The original SAL component was the Seaboard & Roanoke, a nearly straight route between Portsmouth, Va., and Weldon, N.C., whose earliest portion opened for service in 1834. This segment inspired the "Air Line" moniker, which a number of railroads of the time used to claim a line as direct "as the crow flies." By 1900, Seaboard had added a north-south line from Richmond through Raleigh and Hamlet, N.C., to Columbia, S.C., Savannah, Ga., and Jacksonville and Tampa, Florida. The new company also boasted an east-west route from Wilmington to Rutherfordton and Bostic, N.C., crossing the north-south main at Hamlet – a modest town that remained a major junction point, yard, and shop location throughout the Seaboard's existence.

Other key components of Seaboard's early system included important east-west lines from Monroe, N.C., to Atlanta and Birmingham; Savannah to Montgomery, Ala.; and Jacksonville to Tallahassee and Chattahoochee, Fla. (where it connected with the Louisville & Nashville to form a through route to Pensacola and New Orleans). But true to its Seaboard name, traffic was heaviest down the Atlantic coast and into Florida, even though service on the Atlanta and Tallahassee lines always remained a strong presence in the railroad's schedules. By the time of the Florida boom in the 1920s, Seaboard stood shoulder-to-shoulder with competitor Atlantic Coast Line in moving a heavy and growing volume of passengers and freight to and from the Sunshine State.

Most of Seaboard's long-distance passenger service to Florida began in either New York or Washington, and like the ACL, trains started their journey south over the Pennsylvania Railroad from New York to Washington, and via the Richmond, Fredericksburg & Potomac from there to Richmond. Seaboard interchanged its trains at Richmond to the RF&P where SAL trackage ended at Hermitage Yard, about three and one-half miles north of Main Street Station, and motive power was exchanged here. However, long-standing practice called for RF&P crews to operate between Main Street Station and Hermitage using SAL orders and rules.

While Seaboard's north-south mainline began at Richmond as did the ACL's, the SAL took a more southwesterly course south of Petersburg, Va., to Raleigh, Hamlet, and Columbia. From Columbia the line utilized predecessor Florida Central & Peninsular's route south to Savannah, then closely paralleled the ACL into Jacksonville. From Jacksonville, trains ran west on the Chattahoochee line for 18 miles to Baldwin, then turned south on the line to Tampa via Ocala, Wildwood, and Plant City. Beyond Tampa, trains reached St. Petersburg by circling around Tampa Bay. In 1917, Seaboard added an alternate line between Hamlet and Savannah via Charleston, S.C.; the route had lower grades than the line through Columbia and was freight-only except for a few local passenger trains.

Seaboard M2 4-8-2 244 and a 14-car northbound Palmland *make a grand sight on the brick-paved streets of Columbia on June 14, 1942. The big Mountain engines and long strings of heavyweight cars were symbols of Seaboard's steam-powered passenger service to and from Florida before the diesel streamliners usurped them. The train had been recently renamed from the* New York-Florida Limited *and carried coaches and sleeping cars to a number of points on Florida's east and west coasts. (George Votava photo)*

The Miami Extension

Despite its many routes, Seaboard was not satisfied with its Florida map. Under its ambitious president, S. Davies Warfield, the railroad undertook major Florida expansions in the mid-1920s. By far the largest project was building an extension to Miami, letting Seaboard lay claim to the only railroad serving both Florida coasts over its own rails. This expansion included a short segment near Tampa that gave a shortened "cross-Florida" route between Tampa-St. Petersburg and Miami.

Seaboard began constructing its Miami route in 1924 at Coleman, just south of Wildwood on the Baldwin-Tampa line, and extended it southeast to Sebring and across the top of Lake Okeechobee, reaching the east coast at West Palm Beach. From here the line paralleled the Florida East Coast into Miami, usually about a mile inland from the FEC. The line opened to Ft. Lauderdale with great fanfare in January 1925, accompanied by inauguration of Seaboard's storied *Orange Blossom Special*, a winter-season, all-Pullman flyer specifically targeted to wealthy northeasterners who wanted to escape to Florida's balmy resorts. The extension was completed into Miami in 1927. The new Miami route helped cement the importance of winter-season travel to Florida, which for many decades was the most active passenger travel period of the year. The season came to be officially bracketed by timetable changes in mid-December and late April, although additional service sometimes began in November or was adjusted in February.

The *Blossom* ran in the company of a large fleet of other Seaboard named trains between New York and Florida, including the *Carolina-Florida Special*, the *Seaboard Florida Limited*, the *All Florida Special*, and the *Seaboard Fast Mail*. Other notable trains included the *New Orleans-Florida Limited* on the Jacksonville-Chattahoochee route and the *Atlanta Special* and *Atlanta-Birmingham Special* on the line to those cities. The railroad even forwarded a train from Chicago, Cleveland, and Detroit, the *Suwannee River Special*, via the New York Central and the Southern in the 1920s, and the *Florida Sunbeam* over the same route from 1936 to 1949 except during World War II.

The Seaboard also ran many local passenger trains, including the largest fleet of rail motor cars in the southeast, over a thick network of secondary mainlines and branches. The mainlines also had trains with heavy "head-end" consists of mail and express cars. Most later became coach-only and were labeled "Passenger, Mail and Express" in Seaboard's timetables, with the "passenger" portion a distant second in number of cars and revenue. Like other passenger railroads, Seaboard earned significant revenue from its mail business; the Post Office paid well for hauling bulk mail and for sorting first-class letters en route in Railway Post Office cars. Good business also came from the railroad-owned Railway Express Agency, the company that carried nearly all express shipments before the days of UPS and FedEx. Finally, mixed trains (local freights with a passenger car or two added) plied many branches before the 1930s; however, the Depression eliminated most of them by the end of the decade.

The Great Depression also derailed Seaboard's overall financial health, which had been in trouble since the Florida real estate boom burst in the mid-1920s. Soon the railroad became unable to cover its high fixed charges that stemmed from the Miami extension and other recent investments. In December 1930 a creditor brought suit to recover payments owed, and Seaboard was placed in receivership – the first railroad to go bankrupt in the Depression. The receivership was to last nearly 16 years.

In late 1935, Seaboard took delivery of three streamlined rail cars from American Car & Foundry and placed the 57-passenger units in service on three runs, Richmond to Raleigh and two routes in Florida. This colorful brochure announced the cars' service debut in early 1936. (Gary Riccio collection)

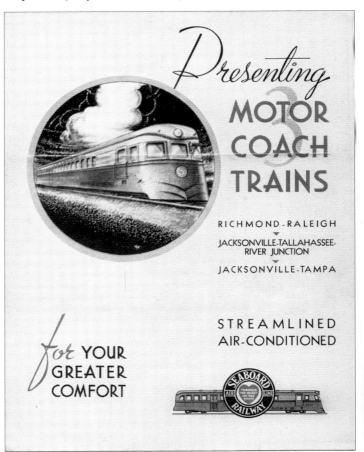

Presenting 3 MOTOR COACH TRAINS

RICHMOND - RALEIGH

JACKSONVILLE - TALLAHASSEE - RIVER JUNCTION

JACKSONVILLE - TAMPA

STREAMLINED AIR-CONDITIONED

for YOUR GREATER COMFORT

Streamliner Envy

The Depression caused Seaboard's revenues to drop sharply, from more than $58 million in 1929 to just over half that amount in 1932. Its passenger trains were soon running with fewer cars, and several long-distance Pullman lines disappeared even though Seaboard's first-class trade to Florida continued to be a reasonably strong market. Although Seaboard had to generally pinch its pennies during the receivership, the receivers pursued any new ideas that might bring in fresh business and hasten the return to solvency – even if they required spending some money. In the 1933-34 winter season, for example, Seaboard and Pullman completely equipped the *Orange Blossom Special* with air-conditioned equipment, claiming the title of the "first air-conditioned train in the south."

The success of the air-conditioned equipment led Seaboard to aggressively expand air conditioning by the following winter to three other trains, the *Southern States Special*, *New York-Florida Limited*, and *Cotton States Special*. The *Atlanta-Birmingham Special* was air-conditioned for the 1935 summer season and renamed the *Robert E. Lee*. By the 1936-37 winter timetable, Seaboard listed "seven fine air-conditioned trains," including a separate west coast *Orange Blossom Special*. By 1940, nearly all of Seaboard's regularly assigned cars were listed as air-conditioned. Other passenger improvements of the period included new colonial-style stations at Camden, S.C., in 1937 and Raleigh in 1942. The Raleigh station was built on the mainline and ended a time-consuming back-up move to the old union depot located on a wye just west of Raleigh Tower between the SAL and Southern mains.

By 1934, the railroads' passenger traffic was slowly recovering, helped by excitement over the new diesels and lightweight trains then appearing on a handful of lines. One of the most sensational was the Chicago, Burlington & Quincy Railroad's articulated, stainless-steel *Burlington Zephyr*. The crowds who stood trackside to watch these trains flash by – and who clamored to ride them – did not go unnoticed by Seaboard management. In November 1934, SAL receivers Legh R. Powell Jr. and Henry W. Anderson began looking into a similar diesel-powered train. Seaboard debated whether various lightweight train possibilities, including "a three- or four-car *Zephyr*-type train," might succeed on short runs like Jacksonville-Miami or Jacksonville-Tampa. The railroad also successfully petitioned the Burlington to send another of its Zephyr trains, the *Twin Zephyr*, on a southern tour mostly over Seaboard rails. The train visited cities along the Richmond-Miami main in 1935, plus the railroad's important Florida west coast cities, and hosted enthusiastic tours at each location.

New and Different Rail Cars

In the meantime, Seaboard expanded its fleet of rail motor cars by ordering in June 1935 three new smoothly styled American Car & Foundry "rail-motor buses," or as SAL often called them, "streamlined motor coaches." The cars (numbered 2024-2026) replaced a steam-powered run between Jacksonville and Tampa and established new round trips between Richmond and Raleigh and between Jacksonville and Chattahoochee. The cars were the first in Seaboard's rail car fleet to have full-length coach seating and air conditioning. Seaboard ads took full advantage of the public's fascination with streamlining, touting the aluminum-painted cars as "The Air-Conditioned Streamliners" and bragging about their quietness and smoothness, individual seats with headrests, and tickets at only 1½ cents per mile. The cars proved unsatisfactory and were out of service within a few years, but were an interesting step toward full streamlined trains.

In a rare action photo, Seaboard "motor coach" 2035 is at Raleigh, N.C., in 1936, on its run from Richmond. The car and two sisters were purchased at the height of the railroad's mid-decade interest in streamlined trains. Seaboard decided the cars were unsatisfactory and had sold all three by 1944. (Charles K. Marsh Jr. collection)

Seaboard was a pioneer in air-conditioning its passenger car fleet. Coach 571, built in 1913 by the Pressed Steel Car Company, stands outside the Portsmouth (Va.) car shops in July 1937 just after being rebuilt with air conditioning and new, smaller sealed windows. The "turtle-back" roof encloses air ducts and other equipment for the new cooling system. The rebuild also included 66 reclining seats in place of the car's original "straight back" seats. (SAL photo, Ron Dettmer collection)

In 1936, Seaboard bought two more rail cars with a somewhat streamlined appearance, Nos. 2027 and 2028. Built by St. Louis Car and powered by 600-h.p. diesel power plants, the cars reverted to Seaboard's traditional pattern of a power unit capable of pulling one or more cars, with a baggage-express section and 15-foot Railway Post Office compartment. But unlike SAL's older rail cars, the SLC units could handle several full-size cars rather than just one or two trailers. The railroad paid $90,000 each for the units but predicted $51,000 annual savings over the steam trains they replaced on the Wilmington-Hamlet-Rutherfordton (N.C.) line, not least because union rules allowed them to operate without a fireman.

While of similar size to Seaboard's older large motor cars, Nos. 2027 and 2028 had shovel noses and a smooth overall profile. Although they seemed clearly inspired by Burlington's 1934 *Zephyr* and similarly styled units, the cars returned to Seaboard's normal passenger color of solid Pullman green. The color was painted on conventional riveted steel, a far cry from the welded stainless steel sheathing that made the *Zephyr* and its kin so glamorous.

Seaboard's next nod to streamlining was its purchase of ten new passenger cars in 1936-37, six coaches and four combines. Built by Pullman-Standard's Osgood-Bradley plant in Worcester, Mass., the cars had a transitional, semi-streamlined design and used several types of lightweight alloys in their construction, making them about 30 percent lighter than equivalent conventional cars. Although the coaches seated 76 passengers and the combines 48, they were still roomy since the cars' restroom areas were small. Other features included air conditioning, reclining seats, and adjustable footrests. They were nicknamed "American Flyer cars" after that electric train com-

pany's models based on similar cars built for the New Haven and several other railroads.

Seaboard signaled its high opinion of the cars by assigning them to the *Orange Blossom Special's* west coast section. (The *Blossom* was still nominally "all-Pullman," and no other segments of the train received coaches.) The American Flyer cars were also used on Seaboard's other premier trains (including, within a few years, the *Silver Meteor* for overflow capacity). They were also the first cars the Pennsylvania Railroad deemed worthy of operation through to New York; in the past coach passengers on Seaboard trains had to change in Washington for points north.

E Units and a Real Streamliner: The *Silver Meteor*

Two years after Seaboard bought its diesel-powered shovel-nose railcars, the railroad's interest in modern power produced a far more dramatic and colorful result: sets of Electro-Motive Corporation 2,000-h.p. E4 passenger units. These locomotives, built to haul heavy conventional trains, were the newest version of similar units that EMC had built for Santa Fe, Baltimore & Ohio, Union Pacific, and several other railroads starting in 1935. They were also the first to incorporate all-EMC components. Once again, Seaboard's receivers justified the purchase on the basis of the diesel's efficiency and lower operating costs – in particular, the locomotives' need for fewer fueling stops and less maintenance.

The new power was dressed in an eye-catching combination of bright yellow, aluminum, and Pullman green with orange striping, which came to be known as the "citrus" scheme. They were built for the flagship *Orange Blossom Special*, and had the train's name affixed to the A units' flanks. In what could have been another example of the *Zephyr* influence, the SEABOARD road name lettering came in a new font very close to that used by the Burlington on its lightweight passenger equipment. This same font would appear on SAL's new lightweight passenger cars a few months later.

The new engines – six A units and three B units – began leaving EMC's LaGrange, Ill., plant in late October 1938. Perhaps taking a cue from the *Twin Zephyr* tour of 1936, Seaboard dispatched the first three units delivered (A-B-A set 3000-3100-3001) on a month-long round of online cities. The "Diesel-Electric Tour Train" promoted both the new locomotives as well as the *Orange Blossom Special*, which would begin its annual winter season in December. The tour train included several of the new American Flyer cars and attracted another round of large crowds. In service, the new diesels soon proved they could keep a 15- or 17-car *Blossom* on schedule, in contrast to the normal limit of 12 cars for Seaboard's 4-8-2 steam locomotives.

The new diesels were shortly followed by yet another Seaboard "first." On the afternoon of February 2, 1939, a sparkling new seven-car streamliner stood ready at New York's Pennsylvania Station to make its first departure for the South. During the previous day and a half, the train had been exhibited to large crowds and had made an appearance at the World's Fair. Dignitaries spoke, champagne christened the new train, and glowing press releases went out. The subject of all this attention was the Seaboard's *Silver Meteor*, the first streamliner between New York and Florida and the first full-length, stainless-steel, lightweight coach train in the South.

The train was the natural culmination of Seaboard's interest in passenger innovations and the growing track record of other lightweight coach streamliners around the country, such as Santa Fe's *El Capitan*. These trains – and now the *Silver Meteor* – were touted as "luxury" transportation, a new concept for coach passengers long accustomed to stiff seat backs, dull colors, and no reserve seating. Orders were placed for a seven-car train from the Budd Company and another E4 locomotive (No. 3006), complete with a *Silver Meteor* nameplate. A naming contest for the new train brought in over 76,000 entries, including 30 who proposed the winning name.

The train departed from New York and Florida every third day, with alternate arrivals at Miami and St. Petersburg – giving the two Florida cities *Meteor* service only every sixth day. (Seaboard also briefly considered running the train to Atlanta-Birmingham on every third trip, but could not get the Pennsylvania to agree.) Its trip frequency was dictated by running times of about 27 hours to Miami and 25 hours to St. Petersburg, combined with time needed for servicing and turning at each terminal. The cars included a 22-seat passenger-baggage-dormitory car (No. 6000), three 60-seat coaches (6200-03), coach-tavern 6300, 48-seat diner 6100, and coach-observation 6400. The widely spaced coach seats reclined to help make sleeping more comfortable; Budd called them "Sleeper-coaches," and Seaboard prominently advertised this description. There were separate men's and women's bathroom lounges at either end of the coaches. The cars also featured bright lighting, pleasing colors, and individual interior schemes.

The *Meteor* Expands

The train was wildly popular right from the beginning, and demand for the *Meteor's* service quickly led to a separate west coast section for every trip the train made. Starting in June 1939, Seaboard ran a separate train from Wildwood to St. Petersburg, giving every-third-day service to both coasts. Wildwood, 4.8 miles north of the Tampa/St. Petersburg line's junction with the Miami main, was Seaboard's traditional switching point for west coast sections or mainline connecting trains. The St. Petersburg section had three cars: coach 6200 and coach-tavern 6300 from the *Meteor* trainset and baggage-coach 285, one of the

Seaboard took every opportunity to promote the new **Silver Meteor***. This 14-page brochure was issued upon the train's inaugural on February 2, 1939, and included fares, schedules, floor plans, and other passenger information on "America's Newest and Smartest Coach Train." (ACL & SAL HS collection)*

American Flyer combines. The combine was repainted silver with black lettering, and with its smooth, low profile made a reasonably good match for the two stainless steel cars. The *Meteor's* other five cars continued to Miami.

Seaboard determined that even the short west coast *Meteor* deserved something more than ordinary motive power, and so with no extra E units available, tapped motor car 2028. The unit had been in Wilmington-Charlotte local service since it arrived in 1936, but was now repainted in the same citrus colors used on the E4 units – complete with a *Silver Meteor* nameplate on its sides. The bright paint combined with No. 2028's smooth lines to make it an adequate stand-in for an E unit, and the motor car handily pulled the run's three cars for more than a year.

St. Petersburg was barely 20 air miles southwest of Tampa, but no railroad crossed the broad expanse of Tampa Bay separating the two cities. Instead, SAL's route first went north to Sulphur Springs, then west to Clearwater, and finally back south again through Belleair and Largo to St. Petersburg, requiring 55 miles by rail. Although the line to St. Petersburg was over a separate subdivision and required a reverse move from Tampa Union Station to reach the junction for Sulphur Springs, the track was considered an extension of the Wildwood-Tampa main and trains continued over it with their same numbers.

The separate west coast train was only the first of several steps Seaboard quickly took to meet surging public demand for the *Meteor*. For the winter 1939-40

season, Budd delivered two more seven-car consists, nearly identical to the first set, allowing the main Miami section to become a daily train. The Pennsylvania Railroad contributed to the car pool by purchasing three of the new coaches; it was the first example of several in which PRR (and after World War II, the RF&P) would share in equipping Seaboard's streamliners.

Riders kept flocking to the *Silver Meteor*, and Seaboard and PRR bought 18 more cars from Budd in time for the winter 1940-41 season. The new equipment was enough for 14-car trains out of New York with daily service and through cars to both coasts. The longer trains carried two diners, more coaches, and a new "feature" car, a coach-buffet-observation (Nos. 6500-02). These cars had 24-seat observation-lounge sections like the 6400 series, but because of the buffet area in the middle, seated only 30 in the coach section. They also differed by having flat observation ends with a diaphragm so they could be placed mid-train when necessary and pointed in either direction.

The additional cars allowed daily service at last to Tampa/St. Petersburg; six cars split off at Wildwood while the rest continued on to Miami. The west coast section originally included a coach-baggage-dormitory, one of the diners, three coaches, and a 6400-series round-end coach observation, while one of the new 6500s was placed on the end of the Miami section. Within a few months the observations were swapped and the 6400s again punctuated the Miami section per original *Meteor* practice.

Seaboard also purchased more E units so that the longer and more frequent trains remained diesel-powered; the passenger unit roster now totaled 20 (14 E4 A units, five E4 B units, and one E6 that arrived in January 1940). The one exception was the lengthened west coast section; motor car 2028 could not manage that many cars, and there were still not enough E units to cover the train. Instead, three Pacific steam locomotives were streamlined to cover the run, Nos. 865, 867, and 868 from SAL's P class built by Alco in 1913. The locomotives were rebuilt at Seaboard's West Jacksonville shops and were given full nose-to-tender shrouding. Like No. 2028, they were painted in the citrus scheme (but without a *Meteor* nameplate).

Pullmans for the *Meteor*

The summer of 1941 brought yet another change to the rapidly evolving *Silver Meteor*: Pullman sleeping cars. Even though the railroads wanted new lightweight sleepers, and a few had been constructed in the 1930s, lightweight Pullmans did not appear in quantity until after World War II. Before the war, the Pullman Company refused to operate most of the cars it did not build, and at the time only the Budd Company had successfully mastered construction of lightweight, stainless steel cars. Pullman's stance led to a 1940 government antitrust suit that eventually forced the sale of most Pullman sleepers to the participating railroads (completed at the end of 1948) and allowed the postwar entry of other carbuilders into the lightweight sleeping car business.

Seaboard thus had to draw from the Pullman pool of heavyweight cars to meet demand for sleeping space on the popular train, but Pullman did paint them aluminum to blend with the stainless train. Available records indicate the cars were painted solid aluminum and probably had black lettering in Pullman's standard extended Roman font. The sleepers included three each of 10 Sec-1 DR-2 Cpt, 6 Sec-6 DB, and 8 Sec-1 DR-3 DB configurations. The group was drawn from cars typically assigned to Seaboard trains, and many would eventually come under Seaboard ownership in the 1948 Pullman breakup. The presence of heavyweight sleepers on the otherwise-lightweight train set a pattern that would last on some of Seaboard's streamliners for nearly 15 more years.

The War Years

Just as Seaboard issued its winter season 1941-42 timetable, the United States entered World War II. The conflict suddenly rearranged the nation's transportation and manufacturing priorities, bringing to a halt any further new passenger locomotives or cars. Thousands of troops quickly began moving by rail, filling much of the available sleeping car and coach space. The new federal Office of Defense Transportation ordered the suspension of winter-season Pullman trains, halting the *Orange Blossom Special* for the duration of hostilities. Seaboard's public timetables, once full of ads for the railroad's many trains and services, suddenly became somber publications noting SAL's dedication to the war effort and reminding passengers to expect difficulty finding their customary accommodations and service. A typical message from a 1942 issue stated firmly that "Uncle Sam and His War Needs Come First."

The conflict altered the operating pattern of the *Silver Meteor* as well. The surge in military and civilian travel led to the establishment in December 1942 of an "advance" section that operated ahead of the regular *Meteor*; it carried cars only for Miami and was combined with the main train south of Wildwood.

Seaboard ordered a single E4 A unit, No. 3006, to power the original seven-car Silver Meteor. *The locomotive poses for it builder's portrait at EMC's LaGrange, Ill., plant in January 1939. The unit joined nine E4s delivered in late 1938 for the* Orange Blossom Special. *The practice of attaching train name plates to the units ended with World War II. (EMC photo, Larry Goolsby collection)*

The largely heavyweight advance section carried nine Pullmans, while the regular section was equipped with the *Meteor's* lightweight equipment and four heavyweight sleepers. One was a New York-Venice (Fla.) 10-1-2 – the first time the train had carried a Pullman for destinations other than Miami or St. Petersburg. The sleeper was forwarded from Tampa to Venice on connecting locals Nos. 507 and 508.

Change came again to the *Meteor* in May 1943, when separate east and west coast sections began operating from New York about an hour apart. The east coast train ran with the lightweight equipment, but the rigors of war had diminished the train's luster a bit. In a tragic accident at Kittrell, N.C., on June 14, 1942, a rear-end collision killed eight passengers and wrecked coach-observation 6400. The absent observation caused Seaboard to end regular assignment of the two remaining round-end observations, and instead run the 6500-series coach-buffet-observations on the east coast *Meteor* and no regular observation on the west coast train. The situation eased a bit when Seaboard had Budd rebuild No. 6400 with a flat end. Still, it appears that both car 6400 and the 6500s were often used as coaches within the trains; another ODT ruling required that nearly all former non-revenue seats, such as those in the cars' observation sections, had to be made available for sale.

Seaboard suffered a number of other serious wrecks during the hectic war years, and the mishaps destroyed three E4 A units (3003, 3012, and 3013). Seaboard originally ran its passenger diesels through to Washington over the RF&P, but the shortage required them to turn back at Richmond. Interstate Commerce Commission reports on the accidents often blamed SAL's sharply increased train frequency combined with busy, unsignaled stretches of mainline such as some of those south of Hamlet.

Although wartime restrictions prevented Seaboard from buying new passenger diesels, the railroad did receive 44 new FT freight diesel units from the Electro-Motive Division of General Motors (the former EMC) between 1942 and 1944. The FT B units came with a steam boiler option, which Seaboard took so the engines could pull passenger trains if needed. Several photos show them doing so, especially on the Passenger, Mail and Express runs. But aside from these limited assists from the FTs, the prewar diesels plus SAL's passenger steam locomotives were left to shoulder the heavy wartime passenger train load. Only in March 1945, near the end of the war, did additional E units join the roster.

Seaboard was also unable to obtain any new equipment for its overworked passenger car roster – which in early 1943 numbered 334 conventional cars and 36 lightweight cars – but the railroad did meet some of the wartime need through rebuilt and second-hand cars. Between 1943 and 1944 SAL added about 25 coaches bought second-hand from various sources. Seaboard also rebuilt several of its older diners into coaches or buffet-coaches. Seaboard helped the *Silver Meteor* out a bit too by modifying car No. 6103, delivered as a diner-lounge seating 42 patrons, to a full 48-seat diner like the other cars in the 6100 series. Finally, the railroad needed more capacity for express and storage mail, and converted 55 steel 18000-series boxcars to box-express cars between 1943 and 1945. Seaboard also rebuilt one of its older motor cars into a baggage-RPO.

As the war effort finally moved toward an end in mid-1945, the Seaboard Air Line looked forward to resuming its modernization efforts and paying attention again to the needs of its civilian passengers. A full-panel message in the March 1945 timetable asked patrons for their continued patience with delays, equipment that was not up to standard, and dining car service that was sometimes compromised by food rationing and hastily trained crews – all of it necessary as the railroad did its part to move troops and military equipment. But the next timetable (July 1945) carried a different message, one promising new

Another early view of the Meteor *shows the train at Savannah Union Station in March 1939, just a month after the streamliner began its every-third-day runs between New York and Florida. An onlooker examines E4 3006, which was bought specifically to power the train. All Seaboard and ACL trains had to back into SUS, which was located in downtown Savannah about two miles east of both companies' north-south mainlines. (Hugh M. Comer photo)*

Seaboard trains that "… will far surpass anything previously offered – in luxury and style, comfort and service." Postwar manufacturing delays would keep these plans from becoming reality for a few more years, but the trains and services that finally emerged would define Seaboard's prominent place among U.S. passenger carriers for the next two decades.

Coach-observation 6400 brought up the rear of the Meteor; the camera faces the car's boat-tail end. A little more than three years after this builder's photo, the car was involved in a fatal rear-end collision at Kittrell, N.C., on June 14, 1942, and was rebuilt with a flat end the next year. (SAL photo, ACL & SAL HS collection)

Flat-end observation No. 6500 was among the equipment Seaboard purchased in 1940 to expand the Silver Meteor's service to daily 14-car trains. The car was placed mid-train so that both the Miami and St. Petersburg sections could have an observation car on the rear after they split at Wildwood. The 1940 cars had fluorescent ceiling light fixtures rather than the incandescent lamps used on the original consist. (SAL photo, TLC Collection)

To power the Tampa/St. Petersburg section of the Silver Meteor, which began service in June 1939, Seaboard drafted motor car 2028. The car had been holding down Wilmington-Charlotte (N.C.) Trains 13-14, but was dressed up in the citrus scheme and moved to Florida for its new and much more glamorous job. The unit is shown shortly after beginning Meteor service; just visible behind it is "American Flyer" combine No. 285, which was painted silver to match the otherwise-stainless steel consist. (George W. Pettengill Jr. photo, Charles K. Marsh Jr. collection)

Pacific No. 868 was one of the three streamlined steam locomotives assigned to the Meteor's expanded west coast section for the winter 1940-41 season. The engine's number style was among the subtle painting variations that each of the three had; unlike their diesel brethren, they did not carry Silver Meteor nameplates. (SAL photo)

Seaboard reaped more publicity when one of its new EMD E6 locomotives was exhibited at the New York World's Fair in late 1939; it was posed at the General Motors pavilion in a special color scheme but with Seaboard lettering. The A unit, built in November 1939 but not delivered until January 1940, wore number 1939 for the display but became No. 3014 when placed into service. The B unit went to another railroad. (SAL photo, ACL & SAL HS collection)

Among the changes Seaboard made for the expanded, daily Silver Meteor effective with the winter season of 1940-41 were special caps for on-board crew members, like this one worn by the bar attendant mixing a drink. It proclaims "Fourteen-car Silver Meteor First Trip out of New York Dec. 1, 1940." (SAL photo, TLC Collection)

This undated scene at the old Raleigh Union Station was probably taken about 1941, after Seaboard had purchased enough diesel passenger units to power several of its other name trains besides the Silver Meteor and the winter-only Orange Blossom Special. The train may the northbound Southern States Special taken early in the morning. Seaboard opened a new station astride the mainline in 1942. (Henry Kitchen photo)

Right: This rare photo shows the Silver Meteor in February 1942 at Sebring, Fla., shortly after the United States entered World War II. The train had added heavyweight Pullmans the previous summer. E6 3015, an E4 B unit, and about nine lightweight cars round out the consist. (Sam R. Appleby Jr. photo)

Below: Seaboard's FT units sometimes pulled passenger trains during the mid-1940s. An unidentified A-B set is on Train 191, the southbound Palmland, as it leaves Raleigh in 1943. The third car is an American Flyer coach. (Wiley M. Bryan photo, Larry Goolsby collection)

Below Right: Servicemen were still returning from duty in large numbers when this photo was taken at Seaboard's Hamlet station on September 14, 1945. The distinctive building has been restored and still functions as an Amtrak passenger station, although it has been moved to the corner where the baggage cart stands. (Jay Williams collection)

With the end of World War II, the Seaboard Air Line at last had a chance to resume adding cars and diesels to its premier passenger runs and to make other improvements that had been on hold for nearly four years – going forward with its plans for "trains that will far surpass anything previously offered." Wartime restrictions on equipment orders were lifted, allowing manufacturers to return to domestic production. Seaboard's long receivership also ended on August 1, 1946, and in the process changed its name from Rail*way* to Rail*road*. Seaboard was ready to modernize its war-weary roster and physical plant.

Among the first concrete results were new locomotives and lightweight passenger cars that had been planned and ordered during the war years. New passenger power from Electro-Motive Division began arriving in March 1945, four E7s numbered 3017-3020. Ten additional E7s (3021-3030) soon followed, and five more (3031-3035) came in 1946, bringing the Seaboard passenger diesel roster total to 38 units.

EMD products dominated Seaboard's diesel passenger roster but did not have a monopoly. Seaboard liked sampling other diesel builders, and received three Baldwin "baby-face" model DR6-4-1500 passenger locomotives in September and December 1947 (Nos. 2700-2702). Shorter and less powerful than E units, the units were placed into light-duty service such as the connecting train between Tampa and Port Boca Grande, Florida. Seaboard had earlier (1945) purchased a much larger cousin of the "baby-faces," Baldwin's DR12-8-3000 "Centipede." This 24-wheeled, 6,000-h.p. monster came with a steam generator for passenger service and was advertised as a dual-service locomotive. Numbered 4500, the engine was dressed in a version of the passenger citrus scheme and posed for a photograph pulling the *Silver Meteor*. The locomotive was reportedly assigned to the west coast *Meteor* and other Florida runs but apparently lasted only a short time in regular passenger service. Seaboard bought additional Centipedes in 1947, all for freight service.

Seaboard's steam roster continued to see use on secondary passenger trains while the new diesels were arriving; in late 1945, steam still pulled the Atlanta-Birmingham segment of the *Cotton States Special* and the Wildwood-St. Petersburg sections of the *Silver Meteor* and *Sun Queen*. The Wildwood-St. Petersburg *Meteor* was in the charge of the three streamlined P-class Pacifics as the war began, but when the separate through west coast *Meteor* was established in 1943, they were replaced by M-class Mountains. The three Pacifics had their shrouding removed by late 1945. For the 1946-47 winter season, Seaboard advertised that both sections of the *Meteor* were fully dieselized. However, it would be several more years before all the named trains would be completely dieselized, and steamers kept pulling some local runs as late as 1950.

The 6600-series observations were frequently posed for publicity scenes such as this one, somewhere in south Florida, of the Silver Meteor's *Miami* section. The photographer has placed an orange bough in view to remind prospective passengers of the Sunshine State's most famous citrus product. The train features two E units, three heavyweight Pullmans, and eight lightweight cars. (SAL photo, Larry Goolsby collection)

Not long after the locomotive's arrival in December 1945, Seaboard posed monstrous No. 4500, a Baldwin "Centipede" diesel, with the Silver Meteor for this publicity picture. It appears the engine may have pulled the Meteor and other trains in Florida for a time, but it had no further regular passenger assignments. In addition to the train's lightweight coaches and lounge and dining equipment, the photo reveals four heavyweight Pullmans, an American Flyer coach, and a Tuscan red Pennsylvania coach. (SAL photo, TLC Collection)

The "Streamline Super Trains"

Seaboard finalized plans in 1944 and 1945 to substantially enlarge its passenger car roster and equip what it referred to internally as three "streamline super trains" – two lengthened daily coach-sleeper trains between New York and Florida, and a third train between New York and Atlanta/Birmingham. The Pennsylvania and Richmond, Fredericksburg & Potomac joined Seaboard in placing a large order with Budd in 1945 for 30 coaches, nine diners, three baggage-dormitory cars, and six round-end observation cars; PRR's share was ten cars and RF&P, eight. The new coaches arrived in early 1947 while the remaining cars came that summer.

Seaboard and its two partners also placed a large order for lightweight sleeping cars, but they would not be delivered until two years after the other equipment. The order was originally for 12 10 Rmt-6 DB cars, three 6 DB-buffet-lounges, and 19 16 duplex roomette-4 double bedroom cars. These last cars, with their heavy proportion of single rooms, were aimed at businessmen traveling alone – long a mainstay of Pullman's clientele. But tastes were changing rapidly, with vacationing families rapidly taking over as the primary Pullman customers. By May 1946, Seaboard had replaced plans for the duplex cars with additional 10-6s; the three railroads eventually received a total of 26 of the cars in mid-1949. Budd and Pullman-Standard (the carbuilding arm of the Pullman Company) shared the 10-6 order, while American Car & Foundry built the bedroom-lounge cars.

The two New York-Florida "super" trains were not entirely new, of course, but were to be improved versions of the two *Silver Meteor* sections that had operated throughout the war years. However, the third train would be a new streamliner on the Atlanta/Birmingham route and would debut in May 1947 after delivery of enough new equipment for a mostly lightweight consist.

Seaboard pinned great hopes on the appeal of the new equipment and trains. In its 1946 annual report, the company noted that passenger revenues had dropped sharply with the end of the war, from over $38 million in 1945 to just above $21 million in 1946. Seaboard said the new capital investments were designed to appeal to a public the railroad knew would be returning to widespread private auto use with the end of wartime shortages and restrictions. SAL's confidence was not misplaced, but the railroad would have to continuously improve to stay ahead of the postwar passenger environment's many challenges.

The Postwar Changes Begin

Seaboard's winter season 1946-47 schedules were the first with noteworthy modifications of the wartime lineup. The *Silver Meteor*, instead of running in solid east and west coast sections from the north as in the later war years, reverted to its original scheme of a single afternoon train carrying equipment for both coasts of Florida and splitting at Wildwood. The railroad kept the second through train but renamed it the *Advance Silver Meteor*, with morning departures but otherwise similar to the regular *Meteor*, including equipment for both coasts. The two trains did have their differences: the southbound *Advance Meteor* bypassed Savannah and Jacksonville (the west coast *Meteor* had begun bypassing Savannah during the war), and the regular *Meteor* had a through sleeper for Sarasota and Venice while its *Advance* counterpart had through west coast cars only to St. Petersburg.

The two Florida trains rotated consists with a lightweight 6300-series tavern-coach and 6400-series observation-coach on the end in one, and a heavy-

Seaboard began operating a separate west coast Silver Meteor *from New York in 1943. The railroad owned enough diesels to power both trains between Richmond and Jacksonville, but had to assign steam to the west coast train between Jacksonville and St. Petersburg. A streamlined P-class 4-6-2 was able to handle the earlier Wildwood-St. Petersburg section, but the full separate west coast train was much longer – at least a dozen cars in this March 1946 photo. So instead Seaboard assigned its powerful M-2 class 4-8-2 engines (such as No. 248 here), which had handled the* Orange Blossom Special *until 1938. Enough E7s had arrived by the end of 1946 to dieselize both* Meteor *sections over their entire routes. (M.B. Cooke photo)*

weight 10 Sec-lounge car and 6500-series buffet-observation-coach on the other. The lightweight observations had been removed from their end-of-train assignments during the later war years but returned about December 1945. Both trains had a substantial complement of heavyweight sleepers with a variety of accommodations, much of it sections.

Seaboard made sure the public knew that its streamliners and other prominent trains were pulled by diesels. With 41 units now on hand, SAL now had most of its name trains behind internal-combustion power and prominently labeled their timetable entries "diesel powered." Curiously, the "diesel powered" label remained in the timetables until mid-1964, long after every steam locomotive had gone to scrap.

The Silver Fleet

The real beginning of Seaboard's significant post-war changes came with the May 18, 1947, timetable. That date marked the inaugural of the *Silver Comet*, a New York-Birmingham streamliner that replaced the conventional *Cotton States Special* on the same route. The arrival from Budd of sufficient new lightweight cars made the *Comet's* debut possible; the train was a near-match of the *Silver Meteor*. The 48

cars Budd delivered during 1947 also allowed upgrading of the *Meteor's* consists as well. With the *Comet* now in the lightweight train stable, Seaboard began calling its streamliners the "Silver Fleet."

Seaboard dropped the *Advance Silver Meteor* at the end of the 1947 winter season, so the summer months saw only the main *Silver Meteor* and the new *Comet* in the timetables. However, Seaboard had one more member of the Silver Fleet to roll out – a train that was "something old, something new." The equipment and schedule of the *Advance Silver Meteor* returned with the December 12, 1947, winter timetable, but under a new name, the *Silver Star* – in keeping with Seaboard's "silver astronomy" theme. The three trains together headlined Seaboard's passenger fleet throughout the railroad's postwar years.

The Silver Fleet's trains were defined as much by their equipment as by their names. Seaboard owned the majority of the large group of 1947 cars: three baggage-dorms (6050-6052); nine diners (6106-6114); 12 coaches (6215-6226); and, delivered in July, six striking tavern-observations, 6600-6605. The 6600s, with 34 tavern seats and 24 in the observation area, were Seaboard's first lightweight observation or lounge cars that had no coach seats. They were otherwise similar to Seaboard's original 6400-series cars of 1939 except for the large red signal light faired into the roof of the long rear taper. Three of the cars went to the *Silver Meteor* and three to the *Silver Comet*; all were complete with a dark blue and white, illuminated tail sign with the appropriate train name.

The 18 new PRR and RF&P coaches in the 1947 group (PRR 4058-4067 and RF&P 850-857) followed the exterior pattern of the pre-war equipment, with stainless-steel construction and fluting on the sides and roof. Lettering was black; Pennsylvania used its own serif font, and RF&P applied the super-extended Gothic style it patterned after the Atlantic Coast Line.

The 1947 cars' interiors had several new features compared to the prewar lightweights, noticeably speaker systems with speaker covers shaped like lyres. The systems included radio sets in the nine new dining cars and the observation-lounge cars, plus a public address system. (Seaboard's lightweight lounge and observation cars had radios before the war, but not its prewar diners.) Another prominent difference was fluorescent lighting; all prewar coaches had incandescent lighting only.

Meanwhile, SAL continued equipping all three Silver trains with heavyweight Pullmans; continuing material delays kept pushing back the new sleepers' delivery date despite Seaboard ads promising as early as November 1946 that the new cars were "under construction." The railroad had to supplement the Silver trains with other non-streamlined equipment too, particularly before the 1947 Budd deliveries but also afterwards as overflow demand required. Examples included heavyweight diners, American Flyer coaches, and standard heavyweight coaches. Among the latter, Seaboard selected a group of rebuilt standard coaches and applied a light silver-gray paint scheme

that helped them blend with lightweight consists. Some of these cars were extensively rebuilt in 1953-54 with wide streamlined-style windows, updated air-conditioning systems, and large bathroom lounge areas. The railroad also tapped additional lightweight cars from the Pennsylvania's Tuscan red fleet, which while not normally assigned to the Florida route did often appear on both Seaboard and Atlantic Coast Line trains.

Another highly publicized Silver Fleet feature was the presence of on-board registered nurses. The nurses, who doubled as hostesses, first appeared on the pre-war *Silver Meteor* and now staffed all three of the postwar streamliners. Seaboard promoted the assistance the "smartly uniformed" nurses could provide to children and families – another nod to the growing family vacation volume. The nurse/hostesses were a distinctive addition to the traditional passenger service agents and coach attendants (porters). The women were of course provided with separate sleeping spaces; hostess bedrooms were included in the pre-war 6300-series tavern coaches and 6500-series coach observations, plus the postwar 6600-series tavern observations. Most onboard male crewmen slept in the dormitory area of the baggage-dormitory cars. Coach attendants slept on the couches in the men's bathrooms, and Pullman car porters slept in an empty sleeping car space or in a special porter's berth found on most postwar cars.

The Silver Meteor

Most of the new 1947 Budd cars were assigned to the *Silver Meteor*, the original and still "premier streamliner" (to quote Seaboard's ad copy) in the Silver Fleet. The train received several of the new 52-seat coaches along with the new baggage-dorms and dining cars. Capping the consist were the 6600-series tavern-observation cars, which replaced the 6400-series coach-observations and the 6500-series buffet-

The northbound regular section of the Silver Meteor *is at Richmond's Main Street Station about 11 in the morning on a spring 1947 day. The train's lightweight coaches show prominently on the rear of the train, capped by tavern-coach 6501 carrying the* Meteor *tail sign. The streamlined equipment is augmented by an American Flyer coach next ahead of No. 6501 and by heavyweight Pullmans at the front of the train. (Sam A. Appleby Jr. photo)*

lounge-coaches that had previously alternated on the ends of the *Meteor* and its *Advance* counterpart.

Aside from the new "silver" equipment, the train still carried its normal assortment of standard-design Pullman cars; the six regularly assigned cars for the winter 1947-48 season offered a total of 42 sections, ten compartments, six drawing rooms, and 14 double bedrooms. Although the *Meteor's* earliest assigned heavyweight Pullmans had been painted silver, that practice had fallen away during the war, and postwar Pullman assignments were usually filled by cars in standard Pullman green. However, Pullman had developed an attractive two-tone gray scheme for many of its modernized cars, and they were standard on the *Silver Comet* when that train was first introduced. They may have also run on the *Meteor* and *Star* at times.

The postwar *Meteor's* sleeper lineup included a 10 Sec-1DR-2 Cpt New York-Tampa-Venice sleeper that had run for a time on the train during the war. The car then rode on the *Sun Queen*, a conventional train (later renamed the *Camellia* and *Sunland*) that left New York earlier than the *Meteor* but arrived at Tampa nearly an hour later. The shift back to the *Meteor*, effective December 1946, was accompanied by a renumbering of the Tampa-Venice connecting train from 507-508 (which had been derived from the *Sun Queen's* west coast section numbers, 107-108) to 257-258 for consistency with the west coast *Meteor's* numbers, 157-158. No through coach service was offered, just an across-the-platform transfer to Nos. 257-258's local car.

Since Tampa was a stub-end station for Seaboard trains, the Venice connecting trains (and St. Petersburg sections and trains to Boca Grande) all departed in the opposite direction from which their southbound mainline connections had arrived. Trains for Venice retraced the route of the mainline trains as far east (timetable north) as Valrico, where they continued on the Valrico Subdivision to Durant. They then turned south on the Sarasota Subdivision to Bradenton, Sarasota, and Venice. Connecting trains for Boca Grande kept going east to Edison, then turned south on the Boca Grande Subdivision. Trains to St. Petersburg – shortened versions of the same mainline trains that had arrived southbound at Tampa – returned to Gary, 1.7 miles east of Tampa Union Station, and used the Tampa Subdivision circling Tampa Bay to reach St. Petersburg.

Advertising the Silver Fleet

The Silver trains were the beneficiary of a stepped-up advertising campaign as private automobiles and commercial airplanes became the railroads' serious competitors in the late 1940s and early 1950s. As these modes increasingly took away business travel, Seaboard and other railroads began to aggressively highlight Florida as a year-round vacation destination, not just a winter escape from the north's cold and snow. A brochure issued in April 1953 noted that Florida hotel rates were lower in spring and summer, and that those two seasons offered "exotic flowers" and "sunshine and cooling breezes," respectively. Seaboard also promoted its "Route of Courteous Service" slogan, which began appearing on the sides of boxcars after the war and on timetable covers in 1955.

Seaboard also advertised other attractive destinations on or near its routes, including those accessible by connecting bus or taxi service. One example was Thalmann, Ga., the stop for the Georgia coastal resorts of Brunswick, St. Simons Island, and Sea Island. Others included Ocala (the station stop for Silver Springs), Winter Haven (Cypress Gardens), and West Lake Wales (the Bok Singing Tower). Passengers could also use Seaboard's heavily promoted "Circle Tour" option in Florida, which let travelers with round-trip tickets to Miami return north via Tampa or St. Petersburg, or conversely, without additional rail ticket costs. Circle Tour passengers could use the railroad's "Cross Florida Service" between West Lake Wales and Tampa/St. Petersburg, which offered year-round daytime connecting bus service as well as nighttime train service in the 1950s.

Seaboard even extolled its inland route through Florida. The railroad was far away from the state's beaches except at Jacksonville and the final portions of the St. Petersburg and Miami routes, but SAL ads pointed out there were still attractive sights along the way: "A [Seaboard] trip has ... wide-window views of ... orange groves, palm-fringed lakes, and real cattle ranches." The number of passengers who were impressed by the cattle ranches may be debatable, but without question the orange groves and lakes certainly said "Florida!" to many a northern tourist.

Speed was another Seaboard hallmark, although postwar advertising did not emphasize it as much as some of the railroad's other improvements. Several of its lines, particularly some long straight stretches in Florida, had official 75 m.p.h. limits, and engi-

neers routinely ran well above that. Many portions of the mainline were raised to 79 m.p.h. once block signal systems and Centralized Traffic Control were installed, an advance that Seaboard adopted during the World War II years for some of its most congested lines but rapidly applied elsewhere around the system once the war was over. CTC made SAL's mostly single-track main far more fluid than it once was, and let the railroad move trains in volumes that rivaled its double-tracked competitors Atlantic Coast Line and Southern.

Seaboard's valiant efforts kept passenger loadings at a respectable level, but as with other lines around the country, volumes fell far below the peak war years. In 1945, Seaboard took in nearly $43 million in passenger revenue and boasted almost two billion passenger miles (one passenger carried one mile), but in 1946 those figures dropped almost by half. By 1950, revenue was down to just $14 million and passenger miles had dropped to 574 million. The numbers declined somewhat further through mid-decade, but finally had a modest uptick in 1955.

Sleepers: Newly Built and Newly Purchased

Seaboard finally received its first group of lightweight sleeping cars in early summer 1949. Most were 10 roomette-6 double bedroom cars named after online cities (the *Atlanta* class), split between Pullman-Standard (13 cars) and Budd (six). RF&P also contributed three 10-6s from P-S and Pennsylvania purchased six from Budd. The RF&P cars were named for Virginia counties along that railroad (*Chesterfield*, *Essex*, *Lancaster*), but the PRR cars

A few months after the 1947 group of lightweight cars arrived, a long southbound Silver Meteor speeds through North Jacksonville, Fla., in March 1948 with E4 3002 and two other units. No fewer than seven heavyweight Pullmans trail the two lightweight cars up front. Standard Seaboard practice was to run three E units on the train to Wildwood, where two would forward the Miami cars and the third would handle the shorter St. Petersburg section. (David W. Salter photo)

and the other companies lacked any equivalent know-how. Their welding techniques resulted in almost immediate warping of the roof sheets, although as long as the problem remained a cosmetic one, SAL let the cars continue to serve as they were. The P-S and ACF welding processes also typically produced long-term corrosion under the side sheets.

A final group of new Pullmans came in August 1949 when American Car & Foundry supplied three 6 double bedroom-buffet-lounges, *Kennesaw Mountain*, *Red Mountain*, and *Stone Mountain*. As their north Georgia and Alabama names implied, the cars had been ordered for the *Silver Comet*, but they too were instead given to the *Meteor*. The *Mountain* cars were the only lightweight passenger cars ACF built new for Seaboard, even though the railroad had been a regular ACF customer for conventional passenger cars. The deliveries boosted Seaboard's lightweight fleet to 88 cars at the end of 1949.

With the new sleepers on hand, the *Meteor's* consist became almost all-lightweight effective with the September 25, 1949, timetable change; a 6 Sec-6 DB Miami car and 10-1-2 to St. Petersburg remained the

carried names of Seaboard points (*Athens, Bradenton, Chester, Clinton, Elberton, Greenwood*). Even though all names in the PRR group except *Bradenton* were locations on the *Comet* route, most of the new 10-6s were went to the *Silver Meteor* and *Silver Star*. Seaboard diverted a number of new cars intended for the *Comet* to the two Florida trains, which with their longer hauls and more attractive destinations were now making the most money and requiring the best equipment. Incidentally, the six Pennsylvania sleepers were the last cars that railroad bought for Seaboard pool service, although RF&P would add two coaches to its Florida service roster in 1955.

Seaboard liked the Budd "all-over" fluted stainless steel look. To keep new cars consistent with its all-Budd prewar roster, SAL rejected the flat-panel roof that Pullman-Standard and ACF normally applied to their lightweight passenger cars and instead told the builders to duplicate the Budd-style fluted roof. Unfortunately, Budd had patented its "shotweld" stainless steel fabricating process

The northbound Miami section (No. 58) of the Silver Meteor arrives at Wildwood about 1948. The train is pulled by E7 3029 and a B unit, and will soon join the St. Petersburg section (No. 158) for the trip to Richmond. The Miami section arrived after the west coast train, and the diesel from No. 158 was normally placed on the point north of Wildwood. Seaboard rebuilt Wildwood's station building and trackage in 1947. (Sam A. Appleby Jr. photo)

Richmond, Fredericksburg & Potomac Budd coach 856 gleams at Sunnyside Yard outside New York City on May 2, 1948. The year-old car was one of eight owned by RF&P and assigned to Seaboard's Florida trains. These and similar RF&P cars could creditably claim the title of longest road name letterboard. (George E. Votava photo, ACL & SAL HS collection)

only regularly assigned heavyweights. For the 1950-51 winter season, SAL rearranged car assignments to finally make the *Meteor* completely lightweight, with every sleeper line covered by the 10-6s plus the New York-Miami *Mountain* sleeper-lounges. Seaboard also listed by this date its new 52-seat cars for all regular coach assignments on the three Silver Fleet trains, with the prewar cars filling in as necessary. As always, the *Meteor* continued to have first dibs on the newest cars.

Just a few months prior to the lightweight sleeper deliveries, Seaboard and other major railroads were parties to another significant sleeping car change. The government's long-running anti-trust suit against the Pullman Company was finally settled in 1947 on the condition that Pullman sell its sleeping car division to 57 railroads. On December 31, 1948, Seaboard purchased its allocation of 31 heavyweight sleeping cars, largely the same cars that Pullman had regularly assigned to SAL trains, and leased them back to Pullman for operation and maintenance. They included three 8 Sec-5 DB cars; seven 6 Sec-6 DBs; six 8 Sec-1 DR-3 DBs; 11 10 Sec-1 DR-2 Cpts; and four of the 10 Sec-observation lounge cars in the *Columbia* series.

It appears the heavyweight cars remained in the colors Pullman had already been painting them: primarily standard Pullman green but with some room cars in the two-tone gray scheme used for many rebuilt cars. A few cars, including the *Columbia* lounges and at least one 10-1-2, had the "shadowlining" scheme (aluminum body with painted faux fluting lines) that imitated the look of lightweight cars. After the purchase, Seaboard replaced PULLMAN on the letterboard with its own name in all the schemes. SAL also stenciled a small number in the 1200 series on the car sides, but normally referred to the cars by their names.

More New Diesels

Meanwhile, Seaboard was busy seeing that its Silver trains were supplied with the newest passenger diesels. After the first wave of postwar passenger units arrived between 1945 and 1947, the railroad resumed buying E units and remained an exclusive EMD customer from then on. The new deliveries began with more E7s, 12 in 1948 (A units 3036-3044, Bs 3105-3107) and four more in 1949 (3045-3048). Starting in 1950, Seaboard added EMD's new E8 model, which had 2,250 h.p. per unit compared to 2,000 for the older locomotives. SAL acquired six E8s in 1950 and five more in 1952, numbers 3049-3059.

These locomotives completed Seaboard's passenger power roster through the 1950s, but the railroad bought a number of road-switcher and general-purpose units with steam boilers for possible passenger service as needed. Many went right to work as passenger station switchers, while others subbed on secondary runs or were coupled with E units when needed on long trains. This fleet included three Alco RSC2s in 1949, Nos. 1529-1531; eight Alco RCS3s in 1950, 1532-1535 and 1537-1540; 15 Alco RS3s in 1951-52, 1665-1679; ten Baldwin RS12s in 1952-53, 1466-1475; and eight EMD GP7s in 1950 (1704-1711) and 25 more in 1950-51 (1745-1769).

Seaboard's E8s were delivered with 98 m.p.h. gearing rather than the 117 m.p.h. top speed of earlier E units. With their increased pulling power, the E8s were sometimes seen on secondary or even branchline trains, where their ability to accelerate trains up to track speed after frequent stops was useful in staying on schedule. They were also common on the *Silver Comet* since their lower gearing was a distinct advantage on the hilly line to Atlanta and Birmingham. Meanwhile, the faster E4, E6, and E7 units continued to dominate the *Silver Meteor*, *Silver Star*, and other Florida trains. Starting in the 1950s, the older units

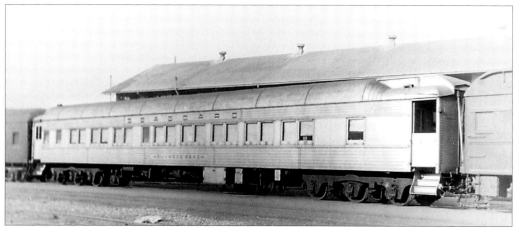

The first Pullman on Seaboard's roster named Hollywood Beach was this 10 Sec-1 DR-2 Cpt car, which was painted aluminum with shadowlining so it would blend with streamlined consists. All the Silver trains carried 10-1-2s before enough new lightweight sleepers were on hand. This photo shows the car, whose name was later given to one of the 1956 Sun Lounges, at New Orleans in 1951 in Pullman pool service. (Elliott M. Kahn photo, Charles K. Marsh Jr. collection)

Pullman-owned Columbia Canyon was a sister car to the four similar 10 section-observation lounge Columbia-series cars that were transferred to Seaboard ownership (Bridge, Basin, Bluffs, and Lake). While the cars had an exterior platform on the observation end, its small size made it largely decorative. Columbia Canyon is shown at Hamlet on October 6, 1951, in aluminum with shadowlining. (Bob's Photo collection)

suggested the new name. Also like the *Meteor*, the *Star* had a separate section that split at Wildwood for Tampa and St. Petersburg; the regular west coast portion consisted of two coaches, two sleepers, and a dining car. The *Star* received certain cars from the 1947 Budd order, including a diner and several 52-seat coaches, but carried one of the prewar 6400-series coach-observations on the end. The train also had a 6300-series tavern-coach. The balance of the *Star* was largely heavyweight, including six standard Pullmans.

The *Star* also adopted the *Advance Silver Meteor's* schedule pattern, leaving New York at mid-morning (four and one-half hours before the *Meteor's* 2:35 p.m. departure) and Miami at 4:40 p.m., more than eight hours after the *Meteor*. The *Star* also used the southbound *Advance Silver Meteor*/ northbound *Silver Meteor* Baldwin cutoff route to bypass Jacksonville during the winter season, allowing it to better the *Meteor's* trip time by more than an hour. The bypass route avoided a slow back-up move into Jacksonville Terminal Station and saved 12 track miles as well. The *Star's* Baldwin servicing stop was not listed in the passenger timetables, but Seaboard in fact allowed passengers to board there, and many from Jacksonville and the surrounding area did so.

The northbound *Silver Star* also bypassed Savannah Union Station, stopping only at West Savannah, two miles west of downtown on the Seaboard mainline. West Savannah was a small stucco station located where Seaboard's main crossed Telfair Road, not far south of Louisville Road. The station and a bypass route were built when the *Orange Blossom Special* was inaugurated in 1925 so that train could avoid the time-consuming moves necessary to reach Union Sta-

were gradually re-geared to match the top speed of 98, although the changeover was not completed until the mid-1960s.

The *Silver Star*

The *Silver Star* made its inaugural run on December 12, 1947, taking over the schedule and equipment of the *Advance Silver Meteor*. As Seaboard had done for the *Silver Meteor*, the railroad held a contest to name the *Star* and reported that over 1,000 persons

tion downtown. With the Savannah and Jacksonville bypasses, the *Star's* New York-Miami timings were 25 hours 45 minutes southbound and ten minutes shorter northbound.

The *Star* ceased operation effective with the April 25, 1948, timetable, but came back on August 1 and remained thereafter as a year-round train. For the winter 1948-49 season, the train picked up the New York-Port Boca Grande sleeper that had been previously carried by the *Palmland*. In the summer of 1949, the *Star* was trimmed to nine regularly assigned cars and dropped its west coast section. And although it resumed stopping at Jacksonville, the train continued to bypass Savannah southbound. This operating pattern became the train's norm; however, effective in summer 1950, four of the *Star's* nine regular sum-

mer cars were cut back to Washington-Miami, including its diner and tavern-coach.

While most of the long-awaited new lightweight sleepers went to the *Silver Meteor*, the *Star* was by no means overlooked. Effective September 25, 1949, 10 Rmt-6 DBR cars from the *Atlanta* class took over both of the *Star's* New York-Miami sleeper lines, making the train's regular equipment all-lightweight except for its *Columbia*-series 10 section-lounge. However, for the winter 1949-50 season, the train's additional seasonal sleepers were again heavyweights, with four such cars added to the regular consist. The winter schedule also saw the return of the train's west coast cars; this winter-season-only operation of the west coast section would continue in place throughout the Seaboard years. For the 1953-54 winter season, the

"The most beautiful and luxurious of any in Florida service..."

David Salter made available correspondence from the late Sam Appleby about Seaboard trains and equipment that Appleby documented at New York's Penn Station in 1950 and 1951. Appleby reported that passengers were extremely excited when Seaboard began placing in service the ex-Chesapeake & Ohio 6227-6234 series coaches in the early fall of 1950. This is an edited composite of several Appleby dispatches between September 23 and October 28, 1950:

FLASH!! SURPRISE OF SURPRISES!! Seaboard coach No. 6232 was in the consist of the *Silver Meteor* – one of the praiseworthy, luxurious, 36-seat former C&O Budd-built coaches. Lettered with the familiar modernistic SEABOARD, the 6232 has taken the place of Pennsy's No. 4057, which was operating in this section of Trains 57-58. Fresh from the shops, the coach is now the most beautiful and luxurious of any in Florida service, in my opinion. As the passenger enters the coach from the front, he presses a small square in the door lettered PUSH, whereupon the door slides (instead of swinging) open. After passing the ladies' lounge, he enters the main body of the coach alongside an eight-seat lounge, set off by a curved, varnished wooden wall topped by a stainless steel handrail. The green leather chairs and sofa fit with the green and cream color scheme of the car, as do the soft green carpets running the length of the car.

Each wide window is fitted with double cream-colored Venetian blinds. Seats are of the Sleepy Hollow type with adjustable footrests, coat racks,

individual ashtrays, small pocket for timetables, and individual reading lamps. Luggage racks are wide and solid. The rear of the coach has a small writing desk with a yellow leather chair. Lockers with free individual keys are provided for baggage, and photos and paintings complete the bulkhead decorations. The attendant said that northbound passengers from Florida kept asking him how they could get reservations for "that car" on their return trip.

Other features that I spotted for the first time: Windows are wider than on previous coaches, either SAL's 6215-6226 series or ACL's 228-247 group [of new Pullman-Standard coaches]. The writing desk is on springs so it can remain steady even when the train sways suddenly on a curve or rough track. The cabinet under the photo mural at the rear has shelves for extra paper cups, writing materials, etc. Wells to hold potted plants provided at each end of the coach section, two of them, are presently covered by stainless lids similar to automobile hubcaps. Color schemes seen thus far were cream and green with yellow desk chair and gray, maroon-tinged upholstering (6232, 6234) or blue and beige, with brown leather lounge seats and desk chair (6227, 6228), blue carpets and upholstering.

Even the best have some disadvantages, however; these cars have only three public address system speakers, two in the coach end and one in the lounge end. Doors could operate faster, openings should be provided in the seat arms so attendant could handle overhead baggage more easily (as on previous 6200s), and lighted car markers should be installed.

Passengers study their Silver Meteor *menus aboard one of the new Budd 48-seat dining cars in charge of steward E.S. Burlingame, standing at rear. A lyre-theme speaker cover shows prominently at the top of the end bulkhead. The glass dividers toward the rear were used, together with curtains, to set apart a banquette section where crew members or African-American passengers could eat and be separated from the other patrons. (SAL photo, TLC Collection)*

Members of a Seaboard dining car and lounge crew pose with diner 6107 at Sunnyside Yard outside New York City. Behind the steward (in coat and tie at center) are four cooks at left (with caps), six waiters, and at right, the bartender or senior lounge attendant. Segregated hiring practices assured that only the cook and waiter positions were open to black employees, but the positions offered better opportunities than many other jobs available to them in that period. (SAL photo, TLC Collection)

ginning to realize the distinct advantages of riding the *Silver Comet*."

The *Comet* began with 15 regularly assigned cars, almost all operating the entire way from New York to Birmingham. Leaving New York, the train included eight lightweights: a passenger-baggage-dormitory, diner, five coaches, and the tavern-lounge-observa-tion. The train's streamlined car complement was, for the moment, nearly a match for the *Silver Meteor* – a circumstance that would last only briefly. The *Comet* also had three heavyweight sleepers and a heavyweight 10-section lounge car (normally from the *Columbia* series). It picked up another standard Pullman in Washington (for Atlanta) and another at

Hamlet (from Portsmouth, for Atlanta). At Hamlet the *Comet* also picked up the Portsmouth-Atlanta coach – now also a new lightweight car.

The *Comet's* Portsmouth-Atlanta Pullman, another inheritance from the *Cotton States Special*, was a sleeper line that dated back to Seaboard's early, pre-Florida days when its premier passenger service ran from Washington and Portsmouth to Atlanta. The cars originated on a connecting local at Portsmouth that ran to Norlina, N.C., the junction of the Portsmouth Subdivision with the mainline. They were forwarded from Norlina to Hamlet in the *Sun Queen* (later the *Camellia* and *Sunland*). At Hamlet, the cars were added to the *Comet's* consist for the run to Atlanta. The same procedures were employed in reverse northbound.

The *Silver Comet's* size and consist remained largely the same at first, but by the December 1949 timetable the train began a gradual metamorphosis into one focused increasingly on the Washington-Atlanta core of its route. The number of New York-Birmingham cars was reduced to six, although a new 10-6 lightweight sleeper was now assigned in place of the line's original 10-1-2 heavyweight; a second 10-6 was added in 1950. After a few minor changes over the next couple of years, the April 1953 consist further reduced the train's New York cars to just four, and by December, only two of the four – a 10-6 sleeper and a coach – continued past Atlanta to Birmingham. The train's other cars originated in Washington, and most terminated in Atlanta. The *Comet* also continued to carry the Portsmouth cars – now originating in an upgraded train called the *Tidewater* – plus a winter-season Raleigh-Atlanta heavyweight 10-1-2 sleeper.

Despite the reductions at the extreme ends of its route, the *Comet* still carried a respectable ten regularly assigned cars into Atlanta. In fact, Seaboard's Atlanta ticket sales in the late forties and early fifties were reportedly second only to Miami. Some of the train's observers also noted that African American customers heavily patronized the Atlanta-Washington segment of the route, sometimes requiring as many as three segregated coaches set aside for their use.

In the summer of 1954, the *Comet* suffered a further indignity: its 6600-series tavern-lounge-observations were removed and reassigned to the *Silver Star* the following winter, further confirming the Florida trains' greater importance. In trade, the *Comet's* coach passengers gained the 6300-series coach-taverns that had previously been on the *Star*.

The *Silver Comet's* Pullman passengers still had use of the heavyweight *Columbia* 10 section-lounges, one of several heavyweight sleepers on the *Comet* through the mid-1950s (others included the Portsmouth-Atlanta sleeper and the winter-only Raleigh-Atlanta sleeper). These continued even after the railroad received new lightweight sleeping cars in 1955 and 1956. For the winter 1956-57 season, the *Comet's* consist still included a *Columbia* car; a Pullman-owned *Elm*-series 12 Rmt-2 SB-3 DB (Portsmouth-Atlanta); and an 8 Sec-1 DR-3 DB (Raleigh-Atlanta).

In the summer of 1957, the *Silver Comet's* regularly assigned New York-Birmingham cars became all-lightweight. Sleeper lines from both New York and Washington to Birmingham were covered by 10-6s, and the heavyweight 10 section-lounges were discontinued. But for the next two winter seasons, 1957-58 and 1958-59, regularly assigned heavyweight Pull-

Sleeping car Petersburg, *one of 19 such 10 roomette-6 double bedroom Pullmans delivered to Seaboard in 1949, was among the 13 cars built by Pullman-Standard; Budd constructed the remaining six. The car posed at Hamlet on November 17, 1958. (Bob's Photo collection)*

mans made once last appearance on the train. The Portsmouth-Atlanta sleeper was covered by a 12-2-3 car, then the next year by a 12 Rmt-1 SB-4 DB car like the Pullman-owned *Oak* series. At long last, for the winter 1958-59 season, a lightweight 10-6 replaced the heavyweight car. The *Comet's* regularly assigned passenger cars were finally all-streamlined from that point on, although the train usually carried several heavyweight head-end cars.

More New Lightweight Cars Arrive

Seaboard's 1947-49 lightweight cars served the railroad well and certainly provided complete justification for the Silver Fleet name, but were still not enough to replace all the heavyweight Pullmans on the *Silver Star* and *Silver Comet*. To be sure, the older sleepers were modernized, had mostly room space, and were often considered quieter and more comfortable than their newer counterparts. However, the traditional cars remained inconsistent with the modern image Seaboard wanted, and even with two-tone gray or shadowlining paint, did not satisfactorily match otherwise-lightweight consists.

Seaboard's prewar lightweight cars had also seen heavy use for more than a decade. Even with interior refurbishing, some of them still lacked post-war features such as fluorescent lighting and radio reception equipment. One early remedy was Seaboard's purchase of eight Budd coach-lounges (6227-6234) in August 1950 from the Chesapeake & Ohio Railroad. Although built in 1948, the C&O cars had barely turned a wheel; they had been purchased for the C&O's planned *Chessie* streamliner and other expanded services, but the train was canceled just as the huge order of new cars began arriving. C&O was happy to sell its surplus new equipment to interested buyers like Seaboard, Atlantic Coast Line, and Illinois Central. The cars had 36 reclining seats in their coach section along with a small eight-passenger lounge at one end. SAL rebuilt five cars to full 50-seat coaches while the other three retained their lounge spaces, which Seaboard promoted as another special feature for its growing volume of coach-class passengers.

To cure the shortage of lightweight Pullman equipment, Seaboard went back to Budd and Pullman-Standard for 15 full sleepers in three configurations and three sleeper-lounge cars. The railroad filled out the order with seven 52-seat coaches from P-S with 10-seat center lounge. RF&P also contributed two similar coaches, Nos. 861-862. The total SAL/RF&P group of 27 cars, delivered in late 1955 and early 1956, was an unusually large purchase this late in the postwar era – a time when a number of other railroads were already beginning to curtail their passenger train offerings.

True to SAL practice, the *Silver Meteor* received most of the new cars. While the coaches and sleepers were assigned to both the *Meteor* and the *Silver Star*, the *Meteor* had exclusive use of the sleeper-lounge cars. Constructed by Pullman at its Chicago plant and dubbed "Sun Lounges," these distinctive cars were the only three ever built to this plan. Their names were carefully chosen to identify South Florida's best-known beaches: *Hollywood Beach* (appropriated from a 10-1-2 heavyweight), *Miami Beach*, and *Palm Beach*. They featured a glassed-in roof over a large, ceiling-height lounge area with high solarium windows and a special Florida-motif interior décor, down to special sand-colored carpeting with seashell images. Seaboard said the lounge space provided a glass roof and expanded visibility like a dome car, yet fit within the tight clearances from Washington northward. The cars were filled out with five double bedrooms, and the lounge was reserved for Pullman patrons only.

The new full sleeping cars were heavy on room accommodations. Pullman-Standard built six 11 double bedroom cars (the *Avon Park* class, for the *Meteor*) and three cars with five double bedrooms, two com-

This interior publicity view of a new 10-6 Pullman shows a double bedroom arranged for daytime use. The post-war double bedroom accommodation featured a compact, private bathroom; the passenger at left is standing in its doorway. (SAL photo, TLC Collection)

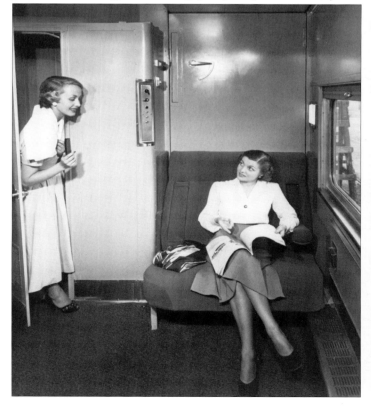

partments, and two drawing rooms (the *Boca Grande* class, for the *Star*). Budd built six cars (the *Bay Pines* class) for the *Star* that also had a substantial number of room accommodations – four roomettes, five double bedrooms, and one compartment. These cars also had four sections, with the same "uppers" and "lowers" that Pullman travelers of more modest means had known for decades. New cars with sections were unusual by this date but several railroads ordered them primarily for military and other government personnel, who were allowed to pay only for a lower berth space. Similar new cars appeared on several other railroads in the South (where military bases were plentiful), including ACL, Florida East Coast, and Louisville & Nashville.

An interesting footnote to the 1955-56 Pullman-Standard order was that Seaboard no longer demanded Budd-style corrugated roofs on the cars; problems with the P-S and ACF corrugated panels applied to the 1949 sleepers were quite evident by this time. These newest Pullman-Standard cars came both with the builder's standard flat roof panels and with stainless steel framing that was designed to prevent the corrosion now plaguing other P-S cars with early applications of corrugated panels. Both they and the Budd cars in the order also were delivered without the full-width diaphragms that had been standard on the earlier postwar equipment; they had proved difficult to maintain and were being removed from the older cars as they were shopped. The cars did retain their traditional side skirts, but Seaboard also later removed this trim from most lightweight coaches.

Pushing for Passengers

Large ads in Seaboard's December 1955 public timetable proclaimed that the new equipment order offered many "delightful innovations," and promised passengers new heights of comfort and luxury aboard that winter's trains. SAL emphasized that with the coach-lounge cars available, both coach and Pullman passengers would have nearby lounge space.

Although the coach-lounge areas were smaller and plainer than those in the Sun Lounges, the railroad noted that coach passengers could also take advantage of the "additional splendid lounge facilities" in the tavern-observation car.

One other prominent Seaboard passenger inducement during this period was reasonably priced dining car meals. In 1956, Seaboard reduced dining car prices (with a top price of $4.75 for a full-course sirloin steak dinner), added fresh flowers in diners, and offered a complimentary coffee and orange juice during a mid-afternoon "hospitality hour." These followed several similar moves in dining car operations and services over the previous few years. The December 1953 timetable had announced "new, delicious" Travel Budget meals, price at 70 cents for breakfast, $1.25 for lunch, and $1.35 for dinner. In 1954, the railroad promoted special children's menus along with paper bibs with a colorful drawing of a passenger train and a puzzle of the six states SAL served.

For a while, Seaboard's promotional efforts and its new equipment had a salutary effect on passenger train performance. The railroad reported about 1,090,000 passengers carried in 1956, a modest increase over 1954 and 1955, and a somewhat stronger upturn in passengers carried one mile – signaling that riders were taking longer trips. Total passenger revenues also were about 10 percent ahead of 1955. The improved showings proved short-lived, however, as the recession of 1957-58 reduced passenger demand and the twin competitive pressures of the automobile and airplane continued making their inevitable inroads. The economic downturn would combine with major changes sweeping the rail passenger industry to strongly challenge Seaboard's decades-long commitment to quality passenger service. But the railroad remained confident that its high-quality equipment, aggressive marketing, modern physical plant, and "Courteous Service" ideals would keep passengers loyal to its trains.

Attractive stations like this new one at Winter Haven, Fla., photographed in December 1947 not long after its completion, awaited Seaboard's patrons at the end of their journeys south. The building's Mediterranean Revival architecture matched that of most other Seaboard stations along the Miami extension, with pink stucco walls and clay tile roofs. (SAL photo, TLC Collection)

Another appealing station was the classic structure at West Palm Beach, the first Seaboard stop on the south Florida coast after the mainline's run through the center of the state. This street-side view highlights the Railway Express section at left. The station was one of many built in the mid-1920s as part of Seaboard's Miami extension. (H.A. McBride photo)

This photo perfectly captures the Silver Star at its postwar peak: two southbound sections of the train, each with an observation car and tail sign, pause at Washington Union Station around 1950. The final car at left is round-end 6401, one of the original 1939 Meteor cars, while 1940-vintage flat-end observation 6500 caps the second train's consist. (Sam A. Appleby Jr. photo)

Seaboard E7 3043 and a B unit, both in the citrus scheme, lead what appears to be the summer-season Silver Star into the Miami station about 1952. The Star's summer service had only a Miami section at the time and ran its coach equipment first, followed by Pullmans. Just visible among the train's complement of heavyweight sleepers is a Chinese red and gray car (eighth back) painted for use on the winter-only Orange Blossom Special. If on time, the train is arriving at 11:00 a.m. (Bob's Photo collection)

It's about 10:15 on a sunny morning at the Portal, N.J., drawbridge, outside the tunnel to Penn Station, and the southbound Silver Star has just left New York in charge of a Pennsylvania GG1 electric locomotive. The elegant Seaboard coach-observation car gliding past the home signal and smash board is No. 6401 with its white-on-blue tail sign. The year is probably around 1952 or 1953; the Star still carried a brace of heavyweight Pullmans, visible just ahead of the nine lightweight cars on the rear. The three original 6400-6402 series cars were round-end observations; No. 6400 was rebuilt with a flat end after a wreck and the other two had rear diaphragms added in the mid-1950s. (M.D. McCarter collection via William E. Griffin Jr. collection)

The southbound Silver Star rolls out over the James River in February 1956 just after leaving Richmond's Main Street Station, visible over the train at left. For a few years, it was possible to see Seaboard E units in both their old and new colors; the new "mint green" scheme, worn only by the trailing unit here, was adopted at the end of December 1954. First up in the train's consist are a heavyweight 180-series baggage-dorm, substituting for the normal lightweight car, and a Tuscan red Pennsy Pullman. (H.H. Harwood photo, William E. Griffin Jr. collection)

Actress Jean Parker christens the new Silver Comet at New York's Penn Station on May 18, 1947; standing in front of the onlookers are Seaboard board chairman Henry W. Anderson (left) and President Legh Powell. Although the Comet was inaugurated as soon as Budd delivered enough lightweight cars to equip most of the train, the Comet's 6600-series observations did not arrive until July. The train thus had to briefly use other cars like the 6400-series prewar observation shown here. (SAL photo, TLC Collection)

The Silver Comet rolls into Atlanta near Northside Drive in this August 3, 1947 scene. Diesel units 3033, 3032, and a third E7 lead a 16-car train with six heavyweight Pullmans in the middle. The signal is part of Seaboard's extensive automatic signal and Centralized Traffic Control installations on its busiest lines during the 1940s. (David W. Salter photo)

Seaboard E7s 3035 and 3040 lead the Silver Comet *into Birmingham at 41st Street, about ten blocks before entering Birmingham Terminal Station trackage, late on the morning of May 23, 1948. Although No. 33 is southbound by timetable, it has been moving west by compass since it left Atlanta. The* Comet *carries a baggage-RPO painted aluminum to match the train, eight lightweight cars, and three heavyweight sleepers in traditional Pullman green. (Frank E. Ardrey Jr. photo)*

The inbound Silver Comet *whips through Weems, Ala., on April 4, 1948 on its way to Birmingham. Note that the heavyweight Pullmans are all in the two-tone gray scheme; the* Comet *frequently carried the gray sleepers in its first years. (Frank E. Ardrey Jr. photo)*

This 11-car, five-month-old edition of the southbound *Silver Comet* is at North Philadelphia, Pa., on October 12, 1947, with three heavyweight Pullmans and an otherwise-lightweight consist. Among the train's new stainless steel cars are tavern-observation No. 6601 bringing up the rear and, next ahead, RF&P coach 851. Within a few years, the train would carry only a handful of through New York cars. (George Votava photo, Bob's Photo collection)

Opposite: These two interior views of the Sun Lounge look toward the bedroom area and the car's end, respectively. The special interior décor, including driftwood lamps and beach-theme carpeting, shows clearly along with the bright atmosphere made possible by the large side and overhead windows. (SAL photos, TLC Collection)

No lightweight passenger car was more synonymous with Seaboard than the Silver Meteor's three unique Sun Lounges. This broadside view of Miami Beach, taken at Pullman-Standard's Chicago plant on January 24, 1956, shows the glass-encased lounge area that combined advantages of a dome car and solarium yet remained within the tight clearances required over the Pennsylvania's electrified Washington-New York run. (Pullman-Standard photo, Ron Dettmer collection)

On the morning after Christmas Day in 1953, the southbound Silver Comet is at Howell's Yard (Atlanta) behind E8 3054 as it gets under way to Birmingham after its Terminal Station stop. Seaboard's 11 E8s were common on the Comet after their delivery in 1950 and 1952. The train has just backed northward the three miles from Terminal Station. Seaboard's standard operating practices for reaching Terminal had all trains from the north heading into the station and through trains backing out to Howell's, where they wyed and then continued to Birmingham. Trains from Birmingham backed into the station so they could leave northbound without a delay at the yard. (Oscar W. Kimsey Jr. photo)

On the afternoon of January 7, 1954, Seaboard GP7 1783 pulls the Silver Comet's Atlanta cars south toward Terminal Station past Southern's North Avenue coach yard (out of sight to the left). Behind the "geep" and coach-baggage combine 264 are three heavyweight Pullmans in three paint schemes: SAL 10-section lounge Columbia Basin, painted in the shadowlining livery; Pullman 10 sec-1 DR-lounge New Waterford in the two-tone gray scheme; and what appears to be RF&P (but "Pullman"-lettered) 8 Sec-5 DB Clover City in traditional Pullman green. These cars, typical of the diverse heavyweights the Comet still carried into the mid-1950s, will be added along with lightweight cars to the incoming Birmingham section for the train's scheduled 7:05 p.m. northbound departure. (Oscar W. Kimsey Jr. photo)

Fort Lauderdale was one of three 5 DB-2 Cpt-2 DR cars Pullman-Standard turned out in January 1956 for assignment to the Silver Star. The small number that Seaboard applied to its sleepers in addition to names – here, 61 – shows on the car's side at lower left. (SAL photo, TLC Collection)

Southern Pines was one of six sleepers Budd delivered in Seaboard's 1955-56 group. They offered the unusual configuration of four roomettes, five double bedrooms, one compartment, and in a throwback to Pullman's earlier days, four sections – the latter typically used by military personnel. The cars were placed on the Silver Star, allowing that train's through consist to become all-lightweight at last. (SAL photo, TLC Collection)

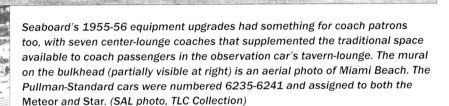

Seaboard's 1955-56 equipment upgrades had something for coach patrons too, with seven center-lounge coaches that supplemented the traditional space available to coach passengers in the observation car's tavern-lounge. The mural on the bulkhead (partially visible at right) is an aerial photo of Miami Beach. The Pullman-Standard cars were numbered 6235-6241 and assigned to both the Meteor and Star. (SAL photo, TLC Collection)

Train time at Fort Lauderdale! A Nash Rambler convertible looks on as the southbound Silver Meteor, No. 57, handles passengers and then gets ready to depart for Miami on December 28, 1956. E7 3031 and a B unit provide the motive power today. Ft. Lauderdale was one of several Atlantic coast stations (starting with West Palm Beach) that Seaboard served on its final 70 miles into Miami. (Bruce R. Meyer photo)

Mary Noble, one of Seaboard's stewardess-nurses, helps children down from the Silver Meteor at West Palm Beach in 1955. Seaboard highlighted the stewardess-nurses as yet another inducement for families to ride its trains to Florida. (SAL photo, TLC Collection)

These two photos show the northbound and southbound Miami Silver Meteors, respectively, passing the Adams Packing Association citrus plant at Auburndale, Fla., about 1955. The trains were scheduled to meet at 12:30 p.m. at the Auburndale siding, just south of this location and the Atlantic Coast Line diamond that was beneath the bridge, but did not make passenger stops here. The plant would not count as lovely Florida scenery, but the boxcars and reefers on the sidings demonstrate its importance to Seaboard's freight revenues. (SAL photos, TLC Collection)

The Silver Fleet streamliners served the Seaboard Air Line's main routes, carried the best equipment, had the strongest passenger loadings, and made the best advertising copy. But the lightweight trains still ran alongside many well-known conventional named trains on SAL's busiest lines, descendants of the railroad's earliest passenger service. At least one, the *Orange Blossom Special*, could stand with some of the country's most esteemed passenger trains.

Even after the lightweight trains arrived, a number of the conventional trains continued to have substantial reputations and clienteles. While they all lost some of their former polish in the 1950s and 1960s, Seaboard nevertheless maintained many of them to high standards and promoted them through large timetable ads and other means. Others, however, declined to eventual "Passenger, Mail and Express" status or disappeared altogether.

The *Orange Blossom Special*

The best-known and most celebrated of Seaboard's conventional named trains was the *Orange Blossom Special*, the winter-season all-Pullman train that began carrying wealthy vacationers to Florida in 1925. Such was the *Blossom's* standing that in the February 2, 1939, timetable that was issued to coincide with the *Silver Meteor's* inaugural, an ad for the flashy new streamliner did not appear until the folder's final panel. But at the front, the *Blossom's* display retained its accustomed opening-pages spot. Seaboard painted the train's famous name on thousands of boxcars, and Pullman gave the *Blossom's* cars their own color scheme in the early 1950s. The train even had a popular bluegrass song written about it in 1938, and Johnny Cash and a number of other singers have reprised the tune in the years since.

Seaboard proclaimed the *Blossom* "Florida's Distinguished Winter Train." The railroad always made sure the train had plenty of premium sleeping equipment with room and lounge space, plus extra dining cars whenever there was danger of overcrowding. The *Blossom* was also the first air-conditioned train to Florida and the first in the South pulled by diesel-electric locomotives. Even after the train came back from its wartime suspension in the winter of 1946-47, it remained a prominent member of the Seaboard fleet. The railroad briefly weighed streamlining the train, particularly when it became clear in 1949 that Atlantic Coast Line was going to field an all-lightweight *Florida Special* – the *Blossom's* competitor for the seasonal first-class winter trade. When Seaboard's new lightweight 10 Rmt-6 DB sleepers became available that year, the railroad assigned one

The Orange Blossom Special *was the flagship of Seaboard's conventional fleet. Inaugurated in 1925, the winter-season, all-Pullman train was also the recipient of the railroad's first diesel-electric locomotives, E4 units delivered by Electro-Motive in the fall of 1938. The* Blossom *was suspended after the 1941-42 winter season for the duration of the war years because Pullmans were badly needed for troop trains. The train is shown pulling away from the Sebring (Fla.) station in February 1942, two months before its last run until the 1946-47 winter season. (Sam A. Appleby Jr. photo)*

of the cars to the *Blossom* during its 1949-50 winter season. But that remained the *Blossom's* only known exception to an all-heavyweight consist.

The *Orange Blossom Special's* new and unique paint scheme, Chinese red and gray, was applied to a refurbished conventional consist beginning with the winter 1951-52 season. The new colors were certainly attractive, and the train never retreated from its tradition of comfort and service. But the *Blossom* was no match for the sleek all-stainless-steel *Florida Special*, nor even for Seaboard's own *Silver Meteor* – all of whose heavyweight sleeping cars had been replaced by new lightweights by the winter 1950-51 season. The *Orange Blossom Special's* final season was 1952-53, and the train made its last run on April 11, 1953.

The *Palmland*

Before the *Silver Meteor* appeared in 1939, Seaboard's premier year-round trains between New York and Florida were the *New York-Florida Limited* and the *Southern States Special*, which had evening and morning departures respectively in both directions and leisurely schedules as long as 36 hours to Miami. The trains featured through sleepers for both coasts of Florida, especially the *New York-Florida Limited*. The trains received diesel power in mid-1940, although steam often returned in the winter season and again became common on the trains during World War II. Effective with the winter 1941-42 season, the *Limited* and *Special* were renamed the *Palmland* and *Sun Queen*, respectively.

Both trains emerged from the war much the same as before the conflict, running frequently behind steam and carrying sleepers for both coasts. Diesels came back to the trains as deliveries of new E7s in 1945 and 1946 allowed, but the Silver Fleet and the *Orange Blossom Special* always had first claim on the units available. The *Palmland* was regularly diesel-powered by the summer season of 1947 except for its separate west coast section; the west coast train continued behind steam each winter until more E7s arrived in 1948 and 1949. While the *Palmland's* sections split in the summer at Wildwood per standard practice, the trains ran separately south of Jacksonville during winters through the 1951-52 season.

The *Palmland* was Seaboard's "two-nights-out" conventional train on the New York-Florida run, with an evening departure from New York and arrival at both Miami and St. Petersburg the second morning. Northbound, the train left its Florida terminals about 9:00 in the evening with a second-morning arrival in New York. Operating as Nos. 9 and 10, the trains ran through the Carolinas in daylight but were largely creatures of the night in Florida. The *Palmland* in fact doubled as an all-stops local train between Hamlet and Jacksonville in the summer season; in winter, a separate Passenger, Mail and Express train handled local passengers on this segment. The *Palmland* also served another significant function: the normal conveyance for pass riders, since employee passes were usually not honored on Silver Fleet trains.

By Pullman to the Golf Course

The *Palmland* and Seaboard's other important secondary trains were equipped with the railroad's large roster of heavyweight head-end cars, coaches, and diners. Heavyweight sleepers came from the group Seaboard purchased from Pullman in 1948 as well as the Pullman Company's own pool. Cars from connections filled out the trains, usually coaches and head-end equipment from the Pennsylvania and Richmond, Fredericksburg & Potomac.

The *Palmland* carried a large number of Pullmans, up to six on the northern portion of its route during the winter. About half terminated at Hamlet

Pullman-owned 6 Cpt-3 DR Glen Island *was among the room sleepers painted in the* Orange Blossom Special's *special Chinese red and gray scheme for the train's last two seasons. The car was part of the northbound* Blossom *at Avon Park, Fla., in March 1952. (Sam A. Appleby Jr. photo)*

Prior to the coming of the Silver Fleet, the Palmland and its companion heavyweight trains were the standard Seaboard conveyances to Florida. In this May 10, 1942, view at Fairwold, S.C., a few miles north of Columbia, southbound No. 191 is in the hands of class M2 4-8-2 267. Behind the powerful steamer are an express car, an American Flyer combine, three coaches, a diner, three Pullmans, and two Norfolk & Western coaches on the rear. (George Votava photo, ACL & SAL HS collection)

to serve the considerable first-class trade destined for the noted golf resorts in the nearby Sandhills towns of Southern Pines and Pinehurst. Through the mid-1950s, Seaboard ads promoted the *Palmland's* morning arrival in the area, accompanied by sketches of smiling golfers on well-groomed courses. The service followed a Seaboard tradition that peaked before the Depression, when solid Pullman trains often ran to the area. Seaboard also highlighted the train's daytime service to Camden and Columbia, S.C., and Savannah and Thalmann, Ga., the nearest SAL point for Brunswick and the lower Georgia coast.

The Hamlet "set-out" sleepers were switched out, serviced, and readied for their return trip on that evening's northbound *Palmland*. Seaboard had a sizeable fleet of switch engines assigned to passenger terminal switching chores; in the diesel era, these included both yard switchers and the boiler-equipped road switchers (especially RSC3s and GP7s).

The *Palmland* also offered an interesting variety of Pullman service into Florida. In addition to through sleepers from New York or Washington to Miami and the west coast, the train forwarded a number of sleeper lines from other cities. Through 1954, the *Palmland* carried a Cleveland-Jacksonville-Tampa car that came as far as Jacksonville on the Southern Railway's *Ponce de Leon*. In the late 1940s, the train also carried a New Orleans-Jacksonville-Miami Pullman south of Jacksonville. Finally, the *Palmland* carried Seaboard's "Cross Florida" (Tampa-Miami) sleeper and coach service.

Although the *Palmland's* west coast section (Nos. 1-2) carried several sleepers, the train had a leisurely overnight schedule and made every local stop along the route. By 1950, both the *Silver Meteor* and the winter-season *Silver Star* had taken over most of these St. Petersburg sleeper lines, and the *Palmland*

was cut back to Tampa effective February 11, 1951. Another *Palmland* winter-season west coast sleeper was a New York-Boca Grande car, but it too migrated to the *Silver Star* effective with the winter 1948-49 season.

The *Palmland's* sleeping equipment remained all-heavyweight until early June 1954, when the train was assigned a lightweight 10 Rmt-6 DB car to cover the New York-Hamlet line during the summer. But more lightweight Pullmans gradually began to appear, even though they were often from other railroads – especially in the winter when Seaboard's own cars were needed for heavy *Silver Fleet* business. For the 1957-58 and 1958-59 winter seasons, lightweight 12 Rmt-4 DBs from the Union Pacific/Wabash/Chicago & North Western *Western* series filled three of the *Palmland's* five sleeper lines. The two remaining heavyweight Pullmans – a New York-Hamlet 6 Cpt-3 DR *Glen* series and a Washington-Hamlet 6 Sec-6 DB *Poplar* car – became the train's last regularly assigned standard sleepers; they were discontinued in April 1959 and November 1958 respectively.

In spite of dieselization and Seaboard's other modernization improvements, the *Palmland's* New York-Miami timing stayed in the range of a day and a half. A major reason was its ongoing function as a local between Raleigh and Jacksonville, which the *Palmland* began doing year-round after the winter of 1952-53. The southbound train took nearly 12 hours to get just from Hamlet to Jacksonville; the *Silver Meteor* made the run in under seven hours.

Grill Cars and Other Equipment

Like all Seaboard feature trains, the *Palmland* offered the railroad's well-regarded dining car service. But as full-service dining car costs rose in the postwar period, SAL began looking for ways to economize while still maintaining an acceptable level of service.

Seaboard E4 3010 and two more passenger A units roll the southbound Palmland *near Savannah, Ga., on Independence Day 1948. The train has about five head-end cars and eight passenger cars. Early the next day, the train's west and east coast sections will be pulling into St. Petersburg and Miami, respectively. (R.D. Sharpless photo)*

After the war, Seaboard offered a full diner only over the Raleigh-Jacksonville portion of the *Palmland's* route. SAL changed the train's service again in December 1953 by placing two coach-grill cars on the Hamlet-Jacksonville segment and further shortening the dining car's run to Raleigh-Hamlet. The new coach-grill cars primarily served lunch sandwiches and other light fare; the full diner continued to offer complete breakfast and dinner service during the two-hour morning (southbound) and evening (northbound) trip between Raleigh and Hamlet. The diner also provided full service to Pullman passengers traveling to and from Southern Pines and Hamlet.

The coach-grill cars (Nos. 849 and 858) seated eight in booths and seven at the counter in the grill section, with 18 spacious coach seats in the balance of the car. They were rebuilt from full coaches that came in a group Seaboard purchased from the Chesapeake & Ohio in 1949 and 1950 and numbered 840-859. The railroad's full dining cars came from two series, Nos. 1007-1009 built in 1922 and 1924 and Nos. 225-243 built in 1925-26. All featured a spacious 36-seat arrangement and large picture windows. The 225-series cars were bought for the *Orange Blossom Special* and carried names of Florida lakes on their sides up until about 1950.

For its coach patrons, the *Palmland* drew from the railroad's substantial fleet of rebuilt heavyweight coaches. They included most of the 807-826 series built by ACF in 1926 plus a good many cars from the 571-598 series built by Pressed Steel Car between 1913 and 1915. The railroad improved other coaches in the 500 and 800 series as well, and by the late 1950s had about 30 updated heavyweights to draw from (including ten of the 800s painted gray for overflow use in the Silver Fleet).

The ex-Chesapeake & Ohio coaches purchased in 1949-50 provided another pool of standard coaches for Seaboard's conventional through trains. C&O had just refurbished these 20 relatively modern "Imperial Salon" cars, many of them with the famed Heywood-Wakefield "Sleepy Hollow" reclining seats. Four cars even had two-one seating, providing spacious accommodations for just 45 passengers – more spacious, in fact, than any of SAL's lightweights. Seaboard's American Flyer semi-lightweight cars also saw *Palmland* service, especially in later years when they were common on the Wildwood-Tampa section.

The *Sunland* – and Predecessors

Seaboard's other through conventional train on the east coast mainline was the *Sun Queen*, Nos. 7-8. Its schedule was roughly the mirror image of the *Palmland's*, with one-night-out, New York-Florida timings in both directions. Southbound, the *Sun Queen* left New York City in the morning and got to Tampa the next afternoon and to Miami at dinnertime. Northbound, a morning departure from Miami or after-lunch departure from Tampa put passengers into New York the next evening. This schedule was a bit faster than the *Palmland's*, with New York-Miami running time about 33 hours each way.

The *Sun Queen's* makeup was similar to the *Palmland's* but with a different mix of sleepers. The train carried only one New York-Miami and one New York-Tampa sleeper after World War II. The *Sun Queen* also forwarded through cars received from Seaboard's Portsmouth connecting train, including cars to both Florida and Atlanta. The latter cars made only a short trip to Hamlet, where they were handed over to the *Silver Comet*. The *Sun Queen* also imitated the *Palmland* by serving as a local on the daylight portion of its run, in this case the territory south of Jacksonville. Both the *Sun Queen's* Miami section and west coast section (Nos. 107-108, which split off at Wildwood) ran as slow-paced, all-stops locals within the Sunshine State.

The *Sun Queen* began undergoing a number of changes not long after the war. Effective with the May 18, 1947, timetable, the train was renamed the *Camellia*. Seaboard proclaimed the *Camellia* a "new" train, and in fact it did receive diesel power over its entire route (rather than just to Wildwood), a Washington-Miami 10 Sec-lounge car, and a couple of the new lightweight coaches just delivered from Budd. The train's west coast Pullman was also changed to a New York-Venice car. However, with the December 1947 timetable change, the train largely reverted to its former self; diesels again operated only to Wildwood, and the upgraded equipment was moved to other trains like the *Orange Blossom Special* and the new *Silver Star*.

The *Camellia's* lounge service and partial lightweight consist returned for the summer of 1948. One of the lightweight coaches traveled only a short distance, the Portsmouth-Atlanta car for the *Silver Comet*, which the *Camellia* handled from Norlina to Hamlet.

One More Name and Other Changes

Effective with the winter 1948-49 season, Trains 7-8's name was changed for the fourth and final time, to the *Sunland*. The new name also brought with it a change in the train's off-season operating pattern. Starting in 1949, the train began running only to the west coast south of Jacksonville each summer. Passengers wishing to go to Miami were advised to transfer to the *Silver Meteor*, which offered a close connection. The Portsmouth-Miami sleeper was cut back to Jacksonville; however, the west coast section continued to provide through coaches and a Pullman to Tampa, although only from Washington.

The *Sunland's* Miami section returned for the winter season of 1949-50, with a

through New York-Miami coach and 10-1-2 sleeper back in service again. In addition, a Detroit-Jacksonville-Tampa sleeper was added later in the season. After this season, all the *Sunland's* cars (both east and west coast) originated at Washington year-round; the *Palmland* now had the New York conventional service to itself. Dining service had also been modified by the summer of 1950 to a full diner from Washington to Hamlet and a parlor-diner between Jacksonville and Wildwood or Miami. In an unusual example of expanded service, the Portsmouth through sleeper was operated beyond Jacksonville to Tampa. But overall, Seaboard continued to trim back the *Sunland's* Pullman offerings, and after the winter of 1952-53, the train offered no Pullman service south of Jacksonville.

Seaboard's November 1953 introduction of the *Tidewater* brought further changes to the *Sunland*. The *Sunland* gained a new through Portsmouth-Jacksonville coach to accompany its traditional Portsmouth-Jacksonville Pullman, although the *Sunland* only carried the cars southbound. But these gains were offset by loss of the *Sunland's* only other sleeper, the Washington-Jacksonville car, and of its full diner. Instead, Seaboard added parlor-dining service between Savannah and Jacksonville.

Seaboard had two parlor-diner cars in the postwar years, 1021 and 1050, which had parlor space plus 24 and 18 dining seats respectively. Like the two grill-coaches for the *Palmland*, Seaboard employed the

A large crowd of passengers is ready to board Seaboard No. 10, the northbound Palmland, *as it pulls into the Columbia, S.C., station on June 30, 1951. E7 3020 and a second E unit lead the long train of heavyweight equipment. Secondary trains like the* Palmland *were heavily patronized by African-American passengers, who at the time had separate coaches assigned to them. (Oscar W. Kimsey Jr. photo)*

cars on medium-length runs with moderate dining service needs. The railroad's diagram books also indicate that the 1007-1009 series diners were sometimes used as diner-lounges. Seaboard tried several other food service variations for the *Sunland*, but the railroad felt that costs remained too high and ended all food service on the train after the winter of 1957-58.

In early May 1956, the *Sunland* received lightweight sleepers for the first time. Both the Portsmouth-Atlanta and the Portsmouth-Jacksonville sleeper lines were upgraded for the summer, the first to one of Seaboard's new 4-1-5-4 cars and the second to a 10-6. Although heavyweight cars returned each winter, the lightweights came back in summer; they became year-round equipment effective with the summer of 1958.

After the winter 1957-58 season, the *Sunland's* stature in Seaboard's passenger lineup faded considerably. The southbound train was eliminated between Washington and Hamlet, and its Washington-Jacksonville coach was transferred to the *Silver Comet* as far as Hamlet. The northbound half remained between Hamlet and Washington, but that train – still numbered 8 and called the *Sunland* – replaced what had been the northern portion of Passenger, Mail and Express No. 6 from Birmingham and Atlanta. In sum, the changes essentially transformed the *Sunland* into a Hamlet-Florida train. The train retained its pattern of running year-round to Tampa but to Miami only in the winter.

The *Tidewater*

Seaboard's 116-mile line between Norlina, N.C., and Portsmouth, Va., was the original component of the Seaboard Air Line system and remained a significant secondary mainline route throughout the SAL's existence – owing in part to the presence of the railroad's headquarters (until 1958) and passenger car shops at Portsmouth. Seaboard's passenger station, which also housed some of its corporate offices, was located at High and Water Streets on the banks of the Elizabeth River. Passengers could take a 15- to 20-minute ferry trip across the river to Norfolk. In mid-1955, bus service via a new highway tunnel replaced the ferry but doubled the scheduled Norfolk-Portsmouth transit time.

Seaboard's postwar service on the line consisted of Nos. 13-14, which were discontinued October 1, 1950, and Nos. 17-18. Train 17 left Portsmouth at 4:30 p.m. and arrived at Norlina at 7:45 p.m., where it connected with the southbound *Sunland*. The train featured a dining car and several through cars that the *Sunland* forwarded south (including a Florida sleeper the *Sunland* kept in its train plus Atlanta cars for the *Silver Comet*). Northbound No. 18 connected with the northbound *Sunland*, and left Norlina at 9:00 a.m. and got to Portsmouth at 12:25 p.m.

On November 1, 1953, the Portsmouth service was upgraded to improve overnight Pullman and coach service between Portsmouth and Jacksonville and provide better coordination with the *Silver Comet*. The formerly anonymous Nos. 17-18 were given a name, the *Tidewater*, and the northbound schedule moved about four hours earlier to provide an early morning arrival in Portsmouth rather than after lunch.

The schedule change resulted in a close connection with the northbound *Silver Comet* and avoided the fairly long layover that the *Comet's* Atlanta-Portsmouth coach and sleeper formerly had to endure. The change also sped up the Jacksonville-Portsmouth sleeper and coach. The *Sunland's* northbound Jacksonville-Hamlet schedule no longer fit the timings Seaboard wanted for the new service, so for this portion of the route the two through cars were transferred to winter-only mail and express train No. 16, then to the *Silver Star* the rest of the year. The northbound *Cotton Blossom* from Atlanta then forwarded the cars from Hamlet to Norlina. The *Tidewater's*

Seaboard class F-7 0-6-0 switcher No. 1129 is pulling a cut of passenger cars north from the Hamlet station (just visible in the left background) toward the yard on a hot August 7, 1950. The cars include coaches from the Pennsylvania and the Richmond, Fredericksburg & Potomac followed by a Pullman; the sleeper may be off the southbound Palmland, which carried several Pullmans that terminated at Hamlet. The heavyweight cars were typical of the foreign-line equipment that often ran on Seaboard's secondary passenger trains. The chunky switcher (Baldwin 1928), noted as one of the most efficient steam switch engines built, is moving past one of Seaboard's rare signal bridges. (Wally Johnson photo)

public timetable listings included the other trains' numbers and schedules north of Jacksonville.

Although the *Tidewater's* schedule was improved, the train continued to offer its predecessor's consist. A typical train carried head-end cars; a through coach and sleeper each for Atlanta and Jacksonville; and a dining car, normally from the 225-243 series. The *Silver Comet's* Atlanta coach was originally the only normally assigned lightweight car. The *Tidewater* gained additional lightweight cars as its through cars for the *Comet* and the *Sunland* were upgraded, such as the 4-1-5-4 Jacksonville sleeper added for a time in 1956. For the 1957-58 winter season the *Tidewater*, like the *Palmland*, carried a lightweight 12 Rmt-4 DB *Western*-series sleeper from the Union Pacific, Wabash, or Chicago & North Western.

Effective with the October 1957 timetable change, the *Tidewater* began operating past Norlina and took the mainline into Raleigh. Coupled with changes that cut the *Sunland* back to a Hamlet-Florida operation, the extension allowed the *Silver Comet* to pick up the Portsmouth-Atlanta cars in Raleigh. The *Comet* also forwarded the *Sunland's* Jacksonville cars to Hamlet, and the *Silver Star* brought the *Sunland's* Jacksonville cars from Hamlet to Raleigh.

Atlanta/Birmingham Trains

Passenger trains were always prominent on Seaboard's route to Atlanta and Birmingham. One of the railroad's earliest feature trains was the *Atlanta Special*, which ran between Washington and Atlanta in the 1890s. By the 1940s the line had two named trains, the *Cotton States Special* and the *Robert E. Lee*, each with through cars from New York and Washington to Birmingham. Both also connected there with St. Louis-San Francisco trains to Memphis.

The *Cotton States Special*, Nos. 17-18, was the flagship of the line, with an overnight schedule of more than 18 hours between Richmond and Birmingham. The train left Richmond in the evening and got to Birmingham at noon the next day; northbound, it left Birmingham in mid-afternoon and arrived in Richmond the next morning. The train carried a variety of New York and Washington sleeping cars, plus two between Portsmouth and Atlanta from the connecting Portsmouth-Norlina trains of the same numbers, as well as a diner. The *Silver Comet* replaced the *Cotton States Special* on May 18, 1947.

The *Robert E. Lee*, Nos. 5 and 6, took its name from the famous southern Civil War general. The train used most of a day and night between Richmond and Birmingham, leaving the Virginia capital just after midnight and getting to Birmingham the next evening. The northbound trip left Birmingham at 7:50 a.m. and got to Richmond at 6:30 the next morning. In 1946 the train carried a dining car and a Washington-Birmingham sleeper and coach. The train made many stops, and served essentially as a daytime local along much of the route. After the *Silver Comet* was inaugurated, the *Robert E. Lee* acquired a new name, the *Cotton Blossom*.

The *Cotton Blossom's* Many Changes

Along with the new name came a series of additional changes. In December 1948, the *Cotton Blossom's* schedule was revised to connect with the *Palmland* at Hamlet and pick up a New York-Atlanta sleeper from that train. But while the Pullman was handed off without delay, the rest of the *Cotton Blossom* arrived early southbound, or waited northbound, so it could meet winter-only Hamlet-Jacksonville locals Nos. 1-2 and exchange mail and express. The resulting layovers at Hamlet were hours long, but at least northbound coach passengers could transfer to the *Palmland* if they wished.

The December 1948 schedule change also saw the *Cotton Blossom* cut back to Atlanta. Its former service beyond to Birmingham was provided by a new separate train, Georgia Division Nos. 15-16, which continued running on the *Blossom's* old schedule – no doubt due to a mail contract – but which now

In late 1953, Seaboard selected coaches 849 and 858 from its ex-C&O 840-859 series and rebuilt them as coach-grill cars for Hamlet-Jacksonville service on the Palmland. Seaboard blanked out several windows on the grill counter side of the cars with this resulting appearance. No. 849 shows the cars' original Roman lettering at Hamlet on December 17, 1958. (Bob's Photo collection)

missed connecting with the *Cotton Blossom* in both directions. Train 15 left for Birmingham nearly an hour before the southbound *Blossom* got to Atlanta, and No. 16 arrived at Atlanta from Birmingham over three hours after No. 6 had left for points north.

Interestingly, photographs and personal recollections confirm that one of Seaboard's parlor-diners regularly ran on Nos. 15-16 and offered light meal service, despite "coach only" listings in the timetables. The *Cotton Blossom* had always offered dining car service all the way to Birmingham, and evidently SAL chose to maintain a degree of food service on the run.

Further change came to the *Cotton Blossom* with the June 1949 timetable, when the train became a coach-only Hamlet-Atlanta train. But in December,

"White" and "Colored"

Segregation of passengers by race was an established practice on all trains in the South, but was most easily seen on secondary and local trains. Many African-American passengers had low incomes and lacked automobiles, and so depended heavily on these conventional trains for much of their travel. They most often had to use the non-reserved-seat coaches and daylight, all-stops schedules that typified these less glamorous entries in the railroads' timetables.

All forms of public segregation had come under increasing attack since World War II. The best-known landmark in the years-long effort was the 1954 Supreme Court decision that outlawed "separate but equal" public education, but there were many other steps along the way. The ruling that most affected railroads was a December 1955 Interstate Commerce Commission decision prohibiting segregation of interstate passengers on trains and buses. The ICC directive put a legal end to a number of long-standing patterns of separate seating and service aboard passenger trains and in stations. The practices included separate cars, or divided areas within the same car, for seating blacks and whites and the use of curtains in dining cars to wall off areas where black passengers were being served.

Not all states complied with the ban, and the separate seating practices did not immediately end. Further, the ICC ruling did not apply to intrastate passengers, so many local trains were free to continue separate seating for those riders. The U.S. government began stepping up enforcement of the interstate ban in the early 1960s, but it was not until passage of the 1964 Civil Rights Act that all segregation on passenger trains was completely outlawed.

On streamliners, the first car was normally a combine whose passenger seats were set aside for African-Americans. After World War II, black patronage on these trains increased to the point where one or more full coaches were often needed for their use. In the late 1940s, both the *Silver Star* and *Silver Meteor* normally had a full coach between the combine and Pullmans for black passengers; the "white" coaches ran at the rear of the train. The Pennsylvania Railroad grew increasingly unwilling to abide by its southern connections' wishes to seat blacks separately on trains leaving New York, and the southern railroads often complained about the PRR's lack of cooperation and the awkward reseating that ensued at Washington when the trains left Pennsylvania rails. Seaboard converted three of its lightweight combine cars to baggage-dormitory cars in 1957, probably because it decided to stop using the combines' coach seats for black passengers in the wake of the 1955 ICC ruling.

Conventional trains carried the bulk of black patrons and often had one or more full coaches assigned for their use – although the cars were sometimes those without reclining seats or air conditioning. Local trains typically had two coaches, one for each race, or a combine for blacks and a full coach for whites. Separation was more easily achieved on sleeping cars for those black passengers who rode Pullmans, since they were already divided into rooms and sections.

In common with other southern lines, Seaboard had many coaches and combines with divided compartments that could be used as segregated cars. The cars had a full partition that walled off about a third to half the car, with a standard door for passage. When used to separate the races, the compartments were labeled "White" or "Colored" with a moveable sign. At other times, the smaller compartment was set aside for smoking, and was so labeled in the railroad's diagram books. Seaboard rostered few center-baggage-section combines with passenger compartments on each end – the traditional "Jim Crow" configuration – and instead favored combines with adjacent partitioned passenger seating areas.

Seaboard again operated the train all the way to Richmond and moved back its northbound departure from Atlanta to allow a connection with No. 16 from Birmingham. After a few more adjustments, in April 1951 the *Cotton Blossom* reverted to its original schedule to and from Atlanta and again became a through train to Birmingham – complete with a through Washington-Birmingham coach. With no further need for separate trains between Atlanta and Birmingham, Nos. 15-16 were discontinued.

Even though the *Cotton Blossom* carried the *Tidewater's* Jacksonville-Portsmouth sleeper for a few winter seasons after the *Tidewater* began service, in general the *Cotton Blossom's* status continued to decline. Seaboard dropped the train's name after the winter 1954-55 season, describing it thereafter as "Passenger, Mail and Express" in the timetables. The train had in fact been making local stops for years on the daylight portions of its runs; its schedules essentially mirrored those of the line's nighttime Hamlet-Atlanta locals, Nos. 11-12 (later changed to 3-4).

The *Gulf Wind* and Other Tallahassee Line Trains

Seaboard's Jacksonville-Tallahassee-Chattahoochee line connected with the Louisville & Nashville at Chattahoochee (River Junction), 43 miles west of Tallahassee. The L&N route continued to Pensacola, then turned north to Flomaton, Ala., where it connected with the L&N's Montgomery-Mobile-New Orleans main. The SAL-L&N route formed a 613-miles through east-west Jacksonville-New Orleans line, and passengers could connect at New Orleans with trains to points as far west as California.

This route was home to Trains 36-37, the *New Orleans-Florida Limited*, and Nos. 38-39, the *Seaboard Mail and Express*. Despite the latter's prosaic name, both trains carried a diner and New Orleans-Jacksonville sleepers in addition to Jacksonville-Flomaton coaches. The *Limited* boasted a New Orleans-Jacksonville-Miami sleeper as well. In the April 1948 timetable change, the *Seaboard Mail and Express* had been renamed the *New Orleans-Florida Express*. Nos. 36-37 took about six hours on their daylight runs, while Nos. 38-39 had somewhat longer nighttime runs. The leisurely, steam-powered trains rated only a small listing near the back of Seaboard's timetables, a sharp contrast to all the attention and improvements showered on the Silver Fleet and other north-south trains.

That all changed on July 31, 1949, when Seaboard and Louisville & Nashville jointly announced a new diesel-powered Jacksonville-New Orleans train, the *Gulf Wind*. The train replaced the *New Orleans-Flor-* *ida Express* in the timetable and assumed that train's numbers and overnight run. However, the *Wind's* schedule was much faster, shaving the Jacksonville-Chattahoochee run from about 6½ to 4½ hours and getting to New Orleans in 15½ hours instead of almost 21. The *Gulf Wind's* diesel – usually a single E7 – was partly responsible, but the train also eliminated many stops from the former schedule. The *Wind* stopped in Florida only at Lake City, Live Oak, Madison, Tallahassee, Quincy, and Chattahoochee.

The new timings had the westbound *Wind*, No. 39, leaving Jacksonville at 4:55 p.m. and arriving New Orleans at 7:20 Central time the next morning; returning, the No. 38 left New Orleans at 5:00 p.m. and got to Jacksonville at 9:00 a.m. The *Gulf Wind* was combined on the L&N between New Orleans and Flomaton with the *Piedmont Limited*, a New Orleans-New York train operated jointly with the West Point Route and Southern Railway.

The *Gulf Wind's* arrival also marked the simultaneous transformation of Nos. 36-37 into a nameless Passenger, Mail and Express run; the sleeper and diner were unceremoniously removed, leaving it coach-only. Trains 36-37 kept their all-stops schedule across the Florida Panhandle and continued to meet a connecting L&N train to Flomaton at Chattahoochee.

Although the *Gulf Wind's* equipment remained all-heavyweight, the train received some upgraded cars. The consist featured bedroom sleepers on the route for the first time, 6 Sec-6 DB cars. A 10 Sec-lounge car, a diner (between Jacksonville and Tallahassee), and reclining seat coaches rounded out the train. However, the *Gulf Wind* did have an entirely new look: all its cars, including those contributed by SAL, were painted in L&N's deep blue with gold lettering and striping. Seaboard cars painted in the L&N scheme included two SAL 6-6 sleepers, *Poplar Road* and *Poplar Springs*, and an American Flyer semi-streamlined combine. One or more Seaboard coaches also no doubt received the new scheme.

It appears that the 10 Sec-lounge cars were normally of L&N or Pullman ownership; Seaboard had cars of that plan as well, but they were kept busy running on the *Silver Star* and *Silver Comet*. Effective with the winter 1951-52 season, the *Gulf Wind* added a third sleeping car during the winters, a 6 Sec-4 Rmt-4 DB car from the Pullman-owned *Fir* series; these cars evidently did not receive the blue L&N colors. However, in May 1953, blue cars did replace the *Fir* sleepers – new L&N lightweight, *Pine*-series 6 Rmt-4 DB-6 Sec Pullmans. The change gave the train its first regularly assigned lightweight car.

53

Effective with the September 1954 timetable change, the *Gulf Wind* received another upgrade, by far its most eye-catching: lightweight, stainless steel 5 DB-buffet-lounge observation cars from the Louisville & Nashville, the *Royal Canal* and *Royal Street*. The cars were properly pointed on the train's rear with an illuminated tail sign, suddenly giving a classy ending to the mostly heavyweight consist. The *Royal* cars, which bumped the 10 Sec-buffet-lounges, migrated to the *Wind* from the New York-New Orleans *Crescent*. They were part of that train's 1950 re-equipping, but became available when L&N withdrew them from the *Crescent's* equipment pool.

While the *Royal* cars were worthy of the Silver Fleet, many of the *Gulf Wind's* cars remained heavyweight, such as the 6-6 Pullmans that continued to run most of the year. For the winter season 1957-58, the 6-6s were replaced by a 12 Rmt-1 SB-4 DB car, drawn from the Pullman-owned *Oak* series. Like the *Fir* series, they were among the cars Pullman had rebuilt with mostly (or all) room accommodations and which continued to see frequent service into the late 1950s and meet overflow needs into the early 1960s.

However, the 12-1-4s lasted only until January 1958 and then were discontinued. They were the last heavyweight sleepers assigned to the *Gulf Wind* and the last time a third Pullman was in the consist. By this time L&N and Seaboard had also ended the practice of an all-blue consist, and SAL's cars in the scheme were repainted into their normal colors.

An interesting *Gulf Wind* footnote is that Seaboard advised eastbound passengers who wanted to connect for south Florida via the *Silver Meteor* to detrain at Baldwin and catch the *Meteor* there. The connection was too close in Jacksonville, and travelers might well miss the *Meteor* if they chose to make the change there. Baldwin was not listed as a stop for either train, but as in the case of the wintertime *Silver Star's* unpublished stops there, a number of long-distance passengers did make use of the small station.

The *Florida Sunbeam*

Although rail passenger travel to Florida was always heaviest from the Northeast, there was a significant volume from the Midwest as well. The majority of trains from the region – primarily Chicago, plus such cities as St. Louis, Detroit, and Cincinnati – used the Illinois Central and Louisville & Nashville to gateways in Alabama and Georgia, where in almost every case the Atlantic Coast Line (sometimes via the Central of Georgia) completed the trains' trips into Florida. A few Midwestern trains used the Southern Railway, including the *Royal Palm*, *Ponce de Leon*, and *Kansas City-Florida Special*; some used SR trackage all the way to Jacksonville while others went as far as Jesup, Ga., or Hardeeville, S.C., and from there used ACL trackage rights into Jacksonville.

There was one other Midwest-Florida route, and the only one that included the Seaboard Air Line. In the 1920s, Seaboard operated the seasonal *Suwanee River Special* to Tampa and St. Petersburg in cooperation with the New York Central and the Southern, with through cars from Chicago, Detroit, and Cleveland via NYC to Cincinnati, where SR took over for the trip to Atlanta. Southern continued pulling the train south to Valdosta, Ga. (over subsidiary Georgia Southern & Florida), and then to the Florida village of Hampton. Hampton was 32 miles south of Baldwin and was the point where the GS&F Valdosta-Palatka line crossed the Seaboard's Baldwin-Wildwood-Tampa line. There the train was handed off to the SAL, which finished the train's journey to Florida's west coast. But with the onset of the Great Depression, the train disappeared from the timetables.

Several new Midwest-Florida trains began to appear as the Depression eased. One of these again plied the SR-SAL "Hampton Route," the winter-season *Florida Sunbeam*. The *Sunbeam* made its first run January 1, 1936, and was similar to the old *Suwanee River Special* (including a two-nights-out, 36-hour schedule). However, the train now had cars to both Miami and the west coast and operated in separate sections to each coast. While the *Florida Sunbeam* name was new to Midwest-Florida service, Seaboard had briefly used it before, during the 1930-31 winter season for a Boston-Miami train.

Like many other seasonal, Pullman-heavy trains, the *Florida Sunbeam* was suspended during World War II so that its equipment could be released for essential wartime travel. The *Sunbeam* returned in the 1946-47 winter season as a Miami-only train. Similar to its pre-war timings, the train arrived southbound at Hampton in the middle of the night, leaving there at 3:30 a.m. and getting to Miami at 11:20 later that morning. Northbound, the train left Miami at 6:30 p.m. and got to Hampton at 2:45 a.m. Its largely nocturnal journey helps explain why no photos of the *Sunbeam* on Seaboard rails have ever surfaced.

The *Florida Sunbeam* operated for only two additional seasons and made its last run on April 30, 1949. The train lasted long enough to rate diesel power over the Southern, and likely had diesels over the SAL as well, at least in its last season or two. Its equipment remained heavyweight to the end, with ten regularly assigned sleepers in a variety of accommodations. One photo of the *Sunbeam* on Southern rails shows a Seaboard American Flyer coach, confirming that SAL participated in the equipment pool.

Patrons get ready to order a light meal in one of the rebuilt coach-grill cars. Those in the scene are identified as (from left) Melvin Thompson, attendant, and passengers Walter Gable, Grace Robinson, E.W. Burroughs Jr., and Margaret Clark at the counter. The grill cars' coach seating area was rebuilt into a spacious two-one arrangement. (SAL photos, TLC Collection)

Seaboard 598 was among the railroad's heavyweight coaches rebuilt with reclining seats and air conditioning starting in the late 1930s. A few cars, like this one, even received silver-gray paint and black lettering for use as extra equipment on lightweight trains. No. 598 is a partitioned car with 68 seats and was at Washington, D.C., on May 28, 1949. Built by Pressed Steel Car in 1915, it was one of Seaboard's oldest cars operating in the postwar period. (George Votava photo, ACL & SAL HS collection)

Coach 808 was one of seven cars modernized in 1953-54 with wide windows, enlarged bathrooms, 48 spacious reclining seats, roller bearings, and other upgrades for use on Seaboard's best trains. The silver-gray car was standing at Hamlet on November 17, 1958. (Bob's Photo collection)

Seaboard 48-seat diner 225 is all elegance and tradition in this 1959 portrait at Hamlet. The 1925 Pullman product was one of a dozen cars delivered that year for the Orange Blossom Special, and once carried the name Lake Istokpoga. SAL heavyweight diners kept their names until about 1950. No. 225 still has Roman-style lettering; Seaboard heavyweight cars began receiving the "streamliner" font lettering in 1956. (George Votava photo, ACL & SAL HS collection)

Lake Borgne, a 10 Sec-1 DR-2 Cpt car, was typical of Seaboard's roster of heavyweight sleepers purchased from the Pullman Company at the end of 1948. The Pullman green scheme was applied to cars that had mostly section accommodations; Seaboard's 11 cars like this one were common on many Seaboard trains. (T.S. Martorano collection)

This July 5, 1946, scene at Tampa shows what is probably the west coast section of the Sun Queen; the train was diesel-powered only to Wildwood at the time. P2 class Pacific No. 826 is in charge of the train, which carried through coaches and Pullmans to St. Petersburg. (Tony Kozla photo, Larry Goolsby collection)

This action scene shows Train 108 racing northward at Rawlings, Va., one morning not long after the end of World War II. The photograph is undated, so the train could be the Sun Queen if taken prior to August 1947; the Camellia between then and December 1948; or the Sunland afterward. The frequently renamed train carried coaches and several sleepers for both Florida coasts. (Wiley M. Bryan photo, TLC Collection)

Seaboard E4 3008 and a B unit are making 70 m.p.h. with Train 8, the northbound Camellia, just out of Hialeah, Fla., on September 13, 1947. The Camellia was advertised as a "new" train in the August 1947 timetable, but was essentially the renamed Sun Queen. However, the train was briefly assigned some of Seaboard's lightweight coaches made available by the 1947 equipment deliveries and the operation of only a single Silver Meteor after the winter season was over. Two streamlined cars are visible toward the rear of the train along with heavy-weight sleepers, a diner, and others including one of the railroad's unusual RPO-coaches. (David W. Salter photo)

The Sunland, the final name for Seaboard's one-night-out conventional train on the east coast route, moves south near Maxwell, Fla., on March 26, 1949 at 9:39 a.m. E7 3043 leads mate 3039 and a third E7 with 13 cars, including five head-end cars (including a baggage-RPO with a 15-foot mail compartment), two combines, and seven passenger cars. Note the train's left-hand running, Seaboard's practice on the double track south of Baldwin that kept northbound passenger trains away from the frequently blocked east mainline adjacent to Baldwin's busy yard trackage. (David W. Salter photo, TLC Collection)

What is likely the southbound Sunland makes it evening stop at Richmond on October 17, 1952. E7 3018 and a second unit have about 12 cars behind them. The train's schedule called for departure from Washington at 3:15 p.m. and from Richmond at 6:15. The elegant station building has been refurbished and is used by Amtrak today, but Interstate 95's bridges now make this panoramic view impossible. (William E. Griffin Jr. collection)

Seaboard's Portsmouth combination office building and station was located at the southeast corner of Hight and Water Streets. This July 4, 1958, view shows the building's north side; the station tracks and platforms are behind it. The accounting departments were housed here, while the railroad's executive offices were in a separate building across the river in Norfolk. The distinctive 1894 building still stands today. (Portsmouth Public Library photo, William E. Griffin Jr. collection)

The Tidewater's immediate predecessors were nameless Trains 17-18. In this April 1951 scene, northbound No. 18 is at Kilby, Va., just west of Suffolk. E7 3030 and a second E unit lead eight cars, including (third from end) the lightweight Atlanta-Portsmouth coach off the Silver Comet. No. 3030 was common power on the run for many years. At left is the interchange track with the Norfolk & Western, which crossed over the Seaboard here. (David W. Salter photo)

The Tidewater's *inaugural on November 1, 1953, was the occasion for these publicity photos.*

Seaboard, Portsmouth, and Norfolk officials gather before E8 3050 with a Seaboard office car in the background. According to the caption, J.R. Getty, SAL's General Passenger Traffic Manager, is sixth from left, and Emory F. Waldrop Jr., his assistant, is eighth. The baskets contain peaches from Georgia; several of the Tidewater's cars went through to Atlanta.

The dignitaries enjoy a good Seaboard meal in dining car 226; the 225-243 series cars were regulars on the run. Getty is pictured at right front, with Waldrop behind him. (SAL photos, ACL & SAL HS collection)

Kilby is again the locale as E8 3049 brings the Tidewater northbound on September 6, 1958. The train carried several lightweight cars by this date, but according to Seaboard timetables, the sleeper should have been a heavyweight Pullman-owned car from the Fir series – perhaps the fourth car back. Note the Atlantic Coast Line box express car behind the engine, an unusual example of ACL passenger equipment on SAL rails before the merger. (William H. Todd collection)

Early on a summer 1940 morning, the southbound Cotton States Special *approaches Atlanta's Terminal Station over Southern Railway trackage. Diesels released from their winter-season duties on the Orange Blossom Special, led by E4 class unit 3000, power the train past Bellwood Tower. The tower marked the junction of the Atlanta, Birmingham & Coast with the SR/Nashville, Chattanooga & St. Louis "railroad gulch" route to Union Station. (Hugh M. Comer photo, Frank E. Ardrey Jr. collection)*

Train 18, the northbound Cotton States Special, *makes its smoky departure from Birmingham's Terminal Station at 3:00 p.m. on October 26, 1946, behind M2 260. The train is pulling a through sleeper and coaches plus a diner, and will pick up additional cars in Atlanta. The green and white Southern E unit at left will shortly leave with the Southerner. (Frank E. Ardrey Jr. photo)*

Seaboard's Emory station in northeast Atlanta served Emory University and let passengers in the area avoid going downtown to Terminal Station. The northbound Robert E. Lee, *No. 6, is slowing for its 2:15 p.m. flag stop on this summer afternoon in 1940. E4 3009 was an example of the diesels that often powered Atlanta-line passenger trains in the pre-war summer seasons. (Hugh M. Comer photo)*

The *Robert E. Lee* has stopped at Cedartown, Ga., on its eastbound (northbound by timetable) run between Birmingham and Atlanta. The M class 4-8-2s, like No. 209 in this April 1947 scene, were common steam power on the train in the early postwar years. (J.E. Jones photo)

Running south of Greenwood, S.C., E7 3020 and a B unit move the southbound *Robert E. Lee's* nine cars on March 16, 1947. Diesels were becoming common on the train by this date, especially in the summer season, but only as far as Atlanta. The silver-gray baggage-RPO was painted to match lightweight cars and has strayed from its normal assignment on one of the Silver Fleet trains. Note the well-manicured ballast and the cleared right-of-way; railroads kept a wide area free of underbrush to minimize fire danger from steam locomotive sparks. (Hugh M. Comer photo)

Steam at 70 per! Dramatic steam locomotive action shots like this one were becoming increasingly rare by the time photographer Salter caught the southbound Cotton Blossom, No. 5, east of Winder, Ga., on January 11, 1948. The nine-car train still boasted a dining car and a Washington-Birmingham sleeper. (David W. Salter photo)

Seaboard E7 3040, delivered just seven months earlier, rolls through Weems, Ala., on September 5, 1948, with the northbound Cotton Blossom. The short but classy train sports two express cars, a baggage-RPO, an American Flyer combine, and – bringing up the rear – one of Seaboard's parlor-dining cars (probably No. 1050) ready to serve breakfast. The Birmingham train has just lost its 12-1 sleeper, which now terminates at Atlanta, but still offers food service between Birmingham and Hamlet. (Frank E. Ardrey Jr. photo)

Another edition of the late-1940s Cotton Blossom is near Atlanta on November 27, 1949. The train features a single E6 unit, No. 3016; a 16000-series box express car immediately behind; a silver-gray baggage-RPO; and what is likely a parlor-diner on the end. (Hugh M. Comer photo, Frank E. Ardrey Jr. collection)

M2 Pacific 239 has paused at Athens, Ga., on its way to Atlanta with the Cotton Blossom on January 7, 1950. Photographer Salter notes that modernized M2s like No. 239 were never used on the Georgia Division until near the end of steam. In the pre-diesel 1930s, the huge engines could be found on the Orange Blossom Special and other SAL flagship trains. The tracks below belong to Southern's Lula-Athens branch. (David W. Salter photo)

Northbound No. 6 is leaving Birmingham (at 41st Street) on Independence Day 1950. E7 3020 is pulling a Frisco wood refrigerator-express, a baggage-RPO, a baggage-express car, a combine, and what appears to be parlor-diner 1050. The photographer's 1949 Mercury is at the left. (Frank E. Ardrey Jr. photo)

This February 19, 1949, view shows the New Orleans-Florida Limited, *Train 37*, between Jacksonville and New Orleans. Powered today by M1 216, the nine-car train is westbound at Olustee, between Baldwin and Lake City, and is carrying a nice selection of head-end cars, coaches, sleepers, and a dining car. A little over five months later Seaboard inaugurated the Gulf Wind on the route, replacing the Limited's *similar nighttime companion train, the* New Orleans-Florida Express. (William J. Husa Jr. photo, ACL & SAL HS collection)

Photos of the Gulf Wind *in its early years are rare. This scene shows the westbound* Wind *arriving at Lake City, Fla., behind E7 3048 on June 25, 1951. The heavy-weight consist was normally all-L&N blue in the train's early years. Just visible to the right of the E unit's nose is an SAL steam locomotive in the siding; it has probably just filled its tender at the enormous wood coaling tower in the background. (Oscar W. Kimsey Jr. photo)

Between 1954 and 1965, the Gulf Wind was graced by one of the Louisville & Nashville's two 5 DB-buffet-lounge observations, Royal Street and Royal Canal, properly pointed on the end of the train and with an illuminated tail sign. This photo, taken at New Orleans, shows what is probably the Royal Street. (Larry Goolsby collection)

This action scene shows the Gulf Wind's typical appearance during the middle years of its existence. E8 3057 is just east of Baldwin with the westbound Wind on April 16, 1964. Coming behind are the train's usual complement of head-end cars, a lightweight coach, a Seaboard heavyweight diner, an L&N Pine-series 6 Sec-4 DB-6 Rmt sleeper, and an L&N Royal-series observation bringing up the rear. (David W. Salter photo)

Southern Railway No. 6, the winter-season-only Florida Sunbeam, is passing Oakdale, Ga., just northwest of Atlanta near Austell en route to Cincinnati. The power is Ps4 1407, a sister to the preserved locomotive at the Smithsonian, and the date is February 23, 1941. The second car is a Seaboard American Flyer coach; SAL carried the train south of Hampton, Fla., and contributed to its consists. (W.T. Reid Jr. photo)

Seaboard's named trains shared the rails with a substantial fleet of other passenger trains that, while not famous or celebrated, had an essential place in the railroad's passenger operations. Some of them were nearly solid trains of through mail and express cars that earned substantial revenue for the railroad. In 1955, for example, gross passenger revenues were about $12 million, while gross mail and express revenues were more than $7.5 million. These "Passenger, Mail and Express" trains were sometimes 15 cars long or more, all head-end equipment except for a combine and perhaps a coach or two.

Seaboard's other nameless passenger trains were all-stops locals that plied secondary lines and branches and that were usually timed to connect with main-line trains. They ranged from a single motor car unit to a locomotive-hauled train with a few head-end cars and coaches. At the bottom of the passenger hierarchy were mixed trains, the term for freight locals with a passenger car (and perhaps express car), usually on the rear in place of the caboose. They had once been fairly common on short branchline runs, but Seaboard had eliminated most of the mixeds by the late 1940s.

Seaboard's small local trains brought in relatively little revenue, but they provided an essential public service for the many households across the rural South who for years either had no car or did not wish to brave the uncertainties of poorly maintained back roads. The trains also often stopped at every small depot to exchange mail and express, serving as a vital (and often only) means of moving these elements of daily commerce. But while Seaboard's through movements of mail and express remained strong throughout the railroad's existence, the short local runs and mixed trains could not survive the steady postwar advances in automobile ownership, better roads, and bus service. Many disappeared in the early 1950s, and all were gone by the decade's end.

Express Shipments

Most Passenger, Mail and Express trains (and a few locals) had one or more express cars manned by "messengers," the term for onboard Railway Express Agency employees who handled loading and unloading of local shipments along the way. These "working" express cars were accompanied by "sealed" cars that carried only through shipments and were not opened until their final destination.

Seaboard's express car movements could rival freight trains for the wide variety of their through routes and destinations. Just like some passenger-carrying cars, many express cars ran beyond Seaboard

Mainline locals 1 and 2 operated from Washington to Jacksonville through about mid-1947. On June 14, 1942, No. 1 has stopped at Columbia, S.C., behind 4-8-2 263, one of Seaboard's large M2 class engines, with seven cars. Two express cars, a full RPO, combine, and two coaches make up the regular consist, while a deadheading lightweight car brings up the rear – an observation-coach, according to photographer Votava's notes. The Seaboard buildings in the background, including the passenger station (tower above the RPO) and the freight station building at right, have been preserved, although the ex-SAL mainline has been relocated to the west. (George Votava photo, ACL & SAL HS collection)

rails over connecting carriers. Some even went directly to places no passenger could go without changing trains; for example, Seaboard express car routes in the mid-1940s included Boston-Atlanta, New York-Mobile, New York-Charlotte, and Portsmouth-Charlotte, and an Atlanta-Memphis car ran in the 1960s. None of these were through SAL coach or sleeper routes.

In a car movement from March 1962, Seaboard picked up a Railway Express Agency express refrigerator car from the Florida East Coast at Jacksonville; the car had originated at Goulds, a small town 20 miles south of Miami on the FEC's Florida City branch. The car likely went north via the *Sunland* over Seaboard and the Richmond, Fredericksburg & Potomac. The Pennsylvania then forwarded the car to New York City in its No. 170, the *Patriot*. From there, the car may have traveled over the New Haven, Boston & Maine, Central Vermont, and Canadian National for delivery to its final destination of Montreal, Canada. The car was probably carrying cut flowers and traveled nearly the entire length of the U.S. east coast and some 40 miles into Canada.

Other typical express shipments included such high-value, time-sensitive perishables as strawberries in refrigerator express cars. Seaboard also rostered horse express cars that ferried race horses to destinations like Camden (S.C.), Tampa, and Miami. But most express consisted of small packages for which shippers would pay premium rates to assure quick, guaranteed delivery. Other express car cargo included storage mail like newspapers and magazines.

The advent of intermodal shipments in the early 1960s brought another type of car to Seaboard's secondary passenger trains, piggyback flatcars and autoracks. These cars appeared on several trains and sometimes outnumbered passenger equipment cars. The time-sensitive intermodal cars brought in substantial additional revenue and helped to defray the increasing expenses of passenger train operation.

Seaboard had a large roster of express cars (nearly 175 in 1948) in both passenger, box, and refrigerator configurations. The cars could occasionally be employed for large shipments of passenger baggage, but personal baggage was normally carried in baggage-RPO, baggage-coach, and baggage-dormitory cars where the baggage space took up about a third to half the car.

Nearly all PM&E trains and locals had a full Railway Post Office car or baggage-RPO combine, which

A short version of local No. 4 is northbound at Apex, N.C., in 1953. E7 3034 leads three express cars, a combine, and a coach. Only Trains 3 and 4 stopped at the small town, located 14 miles south of Raleigh. (R.B. Carneal photo, Charles K. Marsh Jr. collection)

carried U.S. Post Office employees on board to accept and sort mail en route. They also handled the iconic tasks of snagging mail pouches from lineside stands and tossing out filled bags at locations where trains did not stop. Full RPO cars had a 60-foot mail compartment while baggage-RPOs had either a 15-foot or 30-foot section. Most rail motor cars also had a 15-foot compartment. The compartment's length was determined by the volume of mail on a given route. The Post Office strictly controlled car assignments and all other details of the mail operation, including car design specifications.

Railway Post Office cars almost always operated only on their home rails, but there were exceptions. Two on the Seaboard were Washington-Jacksonville, apparently regularly filled by a Seaboard car, and Jacksonville-Flomaton, which L&N cars covered on at least some occasions.

East Coast Mainline Locals

Seaboard's busiest route, the east coast mainline, saw local trains operating together with the line's many through passenger trains. Trains 1-2 and 3-4 were the traditional mainstays of local service between Richmond and Jacksonville. Their trips took the better part of 24 hours, and they ran roughly 12 hours opposite each other. Nos. 1 and 2 ran mostly at night north of Hamlet, making only the major stops, but paused at every station while in daylight south of Hamlet; Nos. 3-4's pattern was the opposite. Both trains also operated to Washington over the RF&P through the war years.

Seaboard began to change both trains' operating patterns after the war. Nos. 1-2 were reduced to winter-only operation and ran only south of Ham-

Train 3 has E7 3032 and an E8 for power with about ten cars on a May day in 1955. The train is at the south end of the Alberta, Va., passing siding, milepost 61. (Bob's Photo collection)

let. They continued serving as all-stops locals on the Hamlet-Jacksonville line, but for the rest of the year, the *Palmland* had to begin making the local stops on this segment. The trains connected with winter-season Jacksonville-St. Petersburg trains of the same numbers; the wintertime Florida versions of Nos. 1-2 doubled as the west coast section of the *Palmland*, but nevertheless retained their local schedules. The result was a very slow, 25-hour trip between Hamlet and St. Petersburg. The Florida train was cut back to Tampa in early 1951. The Florida Nos. 1-2 also operated in the summer, but only from Wildwood to Tampa. In the winter of 1952-53, the shortened Wildwood-Tampa run was made effective year-round.

After the winter of 1948-49, Nos. 3-4 also ceased running south of Hamlet except in winter, with the *Palmland* and *Sunland* able to handle all necessary head-end traffic during the other months. Even the winter runs were further trimmed effective with the 1949-50 season; Seaboard began operating just one pair of local trains between Hamlet and Jacksonville, southbound No. 3 and northbound No. 2; the former schedules of 1 and 4 were dropped. Further, No. 3 became a true express train with no scheduled stops at all between Hamlet and Jacksonville, and was not shown in the public timetables. To cover southbound local service, the southbound *Palmland* continued its summer pattern of making all stops on the route. However, No. 2 did appear in the public timetables with local stops and coach service, and the northbound *Palmland* made only its major stops as in previous winters. This service pattern continued for the winter seasons of 1951-52 and 1952-53.

The "New" No. 16

For the winter season of 1953-54, Seaboard again placed winter-only trains on the Hamlet-Jacksonville run but gave the northbound half of the pair a new role and identity. The former No. 2 was renumbered 16 and left Jacksonville on an earlier, but still overnight, schedule. The train was assigned to carry the through Jacksonville-Portsmouth coach and sleeper for the new *Tidewater*, which initiated a substantially earlier northbound schedule into Portsmouth. The *Sunland* had formerly carried the cars in both directions but now did so southbound only. No. 16 was now even listed in the public timetables as part of the *Tidewater's* schedule.

The southbound schedule for the Portsmouth-Jacksonville cars stayed the same, and so the *Sunland* could continue carrying them between Norlina and Jacksonville as it had in the past. However, Seaboard's public timetables listed only the northbound numbers in the *Tidewater's* summary listing, so that the winter timetable showed train numbers "16-6-18" – for northbound No. 16, the *Cotton Blossom,* and the *Tidewater* respectively. The southbound train numbers, including the *Sunland,* were not listed except in the detailed schedule columns, where a determined traveler could with some time and study interpret Seaboard's system for the train. No. 16's normal consist included the Portsmouth coach, the Portsmouth sleeper, a Hamlet baggage-coach combine, and various mail and express cars. The train left Jacksonville at 5:00 p.m., so photographs are extremely rare. The train's schedule was relatively fast, with scheduled stops only at Savannah and Columbia, getting it to

Hamlet at 12:20 a.m. – only an hour and 40 minutes longer than the *Silver Meteor* and far speedier than the *Palmland* or *Sunland*.

Southbound No. 3 remained hidden from public view. The train offered no public passenger accommodations, and its consist was all head-end equipment except for a baggage-coach rider car on the rear. The train's primary function appeared to be to carry express and sealed mail storage cars to Jacksonville that otherwise arrived on the *Silver Star* in the non-winter months, and of course, to return No. 16's power and combine to Jacksonville. No. 3's run was even more under cover of darkness than No. 16, leaving Hamlet about 8:00 p.m. and getting to Jacksonville around 4:00 a.m. No. 3 was renumbered to 15 about 1956 or 1957; this was, incidentally, at least the third time in the 1930s-1950s that SAL had used the numbers 15-16 for a passenger train.

With Nos. 3-16 no longer serving as winter-season Jacksonville-Hamlet locals, Seaboard simply continued the *Palmland* as a local south of Hamlet all year rather than summer-only. The train took about 10½ hours in both directions between Hamlet and Jacksonville. This pattern stayed essentially the same for the remaining Seaboard years.

The changes south of Hamlet meant that Trains 3 and 4 no longer had their former direct relationship with the Hamlet-Jacksonville locals, and the trains became primarily connections for their Atlanta-route counterparts, Nos. 11-12. The latter trains eventually (in December 1958) changed their numbers to 3 and 4 as well, confirming the Richmond-Hamlet trains' main role as a link in Washington-Atlanta service.

Another local operation on the east coast mainline that lasted into the 1930s was Trains 19 and 20 between Richmond and Raleigh, with a morning departure southbound and a late-evening return to Richmond. Rail motor cars covered this schedule in the 1930s, and the route was one of three to which Seaboard's streamlined ACF motorcars of 1935 were assigned. However, the railroad was not impressed with the cars' performance, and within a year the trains were back in the hands of the older motor cars and a trailer or two. Photos show rail cars 2002 and 2017 among the assigned older units in the later 1930s. The trains were discontinued in 1938.

At least one photo exists showing a solid mail and express train at Raleigh in 1942, southbound No. 45, with a baggage-coach combine visible on the rear. This train and,

presumably, a northbound counterpart appear to have run only during the war years.

Atlanta-Birmingham Trains

Seaboard's mainline from Hamlet to Atlanta and Birmingham hosted all-stops locals in addition to its named trains. The long-time mainstay of local service was Trains 11 and 12, which ran the 325 miles between Hamlet and Atlanta on a leisurely overnight schedule. The trains' primary business was their heavy interchange with mainline locals 3-4 at Hamlet.

Local service on the Atlanta-Birmingham segment was covered by Nos. 5-6 (the *Robert E. Lee*, later the *Cotton Blossom*), with nearly 20 full or flag stops along the way. Between 1948 and 1951, Nos. 15-16 took over this work because of changes in the *Cotton Blossom's* schedule during those years. The *Cotton Blossom's* nameless successor continued to provide Atlanta-Birmingham local service well into the 1960s.

One other local operation on the line that lasted into SAL's middle years was Nos. 29 and 30, which were "gas-electric motor trains" that ran in daylight between Atlanta and Monroe, N.C.; after 1938 the train was cut back to Abbeville, S.C., allowing a single set of equipment to cover the out-and-back run. The only known photo of this operation shows motor car 2023 pulling a single trailer coach. The train was discontinued near the end of 1940.

Railway Post Office cars were standard on nearly every local. No. 3's RPO is catching mail "on the fly" at Bracey, Va., in an undated photo. No. 153, a full-length RPO, is equipped with a moveable arm to snatch mailbags hung on the lineside crane stand. Many smaller stations provided mail service to their communities through this fast and efficient method. (Wiley M. Bryan photo, William E. Griffin Jr. collection)

Rutherfordton-Charlotte-Hamlet-Wilmington

Seaboard operated local train service over its east-west route that traversed most of the length of North Carolina between Rutherfordton, Charlotte, Hamlet, and Wilmington. In the 1940s, Nos. 13-14 ran between Wilmington and Charlotte and Nos. 21-22 between Hamlet and Rutherfordton, overlapping each other on the Hamlet-Charlotte portion of the route. They also shared the mainline between Hamlet and Monroe (junction of the Charlotte/Rutherfordton line) with three Hamlet-Atlanta/Birmingham trains. Train 13 left Wilmington in the late afternoon and took seven hours getting to Charlotte; it started back as No. 14 to Wilmington early the next morning and arrived at lunchtime. Train 21 left Hamlet at 8:30 in the morning and arrived in Rutherfordton six hours later. As No. 22, it quickly turned back and arrived at Hamlet that night.

The trains gained notice in 1936 when they became the first assignment for new rail motor cars 2027 and 2028. The pair apparently pulled the trains into the World War II years, with the exception of about a year in 1939-40 when No. 2028 went south to power the three-car Wildwood-St. Petersburg section of the *Silver Meteor*. Seaboard documents show the units had been shifted to the Hamlet-Savannah locals by November 1944, doubtless because Nos. 13-14 and 21-22 had grown to typical lengths of four to six cars by then – too many for the motor car units to handle. Concurrent timetables show that the Wilmington-Charlotte schedule had grown by an hour, further suggesting that the Wilmington-Rutherfordton trains had returned to steam power. Trains 21-22 were renumbered 19-20 in December 1946.

The Wilmington-Rutherfordton trains regained internal-combustion power in January 1948, when two of Seaboard's three Baldwin DR6-4-1500s were assigned to the pair of locals just after the distinctive locomotives arrived from the builder. By mid-1950, the two diesels had been shifted over to the Hamlet-Savannah locals and held down that assignment for a time before permanently joining the third Baldwin unit in Florida. Steam came back briefly, but photos show that E units were soon pulling the trains. Even Seaboard's most powerful model, 2250-h.p. E8s, often showed up on the short trains.

The Hamlet-Rutherfordton trains (Nos. 19-20) were discontinued on December 10, 1950, leaving only Charlotte-Wilmington Nos. 13-14. Effective with the December 1953 timetable change, the trains were combined with Hamlet-Atlanta locals 11 and 12 between Hamlet and Monroe, apparently altering Nos. 13-14's operations to two disconnected trains, Wilmington-Hamlet and Monroe-Charlotte. Anyone traveling through between Wilmington and Charlotte presumably had to change cars; it seems unlikely Seaboard would have taken the effort to switch a through coach into and out of mainline Trains 11-12 for what must have been only a few passengers.

Above: This handsome set of cars at Hamlet in May 1955, baggage-RPO 86 and baggage-coach combine 259, were used on Trains 3-4. The combine was from the class also often used on mixed trains. Like most older passenger-carrying cars, it had a divided compartment to facilitate segregation of the races. (A.C. Phelps photo, Charles K. Marsh Jr. collection)

Below: Express cars stenciled with a star symbol were equipped for "messengers," or Railway Express Agency employees who handled local loading and unloading en route. Seaboard 389's messenger looks out of the 1926 Pullman product as his train pauses at Providence, R.I., on the New Haven. Express cars often traveled far beyond their home lines. (Bob's Photo collection)

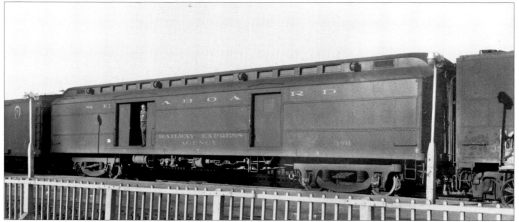

Diesel-electric rail car 2027 may have been placed on the Monroe-Charlotte leg; it and sister 2028 were available after their most recent assignment, the Savannah-Montgomery locals, ended in late 1951. However, No. 2027 was taken off the roster in 1956, so a boiler geep may have taken over in the later years. No. 2028 was assigned to the Hamlet-Charleston local in the mid-1950s, but that unit could have also been used on the Hamlet-Wilmington or Monroe-Charlotte run after the Charleston train was discontinued at the end of 1956.

Nos. 13-14 were discontinued about November 1958. The trains were Seaboard's last truly local branchline runs – that is, with no through cars for connecting trains. After their discontinuance, Seaboard followed its traditional practice of listing the route in the timetable for several years afterward but stating the line now had freight service only and referring travelers to the local bus company that served the same stations. Several bus companies continued to honor SAL through tickets to locations on these branch routes years after the last passenger train ran.

Hamlet-Charleston-Savannah

Seaboard's low-grade line from Charleston, S.C., to Savannah, Ga., known informally among employees as the "East Carolina," hosted daily passenger locals 25 and 26. They made their daylight runs in about nine hours. The trains changed crews and were serviced at Andrews, S.C., about the halfway point and the junction for SAL's important branch to the industrial port of Georgetown. Nos. 25-26 passed through Andrews near each other, and a Georgetown Branch mixed train met both trains there. The trains – usually a rail motor car and trailer – were nicknamed the "Boll Weevil" after the insect that devastated southern cotton crops in the 1920s, particularly along this agriculturally rich "low country" route.

Trains 25-26 grew to two or three cars and drew varied motive power assignments in their later years. By late 1944, diesel rail motor cars 2027-2028 had replaced older rail cars; they in turn were reassigned to the Savannah-Montgomery route after the war, and steam power took over. Diesels made occasional appearances; one photo shows an E7 in 1948. By mid-1950, the trains were in charge of the Baldwin DR6-4-1500 units that were earlier on the Wilmington-Rutherfordton trains.

The Baldwins probably lasted until December 31, 1952, when Nos. 25-26 were cut back to Hamlet-Charleston. The shortened route allowed a single set of power and equipment to cover the run in a sched-

uled ten hours, and it appears motor car 2028 came back as normal power for the train; its previous assignment, the Savannah-Montgomery local, ended in late 1951. However, reportedly a boiler GP7 pulled the trains' final run on December 31, 1956.

Savannah-Montgomery

Seaboard's Savannah-Montgomery line was originally the appropriately named Savannah-Americus-Montgomery Railway, which had built from Lyons, Ga., west to Montgomery by 1891. The Georgia & Alabama Railway took over the SAM in 1895 and completed the line into Savannah; the G&A became part of the Seaboard in 1900. The line ran in a mostly straight line through Vidalia, Cordele, Americus, and Richland in Georgia and Rutherford, Hurtsboro, and Fort Davis in Alabama.

For many years the Savannah-Montgomery route hosted twice-daily local trains over most of the line, but in 1939 Seaboard reduced service to a single pair of locals, Nos. 11-12. The line was long the province of Seaboard's rail motor cars, known as the "Huckety-Buck" or the "Butt-head" along some parts of the line. Trains 11 and 12 took over 12 hours in each direction, from early morning to early evening. At 337.5 miles, the run was the longest pulled by any of SAL's motor car fleet. The trains were scheduled to meet at Cordele just after 2:00 p.m., affording connections to a number of other trains that converged at Cordele's union station around this time from the Atlanta, Birmingham & Coast (ACL after 1946), Southern (Georgia Southern & Florida), and Albany & Northern.

The line was never a significant part of Seaboard's passenger network despite its direct link between Georgia's leading port city and Alabama's capital and the many connections available at both ends. Apparently there was little significant passenger demand between the two cities; rival ACL offered service between the two points as well, but without much competition – its single local took even more hours over a longer route through south Georgia.

SAL motor cars 2027 and 2028 had taken over Nos. 11-12 by 1946. Both were by now in Seaboard's bright citrus colors, a stark contrast to the drab and utilitarian cars the units carried. Photos show Nos. 2027 and 2028 typically pulling two coaches, often from Seaboard's group of trailer cars, and often an express car as well. On weekends or when the railcars were in the shop, the trains could draw a Pacific steam locomotive or even a low-drivered Decapod. The reliable iron horse also had to bring in ailing motor cars when they decided to quit out on the road.

The little trains succumbed to the inevitable inroads of automobile and bus competition in 1951. The Georgia portion was discontinued first, on May 13, followed by the Alabama segment on November 24.

Cuthbert-Tallahassee

Seaboard's north-south line between Richland, Ga., and Carrabelle, Fla., via Bainbridge and Tallahassee was originally the Georgia, Florida & Alabama Railroad, which Seaboard leased in 1928. Seaboard acquired the GF&A to provide a route from Florida toward the Midwest by linking SAL's existing Jacksonville-Chattahoochee line at Tallahassee and its Savannah-Montgomery line at Richland.

Seaboard initially continued running GF&A's daily local service between Richland and Carrabelle, but by 1931 the trains had been cut back to Cuthbert (Ga.)-Tallahassee. Train 18 left Cuthbert in the morning for Tallahassee, and as No. 17 returned to Cuthbert early in the evening. The northern terminus of Cuthbert was apparently chosen because of SAL's active connection there with the Central of Georgia's Smithville (Ga.)-Montgomery line. Prior to 1931, Seaboard (and before it, GF&A) participated in carrying a through winter-season Atlanta-Tallahassee sleeper from the CofG via Macon to Cuthbert.

After the sleeper's demise, Trains 17-18 were put in charge of an SAL rail car. The railroad's older "butt-head" cars always covered the runs; No. 2015 did the honors in Nos. 17-18's last years, since it was the only older car on the roster after the late 1940s. The trains were discontinued on February 11, 1951.

A more enduring legacy of the Georgia, Florida & Alabama was eight steel passenger cars the railroad bought in 1926 from Bethlehem Shipbuilding Corporation. They included three coach-RPOs (Seaboard series 171-173, later rebuilt as baggage-RPOs), two express cars (432-433), and three coaches (682-684). The relatively short, four-wheel-truck cars were ideal for hauling behind Seaboard's rail motor cars and were common on these runs. The coaches disappeared from the roster in the 1950s but the head-end cars lasted throughout the Seaboard years.

Jacksonville-Tallahassee-Chattahoochee

One of the Jacksonville-Chattahoochee line's former named trains, the *New Orleans-Florida Limited*, became a Passenger, Mail and Express train in 1949. Trains 36-37 maintained an all-stops daylight schedule that took about six hours westbound and a little less eastbound between Jacksonville and Chattahoochee. The trains carried a through Jacksonville-Flomaton coach for connecting Louisville & Nash-

ville locals 62 and 63 at Chattahoochee for the trip to Flomaton. At Jacksonville, passengers from Nos. 36-37 could connect with the *Palmland* after waiting for a few hours. Nos. 36-37 typically had about half a dozen head-end cars trailed by a combine and coach.

The most interesting episode in Tallahassee line local service came a few years earlier in 1935, when Seaboard assigned one of its three new American Car & Foundry "streamlined motor coaches" to the route as the *Tallahassee Flyer*. The car left Jacksonville as No. 35 in the morning and sprinted to Chattahoochee in just under four and one-half hours. Returning as No. 34, the car got back to Jacksonville that night.

Like its two roster mates, the ACF car did not perform well. Seaboard discontinued one of the rail cars' other runs (Richmond-Raleigh) in 1936 and moved that unit to Jacksonville to serve as backup for the original car's "irregular operations." The relocated car also backstopped the third assignment, Jacksonville-Tampa. In 1938, the *Tallahassee Flyer* was cut back to its namesake city but kept the same basic schedule to allow a relatively long day trip from Jacksonville to the Florida capital. The ill-fated run was discontinued in 1939. All three ACF cars were sold during World War II.

Jacksonville-Tampa

Jacksonville-Tampa local service was in fact provided by two named trains, the *Palmland* and *Sunland*, which in Florida operated as locals despite the through cars they carried to both coasts. One of Seaboard's three ACF rail cars also briefly served the route; in 1935 the car replaced a steam-powered run and began running as North Florida Division Nos. 15-16. This was an overnight run leaving Jacksonville in the afternoon and returning just before noon the next day. The run was dropped in 1937.

Tampa-Venice

Seaboard served the Florida Gulf Coast cities of Bradenton, Sarasota, and Venice via the Sarasota Subdivision, which went south from the Tampa-West Lake Wales line at Durant, east of Tampa. The branch angled back toward the coast until it reached Bradenton, where it turned directly south and paralleled the Gulf to Venice. For many years Seaboard had operated trains over this line that connected with the *Sunland* and its predecessors and, in the winter, with the *Palmland* as well. These trains had several through coaches and sleepers between the Northeast and the popular west coast resorts at Sarasota and Venice.

By the end of World War II, Seaboard operated only a single Venice train year-round. The train left Tampa in mid-afternoon, timed after the arrivals of the *Sun Queen* and the west coast *Silver Meteor.* Northbound, the train left Venice mid-morning and got to Tampa after lunch. The train's rail route carried it east from Tampa as No. 26, which ran timetable north to Valrico, junction point of the Valrico Subdivision. There the train ran five miles timetable south as No. 507 to Durant, junction point for the Sarasota Subdivision. The train continued south to Sarasota for a total run of about 87 miles. Counterpart No. 508 changed numbers to 25 at Valrico for the timetable-south run back into Tampa.

Effective with the December 1946 timetable change, the Venice through sleeper was handled by the *Silver Meteor's* west coast section in both directions, and the Venice train's numbers were changed to 26-257 southbound and 25-258 northbound in sequence with the *Meteor's* numbers of 157-158. In mid-1949, the Venice line received a new 10 Rmt-6 DB Pullman.

Seaboard was very proud of its three American Car & Foundry "motor coach trains" when they were new in 1935. This company photo's caption brags that the aluminum-bodied cars had an "enormous" gasoline engine and "exceptionally comfortable [interiors with] strikingly eye-pleasing colors." No. 2025 is on display at Raleigh Union Station prior to entering service as Richmond-Raleigh Nos. 19-20. (SAL photo, Larry Goolsby collection)

The ACF rail cars proved unsatisfactory, and Trains 19-20 were soon put back in charge of Seaboard's less attractive but more reliable rail cars from the 1920s. Brill car 2017, which included baggage space and a 15-foot RPO compartment, is bringing a trailer coach into Raleigh as No. 19 in 1936. (Charles K. Marsh Jr. collection)

Seaboard's Baldwin 2700-series locomotives pulled the Venice train after all three of the units were assigned to Tampa about 1952. Then about 1958, rail car 2028 was placed on the train after the peripatetic unit was released from pulling locals out of Hamlet. No. 2028 remained on the train throughout the SAL and SCL years, gaining considerable nationwide fame as the last "shovel-nose" rail car in service. Seaboard sometimes substituted Alco road-switchers, usually one of the boiler-equipped RSC2s or RSC3s like 1533. These units could also be found serving as the Tampa passenger station switcher.

Effective with the April 1956 timetable, Seaboard added a through New York-Venice coach to the *Silver Meteor's* consist, and made the Venice train's through cars all-lightweight. Nos. 257-258 still carried a conventional baggage-coach combine for local Tampa-Venice service and conventional coaches as needed for additional capacity.

Tampa-Port Boca Grande (and Naples)

Connecting passenger trains from Tampa to Port Boca Grande reached their destination over the Boca Grande Subdivision, originally the Charlotte Harbor & Northern, which Seaboard leased in 1925 and fully merged in 1946. The "Cold, Hungry & Naked" was built to haul phosphate from the rich mines in south-

St. Louis Car/Electro-Motive Corporation rail car 2002's face is all function and no form in this 1937 portrait at Raleigh on No. 19 or 20. Note the air whistle and large steam locomotive-style bell. The unit was delivered in 1925 with a passenger compartment at the rear, but the space was converted to baggage use in 1932. (Wiley M. Bryan photo, Charles K. Marsh Jr. collection)

line received a lightweight 10-6 car effective in the winter of 1956-57 season, but lightweight 4 DB-4 Cpt-2 DRs (like the *Imperial* series owned by Pennsylvania and other railroads) served over the next two winters. The lightweight cars were not enough to keep Nos. 321-322 in the timetables, and they made their last runs on April 12, 1959.

The Boca Grande line's history includes a couple of unusual footnotes. In April 1956, an accident at Fort Green Springs heavily damaged PRR lightweight 10-6 sleeper *Elberton*. Subsequent litigation delayed repairs on the car for three years, but ultimately Pullman rebuilt it into an 11 double bedroom car. The *Elberton* was then placed in service on Pennsy's *Broadway Limited* – despite its stainless steel exterior in the otherwise-Tuscan train – but came back to Florida service after the *Broadway* was discontinued in 1967.

The route also included Hull, a point just south of Arcadia that was the junction for Seaboard's Fort Myers-Naples extension – one of Seaboard's several mid-1920s expansion ventures. The Naples extension was opened in January 1927 with great fanfare, and for a short time the *Orange Blossom Special* carried through Pullmans for the branch. But all passenger service on the extension had disappeared by the early 1930s, and in 1942, only 15 years after it was built, Seaboard abandoned most of the line south of Fort Myers. The Atlantic Coast Line took over the segment into Naples and even bought the former Seaboard Spanish mission-style depot, vacating its own facilities in Naples in favor of the SAL building. ACL inaugurated regular trains to Naples, including through cars to New York, and successor Seaboard Coast Line continued the service. Ironically, SCL powered the Naples connection train with motor car No. 4900, formerly Seaboard Air Line 2028, the same unit that had run on the nearby Venice line.

west Florida, and began at Port Boca Grande (located on Gasparilla Island and called South Boca Grande before 1947). From there the line went inland northeast to Arcadia, then turned north to Edison, near Mulberry on the Tampa-West Lake Wales line. Although Port Boca Grande was only about 85 air miles south of Tampa, the rail route took trains on a 126-mile inland journey between the two cities.

As was the case with Venice branch trains, Seaboard's employee timetables gave trains leaving Tampa a timetable-north number between Tampa and Valrico, then a southbound number from Valrico to Edison and beyond. To Port Boca Grande, the train was Nos. 30-321, and to Tampa, Nos. 29-322.

In the winter season, the Port Boca Grande trains carried a through sleeper from New York (usually a 6 Cpt-3 DR, like the mostly Pullman-owned *Glen* series). The car came via the *Palmland* originally, then moved to the *Silver Star* in winter 1948-49. The Port Boca Grande train left Tampa after the *Silver Star* and *Palmland* had pulled in, leaving in the morning and getting to Port Boca Grande just after lunch. Passengers of means could take a connecting yacht beyond to Useppa Island. The northbound run left in the afternoon and got back to Tampa at 6:55.

The Boca Grande train carried a Seaboard parlor-diner during the winter season up through winter 1953-54. The New York-Port Boca Grande sleeper

"Cross Florida" Service

For many years Seaboard provided "Cross Florida"

service, its name for trains and buses that operated from St. Petersburg and Tampa eastward via Plant City, Mulberry, and Bartow to a connection at West Lake Wales with the Wildwood-Miami mainline. The "Cross Florida Day Service" was via bus and connected with the *Sunland*, but the "Cross Florida Night Service" was by rail. (Interestingly, although public timetables used the "Service" label, employee timetables called the trains the *Cross State Night Limited*.) The train operated from Tampa to West Lake Wales and carried a through Tampa-Miami coach and sleeper. At West Lake Wales, the southbound *Palmland* completed the through cars' trip to Miami. Seaboard's public timetables carried a separate table for the Cross Florida service, and the through cars were included as well in the *Palmland's* equipment listings.

The Cross Florida Tampa-Miami schedule took more than eight hours. No. 28-427 left Tampa before midnight and got to Lake Wales about an hour and a half later; the through cars arrived at Miami about 8:00 the next morning. Northbound, the *Palmland* left Miami in the evening, and the through cars got to Tampa (via No. 428-27) early the next morning. Fortunately for Pullman passengers, they could occupy their car until 7:30 a.m.

The cross-state separate train became a winter-only operation after the 1948-49 winter season. The through coach and sleeper did continue in the summer, but took an unusual roundabout route that started from Tampa via the northbound west coast *Palmland* as far as Wildwood. There they were switched out and added to the southbound east coast (Miami) *Palmland*. This summer variation was nearly 100 miles longer than the winter train's direct eastward route but saved a separate train movement.

Seaboard dropped the cross-state sleeper after the 1954-55 winter season and the summertime through coach in the summer of 1956; thereafter cross-state passengers had to make an across-the-platform transfer at Wildwood. Even the winter train service's coach was cut back to a local Tampa-West Lake Wales car beginning in the 1955-56 winter season. Nos. 28-427 and 27-428 ran for one last winter, 1957-58,

and were discontinued on April 24, 1958. Seaboard continued to feature the bus service to West Lake Wales into the early 1960s.

Mixed Trains

Unlike its neighbor Atlantic Coast Line, Seaboard operated relatively few mixed trains in the 1940s, although some of Seaboard's rail motor car runs provided passenger service where mixed trains might otherwise have operated. After the war, Seaboard seldom listed the mixed runs in public timetables, although they did appear in employee timetables and in the *Official Guide*. By the late 1940s, only five known mixed trains remained: Nos. 212-285, Henderson-Durham, N.C. (discontinued in early 1954); Nos. 211-212, Moncure-Pittsboro, N.C. (late 1950); Nos. 35-36, Andrews-Georgetown, S.C. (mid-1949, replaced by a Seaboard-operated bus); Nos. 101-102, Starke-Bell, Fla. (about 1957); and Nos. 607-608, Wildwood-Orlando, Fla. (late 1954).

In the steam era, Seaboard's typical light freight power, such as Ten-wheelers and Consolidations, could often be found at the head of mixed trains. After diesels took over, available photographs show Alco RS3s on mixed runs; these units were normal power on most branchline runs, whether mixed or standard local freights.

The passenger cars used in later years on mixed trains were often from the 254-259 series of divided baggage-coach combines. These cars had the baggage compartment at one end, and the passenger compartment was partitioned for separate seating for blacks and whites. Seaboard had only a few of the "Jim Crow" combines with a baggage compartment in the center, and most were apparently off the roster by the postwar years. Full coaches were also used at times, along with full express cars when volume required. All the passenger-carrying equipment was drawn from older cars that had no air conditioning. Many of these cars had only coal stoves for winter warmth; a few had steam heat that could be activated if a boiler-equipped diesel was coupled to them, and in fact some photos show the passenger equipment next to the locomotive.

Up through the 1940s, local service on the Norlina-Portsmouth line looked much like this trim train at Franklin, Va., on October 10, 1948. P class Pacific 861, a 1912 Baldwin product, has an express car, baggage-RPO, and two coaches in hand as it pauses on No. 13's southbound run to Norlina. (H. Reid photo, Wally Johnson collection)

Seaboard No. 14, the Charlotte-Wilmington (N.C.) local, pulls into Hamlet led by Baldwin unit 2701 on March 25, 1950. The rare diesels powered Nos. 13-14 from about 1948 to 1950. The express car and baggage-RPO appear to be former GF&A cars from the 432-433 and 171-173 series, respectively. (David W. Salter photo)

Northbound Train 26 has just left Savannah for its all-day run to Hamlet, 263 miles distant, on July 4, 1948. E7 3029's paint is beginning to fade even though the unit is only three years old. The combine, apparently from the 250 or 260 series, is clearly not air-conditioned. The train normally carried an RPO car but did not on Sundays – which this July 4 was. (R.D. Sharpless photo, Robert H. Hanson Jr. collection)

It's early morning on a March 1955 day in Hamlet, and two locals have converged at Seaboard's North Carolina crossroads. At left is Train 14, which will leave for Wilmington at 8:20 behind E8 3056 with a combine and coach. Then No. 25 at right, with rail car 2028, will back out to the same track and leave at 8:30 for Charleston. No. 25's route diverges from the Wilmington main just south of the station. Train 25's cars are an interesting pair: baggage-express combine 2045, formerly rail car 2017 before it was de-motored and rebuilt in 1943, and a 500-series coach rebuilt with a streamlined-style "turtleback" roof. The 2045 had been a regular on the Savannah-Montgomery trains before they were discontinued in 1951. (Ed Patterson photo, Old Dominion Chapter NRHS collection)

The Charleston and Wilmington locals returned to Hamlet at 6:40 and 6:45 p.m., respectively, and again offered across-the-platform connections. In another March 1955 scene, No. 26 from Charleston (left) and No. 13 from Wilmington are together for their evening rendezvous. The 2028 is still doing the honors on the Charleston train, but a different E8, No. 3053, is on the Wilmington run. (A.C. Phelps photo, Charles K. Marsh Jr. collection)

It's March 1950, and steam is back in charge of No. 25 as it leaves Hamlet for Savannah behind P class 858. The two-car train includes baggage-RPO No. 113 plus an unusual visitor: an air-conditioned coach, probably from the 571-599 series, painted in silver-gray with black lettering for overflow service on Seaboard's streamliners. (David W. Salter photo)

No. 25 has pulled into the Charleston station from Hamlet on an afternoon in 1955, led by motor car 2028. By this date, all Seaboard regular passenger train service was air-conditioned, and the single coach is probably a partitioned car from the 571-599 series. The attractive station, located on Grove Street, had the same mission styling seen on many Seaboard stations in Florida. (A.C. Phelps photo, Charles K. Marsh Jr. collection)

This rare view shows rail car 2023 leaving Atlanta as No. 30 about 1938 with a trailer coach from the 2051-2069 series. The "gas-electric motor train" left Atlanta in the morning, turned at Abbeville, S.C., and came back in the evening as No. 29. The little train was discontinued in late 1940. (W.J. Rivers photo)

Seaboard M1 221, one of the railroad's Mountains once found heading long, named flyers, has to settle for the short five-car consist of Atlanta-Birmingham local No. 15 about 5:20 in the afternoon on March 5, 1949. The train is a few miles out of Atlanta at Harryat, just across the Chattahoochee River. The consist features three head-end cars, a combine, and – in a gesture to the full diner that once ran on No. 15's predecessor, the Cotton Blossom – one of Seaboard's parlor-diner cars. (R.D. Sharpless photo, ACL & SAL HS collection)

On the evening if May 28, 1949, E7 3029 is taking No. 15 back to Birmingham through the rolling countryside west of Dallas, Ga.; behind the parlor-diner is an extra car that appears to be a 180-series baggage-dorm. The high deck girder bridge in the left background spans Pumpkinvine Creek. (David W. Salter photo)

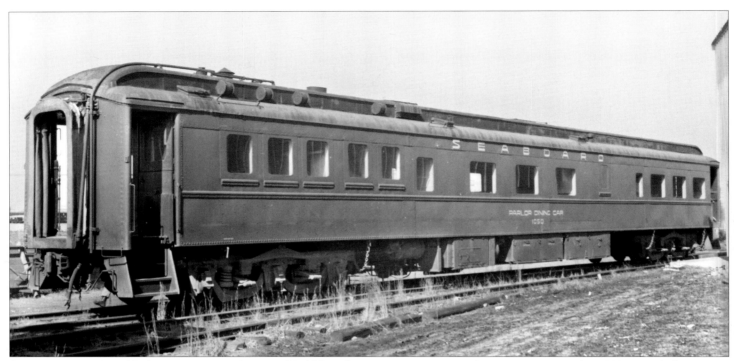

Seaboard parlor-diner 1050, shown here on February 25, 1967, after it was donated to the Tennessee Valley Railroad Museum in Chatta-nooga, was a regular on the Atlanta-Birmingham run in the late 1940s. Originally a Western Maryland café-parlor car, it could seat 18 in its dining section and 12 in the parlor. (Oscar W. Kimsey Jr. photo)

Seaboard's rail car fleet provided basic, economical service on many of the railroad's lightly patronized passenger runs. They also kept labor costs low – the unions agreed the cars needed only an engineer and no fireman. In this scene from July 1942, Brill car 2013 and a trailer coach protect No. 11's schedule at Pitts, Ga., home of photographer David Salter – whose Montgomery-Ward bicycle at right was delivered by the same train a month before. (David W. Salter photo)

Not long after leaving its original assignments in the Carolinas, brightly painted rail motor car 2028 pauses on a sunny December 1, 1946, at Pitts, Ga., with Montgomery-bound local No. 11. Passengers have been boarded and the conductor is ready to swing up as townspeople look on, while the train's RPO clerk is at his post in the rail car's 15-foot mail compartment. Photographer Salter recalls that when he was in Navy boot camp in Illinois, he got mail from his folks in two days if they put a letter in No. 11's mail slot, but in three days if they sent it via air mail! (David W. Salter photo)

Train 11 leans into a curve east of Seville, Ga., at 50 m.p.h. on a September 1947 afternoon. Behind rail car 2028 are express car 432, a 2051-class coach, and business car Savannah with officials who are having a look at the Savannah Subdivision. Note that No. 2028 has acquired a headlight visor since the 1946 photo above.(David W. Salter photo)

Steam returned to Nos. 11 and 12 when motor cars 2027 and 2028 were being shopped or the consist was too heavy. On January 2, 1948, class P4 Pacific 876, a former Western Maryland engine, has an easy time moving Train 11 across the flat Georgia fields east of Pitts – a sharp contrast to the Appalachian grades and curves the engine used to encounter. Baggage-RPO (and former rail car) 2045 and three more cars complete this archetypal scene of Seaboard local passenger service. (David W. Salter photo)

Train 11 drew No. 2027 on September 13, 1949, but photographer Salter notes the unit was "sickly" by the time it came in view of his camera west of Seville, Ga., and had to have Alco RSC2 1503 lend a helping hand. The cars today were express trailer 2041 and a trailer coach from the 2051-2059 series. No. 2027 seems to have disappeared from view in the early 1950s, and the car may have languished in storage until it was officially removed from the roster in 1956. (David W. Salter photo)

Each afternoon just after 2:00, Seaboard Nos. 11 and 12 were scheduled to meet at the south-central Georgia rail junction of Cordele. In this scene from 1948, rail cars 2027 and 2028 wait at the left to depart with their trailer coaches. Meanwhile, the Albany & Northern's small Brill car has arrived from Albany and reached the station over a short segment of SAL trackage rights. The two tracks crossing in front of the A&N car belong to the GS&F, while the ACL's Atlanta-Waycross line angles across the SAL in the background; trains from both these lines also converged at the station around this same time. (W.C. Whittaker photo)

This rare photo shows the Tallahassee Flyer, No. 34, at its namesake city on a late-afternoon run back to Jacksonville sometime in the late 1930s. ACF rail car 2026 has had some significant front-end modifications since delivery in 1935, including broad zebra stripes to increase the car's visibility. What appears to be a police car siren has also been added to the roof to help warn motorists unaccustomed to a train that doesn't whistle and belch smoke. Other changes include louvers on the front windows and relocation of the horn from the center of the nose to the right side of the cab. The car still runs today in excursion service for the California Western Railroad as its M-300. (William Monypeny photo, Louis Saillard collection)

Eastbound Passenger, Mail and Express No. 36 is conducting brisk head-end business at Tallahassee in 1952. E7 3026 leads about five express cars plus a baggage-RPO, combine, and coach. Such trains sometimes picked up and set out express cars en route; a car is on the siding in front of the passenger station's umbrella shed. The two-story building farther back is the freight station. (Tom Solomon photo, Larry Goolsby collection)

Baldwin DR6-4-1500 No. 2700 stands at Tampa Union Station on the evening of March 9, 1955, ready for its 11:20 p.m. departure with No. 28-427 and the railroad's Cross Florida Night Service train. Although these runs were listed in the public timetables only by their service label and train numbers, employee timetables grandly named them the Cross State Night Limited. The winter-only train had a through Tampa-Miami coach and sleeper, but this was the last season the Pullman operated. The train itself was discontinued after the winter season of 1957-58. (Jim Scribbins photo, Larry Goolsby collection)

This fine action scene at Tampa on July 30, 1948, reveals an interesting consist behind P2-class Pacific 819. The train is No. 25/258, the northbound Venice-Sarasota-Tampa run whose last car is the through Venice-New York 10-1-2 sleeper for the Silver Meteor. The other cars include a baggage-RPO with a 15-foot mail compartment, combine, and American Flyer coach. (Sam R. Appleby Jr. photo)

Seaboard's Trains 321-322 served the Port Boca Grande branch and connected with the Palmland at Tampa. This foggy scene is likely from the late 1940s, not long after No. 2700 arrived from Baldwin in late 1947 and went to work on the 126-mile run. The train's winter-season consist included a Pullman and a parlor-diner, and both appear to be present in this photograph. (DeGolyer Library, Southern Methodist University, Dallas, Texas, Ag1982.0232)

The southbound Tampa-Port Boca Grande train, No. 321, has pulled up to the Boca Grande station with Baldwin 2702 on October 5, 1952. The large building was constructed by predecessor Charlotte Harbor & Northern, and today houses restaurants and boutique shops. (George W. Pettengill photo, ACL & SAL HS collection)

This marvelous view looks east-southeast at Seaboard's trackage at Port Boca Grande, dominated by the railroad's large phosphate elevator in Charlotte Harbor and a couple of waiting ships. At left center, Train 322 waits for its 3:00 p.m. northbound departure and will have less than two and one-half miles to go before its first stop at Boca Grande. There was no separate station building here, but SAL employees and others could buy tickets at the railroad's office at top right. The houses in the foreground are company-owned and were rented to Seaboard employees for $11 a month. Port Boca Grande was one of Seaboard's two phosphate sea terminals; the other was at Tampa. (DeGolyer Library, Southern Methodist University, Dallas, Texas, Ag1982.0232)

Starting in 1927, Seaboard ran passenger trains to Fort Myers and Naples, Fla., but stopped when the Depression hit. Seaboard's mission-style Naples station was already freight-only by the time of this February 1936 photo. SAL abandoned the Naples portion of the line in 1942, but ACL took over the trackage two years later and restored passenger trains to the stucco and tile building. Naples continued to enjoy passenger service from that time up until Amtrak. (William Monypeny photo)

Of the few mixed trains Seaboard operated in the postwar years, the Starke-Bell (Fla.) run lasted the longest. Boiler-equipped RSC2 1535 and the train's combine, a car from the 254-259 series, wait at Bell in December 1952 for their return trip to Starke as Train 102. (Charles Waldheim photo, Bill Cogswell collection)

RSC3 1537 is heading east with the Bell to Starke mixed in this scene from 1956, about a year before mixed service was discontinued. The first coach is from the ex-GF&A 682-684 series. The train's second coach is probably needed for the large contingent of Peninsular Railfan Club members who were riding on this date. (Tom King photo, Charles K. Marsh Jr. collection)

Seaboard combine 259, shown here at Hamlet in 1955, was often found on mixed and local runs. Pressed Steel Car Company turned out the all-steel car in 1913, and aside from some window modifications, still looks much as it did when built. The car was donated to the Gold Coast Museum in Miami and later selected by the National Park Service for complete restoration to its appearance as a "Jim Crow" divided car. (A.C. Phelps photo, Charles K. Marsh Jr. collection)

As the Seaboard Air Line entered its last decade of corporate existence, far-reaching changes were under way for traditional passenger railroading. The late 1950s were not a happy time for passenger trains in the United States; the new interstate highway system was expanding, gas and cars were plentiful, and jet airliners had begun whisking travelers between major cities with unprecedented speed. Railroad passengers were leaving in large numbers, and most companies were trying to cut costs – including entire trains – as rapidly as they could. Expensive and aging equipment, outdated stations, and rising labor costs increased outgo just as declining ridership lowered income. With these trends already in place, the significant recession of 1958 was the tipping point for many local and secondary runs. For other trains, the downturn marked the end – or at least the rapid decline – of such amenities as sleepers and diners. David P. Morgan, editor of *Trains* Magazine and acute observer of the U.S. railroad scene, wrote an issue-length analysis in April 1959 with the grim title, "Who Shot the Passenger Train?"

Seaboard was not immune from these changes. Its slimmer timetables reflected the end of the branchline local, the demise of many small-town stops, and reductions in Pullman and dining car service on many secondary trains. The railroad took steps to generate new revenue where it could; for example, in 1959 SAL began assessing seat reservation charges of 50 cents to $1.50 in coaches on the three Silver trains. Yet on the whole, Seaboard's passenger service was managing very well. As the 1960s approached, its primary passenger trains not only held their own in most respects but even saw some improvements.

The railroad's passenger volume hit a low point in 1959, when passengers fell to 894,150 after being at nearly two million a decade earlier. But in 1960, the numbers began to turn around, and passengers carried climbed modestly but steadily every year afterward. Seaboard also reported an 8.5 percent jump in gross passenger income in 1960 over 1959, the highest figure since 1952. Summer vacations were a prominent factor, with warm-season travel to Florida the best since 1947 – owing in large part to aggressive promotion of package tours combining special rail fares and hotel rates. Other reasons included reduced round-trip summer season coach fares begun in 1961 and repeal of the 10 percent federal excise tax on rail passenger transportation in 1962.

Seaboard's resilience was due in no small part to its location and market access. Situated between the populous and prosperous northeast and the nation's favorite vacation destination, the railroad had certainly been dealt a favorable passenger service hand. But SAL maximized this advantage by keeping its trains fast, attractive, and competitive with its rivals – especially, of course, the Atlantic Coast Line. Seaboard's timetables subtly distinguished between its services and ACL's, noting for example that the *Silver Meteor* and *Silver Star* provided "exclusive morning and afternoon streamliner departures to both coasts" from New York – a boast aimed at the *East Coast Champion* and *West Coast Champion*, which each served just one coast.

Seaboard also promoted its other successes and special features, such as registered nurses – something no other southeastern line offered. The railroad also held up its reputation for on-time performance and fast running. *Trains* Magazine ran an annual passenger train speed survey in which SAL frequently placed well and occasionally won. In a memorable anecdote printed in the Second Quarter 2008

Seaboard's passenger numbers dipped in the late 1950s, but the railroad kept its best trains up to high standards. The 20th anniversary of the Silver Meteor, *always SAL's premier postwar train, was noted with a cake and a suitable publicity photo on board one of the train's diners on February 4, 1959. Pictured from left are Miami Mayor Robert Kind High;* Meteor *nurse Patricia High (who held a record 18 years 2 months seniority in her job); and Miami General Passenger Agent Wesley Ficht. (SAL photo, TLC Collection)*

What may be local No. 4 pauses at Richmond's Broad Street Station in April 1963 behind E7 3034. Seaboard moved here from Main Street Station in 1959 to reduce its station costs; the change also placed all of Richmond's north-south trains in one location. Broad Street's track arrangement required SAL trains to face north on the west side of the station's loop, instead of south like ACL and RF&P trains. (Harold K. Vollrath photo, ACL & SAL HS collection)

issue of *Lines South*, David Salter related an early 1960s *Silver Meteor* trip from Tampa to Jacksonville where he timed the late-running train at 103 m.p.h.

Another service Seaboard often employed to keep the public happy – and bring in more revenue – was special trains, especially to sports events. One tradition that lasted well into the 1960s was trains from Atlanta to Athens for the annual fall Georgia Tech–University of Georgia football game. These movements often comprised more than one train, and even for this short trip often had Pullmans or tavern cars for first-class passengers. Another example was a special that Seaboard operated in cooperation with the Pennsylvania and RF&P in November 1960 for the Notre Dame vs. University of Miami game in Miami Beach, complete with a full-color souvenir menu for the "Notre Dame Fans of Philadelphia."

New Stations, More Coaches

The late-1950s downturn didn't stop Seaboard from maintaining the Silver Fleet to high standards. At the height of the recession, in June 1958, SAL went back once again to its favorite supplier of "pre-owned" cars, the Chesapeake & Ohio – this time, ten 52-seat coaches built by Pullman-Standard in 1950. The cars (numbers 6242-6251) had Sleepy Hollow seats and a partial mid-car partition to break up the normal coach "tunnel" look. On the outside, they had flat roofs and side fluting only below the windows; Seaboard painted the balance of the sides silver-gray to blend with its stainless-steel fleet.

Seaboard also made changes in station facilities as the decade turned. Economics drove these steps, but the railroad used several of the occasions to provide new station buildings and improved service. On January 20, 1959, Seaboard opened a new St. Petersburg station at Eighth Avenue South and 34th Street. The move reflected the city's desire to eliminate the street running necessary to access the old station at Second Avenue South and Eighth Street. Many other cities across the country were making similar changes as automobile traffic became heavier and motorists grew increasingly impatient with the blocked crossings and reduced parking that came with downtown stations.

A more substantial station change came four months later. On April 26, Seaboard left its historic Richmond passenger facility, Main Street Station, and moved about 2.7 miles northwest to Broad Street Station, used by the Atlantic Coast Line and Richmond, Fredericksburg & Potomac. Seaboard had shared the aging (1901) Main Street building with just one other tenant, Chesapeake & Ohio, so the move reduced SAL's building rental and maintenance charges. It also put the heavy north-south traffic from both Seaboard and ACL in one location.

Broad Street had hosted the ACL and RF&P since the neoclassical-style building opened in 1919. It was part of an extensive project to take passenger trains out of downtown and avoid a steep grade there, and included a new bypass route west of the city. The station was located just off this bypass, and all passenger movements in both directions entered the station from the north and passed through the complex in a counterclockwise direction using a loop track. But because of Seaboard's track connection west of the area, SAL northbound trains had to pull past the station and back into the west side of the station loop. They ended up facing north at the station, rather than south as did ACL and RF&P trains. Similarly, to enable departure onto Seaboard's main, southbound

RF&P trains destined for the SAL entered the loop clockwise. After Seaboard power replaced the RF&P engines, the train backed out and passed through a portion of RF&P's yard trackage to attain the connection track to Seaboard's main.

A third major station change came on August 16, 1962, when Seaboard and ACL vacated Savannah's downtown union station and moved to a new joint "Seaboard–Coast Line" facility. The name foretold the Seaboard Coast Line merger that had been planned since the late 1950s and that would become reality in 1967. The new building was off Telfair Road west of the city, not far from Seaboard's West Savannah station. SAL trains had to use a short segment of ACL trackage via new connections to access the station, which was about halfway between the north end of Seaboard's freight yard and Central Junction. The station also provided a full-service Savannah stop for the *Silver Star*, ending the train's former stop at West Savannah.

Streamliners to Florida

The *Silver Meteor* remained Seaboard's premier train. While timetable ads also gave plenty of space to the *Meteor*'s "twin," the *Silver Star*, the *Meteor* was clearly the favored sibling. The train's status was always on display in the form of its 1947 Budd 6600-series observation cars, on the end and properly pointed. (The *Star* carried 6600s on the rear during the winter seasons, but its three assigned cars had large end diaphragms for summertime mid-train use.) The other exclusive *Silver Meteor* feature was the train's Sun Lounge cars, whose distinctive high lounge windows always stood out mid-train. The *Meteor* also still offered all-year service to both coasts including through cars to Venice – by now the only branchline passenger service on the system. Finally, almost all the train's through cars operated from New York; the

only exception was a winter-season Washington-Miami 10-6 effective for the 1959-60 season.

The *Silver Meteor* was usually the longer of the two trains, typically 18 cars or more in winter. The winter-season Pullman lineup regularly included a 5 DB-2 Cpt-2 DR *Boca Grande*-class car, one of the *Avon Park*-class 11 DB cars, and several 10-6s. Two diners, two coach-lounges, and full coaches completed the train. Through cars for the Venice connecting train included a coach-lounge and a 10-6. The wintertime *Star*'s consist was close behind the *Meteor*'s lineup, although the *Star* carried a 4 Rmt-1 Cpt-5 DB-4 Sec sleeper (seen on the *Tidewater* in summers) instead of the *Meteor*'s all-room 5 DB-2 Cpt-2 DR and only one coach lounge. Both trains were shorter in the warmer months, especially the *Star*, which in October 1959 had fallen back to just eight regularly assigned cars. The summertime *Star* also did not operate its feature cars and several others north of Washington.

The *Star* did surpass the *Meteor* in one respect– its southbound winter-season timing between New York and Miami. As in past years, the winter *Star* traveled via the Gross-Baldwin cut-off and bypassed Jacksonville, bettering the *Meteor*'s southbound time by an hour or more. During the 1962-63 winter season, the *Star* trimmed its southbound run to only 24 hours and 40 minutes, and in following winters the timing was just ten minutes longer.

Seaboard made a few other adjustments in the *Silver Star*'s feature cars to save money while leaving the train's traditional services essentially intact. After running the 6600-series observations on the rear year-round between December 1957 and April 1960, the cars were again moved mid-train for the warm months. Seaboard also began dropping the *Star*'s normal Pullman lounge (a 6 DB-lounge *Mountain*-series car) in summers; the practice let Seaboard simply use the mid-train 6600 as the train's first-class lounge each summer instead of incurring Pullman charges for the sleeper-lounge car.

Another change, implemented in July 1960, was shortening one of the *Star's* 10-6 sleeper lines to Richmond-Miami. Turning and servicing the car at Richmond allowed the use of one less Pullman to protect the train's schedule. The change also meant placing the car on the rear of the train to simplify switching at Richmond. The summer-season *Star's* sleepers had run on the train's rear during most of its existence, although in the later 1950s the summer sleepers had reverted to the Pullmans' standard position first in the consist. But after the winter of 1961-62, the Pullmans ran at the end all year; this change also permanently relegated the 6600-series observations to mid-train throughout the year.

The *Silver Comet*

As the *Silver Meteor* and *Silver Star* dominated the Florida trade, Seaboard continued to offer a solid array of other premium trains on its main routes. The *Silver Comet* remained the official third member of the Silver Fleet, although the train had lost some of its former luster. Seaboard prominently promoted two other trains, the *Tidewater* and *Gulf Wind*, both of which offered long-distance dining and sleeping car service and had gradually become mostly streamlined.

The *Silver Comet* no longer matched its Florida counterparts in length or features; for example, its registered nurse had been quietly dropped about 1958. But the train still ran as many as ten regularly assigned passenger-carrying cars, including a 10-6 sleeper and coach all the way from New York to Bir-

mingham. Most of the remaining cars operated from Washington or Richmond to Atlanta or Birmingham. The train's regularly assigned tavern-coach also ran the entire route during some peak travel periods. That car was normally from the 6300 series, but sometimes a 6500-series coach-buffet-observation or even a diaphragm-equipped 6600-series tavern-observation substituted.

The train's long-distance consist was completed by the traditional Portsmouth-Atlanta coach and sleeper from the *Tidewater*. Finally, the *Comet* continued to forward several coaches and head-end cars for Jacksonville that were transferred to the *Sunland* at Hamlet. Together with several head-end cars, the *Comet's* regular consist could swell to as many as 15 cars between Raleigh and Hamlet.

The *Comet's* New York-Birmingham route sleeping car lines were regularly filled by *Atlanta*-class 10-6s, but Pullmans for its connecting trains were anything but commonplace. Foreign sleepers in a variety of unusual configurations were regularly used for the cars the *Comet* picked up from the *Tidewater* and for the winter-season Richmond-Jacksonville sleeper the *Sunland* carried south of Hamlet. Portsmouth-Atlanta sleepers could include Wabash *Blue*-series cars or, as in the summer of 1965, a 14 Rmt-4 DB Pullman usually from the New Haven's *Point* series. Other summers saw one of Seaboard's *Bay Pines*-class 4-1-5-4s. The Portsmouth-Atlanta sleeper ran for the final time on November 14, 1966; it was a 6 Rmt-4 DB-6 Sec Pullman like Boston & Maine's *Dartmouth College* cars or New Haven's *Beach* series.

The *Tidewater* and *Gulf Wind*

The *Tidewater* continued to be closely aligned with

This view of the southbound Silver Meteor's east coast section, at Winter Haven, Fla., in April 1960, shows a typical Miami train in Seaboard's later years. E7 3024 and an E4 B unit have about a dozen cars in tow, including the Jacksonville-Miami baggage-RPO the train normally carried. (David W. Salter photo)

the *Comet's* schedule and car offerings as it moved passengers and head-end business from Portsmouth to points south and southwest. In addition to the *Tidewater's* through cars the *Comet* carried to Atlanta and forwarded to Jacksonville, a Portsmouth-Raleigh diner and a baggage-RPO completed the modest but first-class consist. The *Tidewater's* schedule had stayed much the same since the its 1953 debut – a morning arrival in Portsmouth and an evening departure, both timed to connect with the *Comet* at Raleigh.

The *Tidewater's* 1960s consist had become mostly lightweight; the train's sleepers were always normally streamlined. The Portsmouth-Jacksonville Pullman followed the general pattern of the Atlanta sleeper, with a UP or C&NW 12 Rmt-4 DB car in the fall and winter and one of Seaboard's 4-1-5-4s in summer. In November 1962, the summer-season car changed to a Louisville & Nashville 6 Rmt-4 DB-6 Sec sleeper. The Atlanta and Jacksonville coaches were usually lightweight cars. The dining car remained a heavyweight from the 225 series, and the train's baggage-RPO was of course heavyweight as well.

The *Tidewater* had the distinction – perhaps not a welcome one – of being the first known Seaboard named train to regularly add premium freight cars to its consist. Starting in fall 1959, SAL began coupling insulated boxcars from the Suffolk Peanut Company to the train's rear on Sunday nights, since the line's only scheduled freight train did not run on Sundays. Then as early as November 1960, Seaboard also began regularly running auto racks on the train, again often on Sundays. A GP9 usually supplemented the *Tidewater's* standard single E7 when this extra tonnage required additional horsepower. The cars continued to Atlanta and other destinations on freights.

The *Gulf Wind* was the final top-ranked Seaboard train in the 1960s. The overnight Jacksonville-New Orleans train's consist had come to resemble the *Tidewater's*, with lightweight sleepers and coaches supplemented by a heavyweight diner and several head-end cars. The continued presence of an L&N *Royal*-series car also distinguished the *Gulf Wind* as Seaboard's only other train with a regularly assigned round-end rear observation car. The observation and the train's other Pullman, a 6 Rmt-4 DB-6 Sec usually from L&N's *Pine* series, went through to New Orleans along with its coaches. The *Wind's* Seaboard diner ran only from Jacksonville to Tallahassee, but that allowed plenty of time for dinner going west and breakfast coming east.

FEC's Strike, Seaboard's Gain

A pivotal event occurred in early 1963 that greatly affected Seaboard's passenger train fortunes – and largely for the better. On January 23, the Florida East Coast Railway's unions struck the company over its refusal to participate in national wage negotiations. FEC immediately stopped operating all passenger trains, including the Atlantic Coast Line's through streamliners from Jacksonville to Miami, forcing ACL to quickly secure an agreement with Seaboard to handle its trains as part of a new inland route. ACL trains took their own Jacksonville-Tampa line to Auburndale, where ACL crossed SAL's Wildwood-Miami main. There, they used an existing connection track to get onto SAL's Miami Subdivision for the balance of the trip. The rerouted ACL Miami trains included the *East Coast Champion*, the alternating *City of Miami* and *South Wind* from Chicago, and the winter-season *Florida Special*. Charges for trackage rights earned the Seaboard $457,000 in 1963 alone.

ACL expected that the detours would be temporary and even published its April 1963 timetables with the traditional FEC route. However, the strike not only dragged on but became increasingly violent, and it was soon clear that the rerouted trains were on Seaboard rails to stay. The additional trains made the

This August 1966 portrait shows a three-unit, 20-plus-car northbound Silver Meteor cruising at 70 m.p.h. on double track a few miles south of Baldwin, Fla. – although Seaboard trains were known to make up time by passing the century mark. Northbound passenger trains operated on the "left-hand" main to clear freights working the busy yard at Baldwin, located on the east side of the mainline. Lead unit 3060 was Seaboard's only E9 and the only unit delivered in the light "mint green" scheme. (David W. Salter photo)

Auburndale-Miami line a passenger train watcher's paradise; combined with Seaboard's existing eight daily winter-season movements, this trackage now saw 14 passenger trains a day.

Trackage rights charges were not Seaboard's only financial boost from the strike. Two pairs of local Jacksonville-Miami FEC trains were among the strike's victims, and the substantial amount of mail and express they once carried had no rail alternative but the Seaboard. To help move the extra business, Seaboard had by the October 1963 timetable change reinstated the *Sunland's* Miami section year-round; the Miami train last previous non-winter run was 1948. The change no doubt contributed to Seaboard's increased mail revenues in both 1963 and 1964 and express income in 1964.

Finally, Seaboard's streamliners benefited from the strike in a very visible fashion. FEC's exit from the passenger business obviously rendered its passenger car roster surplus, and the railroad began thinning its fleet in 1964. Although the Florida Public Utilities Commission required FEC to reinstate a Jacksonville-Miami day local in mid-1965, that operation required only a few cars. Thus in October 1965, Florida East Coast put up for sale almost all its remaining cars. Seaboard snapped up 36 of them, all lightweights: coaches, diners, observations, a diner-lounge, three combines, and a baggage-express car. The purchase

provided some much-needed extra capacity to serve Seaboard's brisk mid-sixties passenger business, and once again let the railroad improve and modernize its roster at low cost.

The cars fit well with Seaboard's existing light-weight fleet. Most were built by Budd and Pullman-Standard, and all but three had unpainted, corrugated stainless steel sides and roofs. The three exceptions were smooth-side cars painted in Illinois Central colors for FEC's contribution to the *City of Miami*. Two, *Sebastian* and *Lantana* (renumbered 6266 and 6269), remained in their IC chocolate and orange scheme. The third car, *Canal Point* (6267), had Budd-style fluting under the windows and silver-gray paint on the balance of the side; it appears Seaboard may have made this modification after the purchase.

Seaboard did not buy any of the sleeping cars that FEC offered, since its need for extra sleeper space was largely seasonal and doing so would have triggered increased payments to the Pullman Company (as required of all railroads participating in Pullman Company operations). It was cheaper for Seaboard to fill its additional sleeping car needs by drawing from the pool of extra sleepers that Pullman always had available – particularly with so many other railroads dropping sleeping cars from their trains. Florida East Coast later sold its sleepers to Canadian National.

A 19-car Silver Meteor *gets under way after a quick stop on March 26, 1965, at Waldo, Fla., the station stop for Gainesville and the University of Florida. One of the train's signature tavern-lounge-observations, 6602, brings up the markers on this sunny afternoon. (David W. Salter photo)*

Two of the ex-FEC acquisitions were unique to SAL's roster. The first and most interesting was a 1950 ACF tavern-lounge car named *South Bay* (renumbered SAL 6620); it was part of FEC's contribution to the *New Royal Palm*, a Cincinnati/Detroit/Cleveland to Miami train operated by New York Central, Southern Railway, and FEC. The *South Bay* was built as a diner-lounge, but in 1956 FEC converted it to a tavern-lounge by removing a portion of the kitchen and adding more lounge seating. Unlike Seaboard's other 6400- through 6600-series cars, the former *South Bay* did not have an observation end.

The second one-of-a-kind car was the lightweight baggage-express car, No. 501 on FEC and renumbered as SAL 6070. Also a 1950 ACF product, it was

Seaboard's only piece of lightweight head-end equipment. It appears Seaboard placed the car in general head-end car pool service and did not attempt to assign it to the streamlined trains.

The FEC equipment purchase gave Seaboard a greatly expanded pool of lightweight cars to draw from when the Silver Fleet needed overflow capacity. Seaboard was also able to use lightweight cars more frequently on its other trains. However, the railroad made no wholesale reductions in its conventional car fleet, instead keeping most of them on hand for extra capacity if needed. One exception was that SAL halved the number of its remaining classic heavyweight diners, from ten to five. The purchase further boosted the proportion of Seaboard's lightweight fleet obtained from other railroads; for example, the streamlined coach fleet now numbered 75 cars, of which only 34 were bought new by SAL.

The *Palmland* and *Sunland*

By the late 1950s, Seaboard's two mainline secondary passenger trains, the *Palmland* and *Sunland*, had settled into a pattern that would change little into the mid-1960s. Both trains still ran on very leisurely New York-Miami schedules, taking 36 hours or more in both directions and making local stops on the southern ends of their runs. The two still had some classy features, particularly the *Palmland* with its variety of through sleepers (including New York-Hamlet and New York-Miami) and coaches plus dining service over the middle portion of its route.

The *Palmland's* 1960s sleepers were drawn largely from the ranks of 10 Rmt-6 DB and 12 Rmt-4 DB cars. In October 1965, an 8 Rmt-6 DB sleeper (like some of Rock Island's *Golden*-series cars) appeared on the New York-Miami line and ran through the summer of 1966; afterward, 10-6s covered both the Miami and Hamlet sleeper lines. The Rock Island cars were good examples of Pullmans that began running beyond their home roads when their original train assignments reduced or ended service, in this instance the *Rocky Mountain Rocket*.

One distinction the *Palmland* had during these years was that rival Atlantic Coast Line no longer had a through New York-Miami Pullman on its secondary trains, so those traveling such trains (including pass riders) took Seaboard if they wanted first-class passage on the route. The *Palmland* also retained its full dining car between Raleigh and Hamlet and its grill car between Hamlet and Jacksonville.

A common *Palmland* sight through at least 1966 was extra heavyweight Pullmans carrying service personnel to locations such as Fort Jackson, just east

Keeping travelers well-fed was an ongoing Seaboard tradition. This dining car re-supply order, submitted by steward E.B. Ross for the southbound Silver Meteor *of May 29, 1963, certainly illustrates the point. The requests for bacon, ham, sausage, and no fewer than 360 eggs underline the breakfast preferences of the time. The "large felts" are the soft pads that were placed beneath the tablecloths. (ACL & SAL HS collection)*

```
CQB
    COLA SC MAY 29-63

SAL DINING CAR DEPARMENT
                        JAX

  12 LARGE FELTS
 500 GUEST CHECKS
  20 LB BEEF LOIN
  60, 8-OZ BEEF STEAKS
   6 LB PORT SAUSAGE MEAT
   6 LB BACON
  30 LB SUGAR CURED HAM
  30 LB TURKEY
  18 LB LARD
  40 LB TROUT
   6 QT COFFEE CREAM
 360 EGGS                    U S B g
  24 BAKING APPLES
  15 LB CABBAGE              S 1°a
  16 EGG PLANT
  10 BERMUDA ONIONS
  15 F F POTATOES
  12 32-OZ CONSOMME
   1 GAL LIMEADE
   1 GAL TOMATOES
   1 GAL APPLE
   1 NO 10 PICKEE STRIPS
   1 PKG OATMEAL
  20 DOZ ROLLS
  15 LB COFFEE
  20 LB FLOUR
  10 MIX CORN MUFFIN FLOUR
  10 LB GRAD SUGAR
   8 KITCHEN SOAP

   E B ROSS CAR 6110 TRAIN NO 57

                        452AM
```

of Columbia. The Vietnam conflict was the last time the venerable heavyweights saw widespread use, and Seaboard was among the railroads that kept a sizeable roster of such cars on hand just for this purpose. Although Seaboard rarely used the cars in its own revenue service any more, the railroad enjoyed a bit of additional income by keeping them in the Pullman lease system. In 1963, SAL still had 14 heavyweight sleepers on its roster under Pullman lease. (The railroad also rostered 12 other sleepers that year that had been converted to coach service, a change it began making to some Pullmans in the late 1950s.)

The *Palmland* also still served both Florida coasts year-round, although its Tampa connecting train was essentially a mail and express run with only a baggage-coach combine for passengers. That train was the first assignment (1962) for Seaboard's two Flexi-Van flatcars carrying truck vans of storage mail. The *Palmland* and *Sunland* could carry exceptionally heavy volumes of head-end traffic at times, particularly around holidays. One December 1964 consist from Jacksonville Terminal shows a northbound *Palmland* with four locomotives and no fewer than 35 cars. Some were deadheading, but most were in-service mail storage and express cars.

The *Sunland* remained the approximate schedule counterpart to the *Palmland*, about 12 hours apart, but otherwise was clearly the lesser of the two. While passenger timetables showed the *Sunland* running south from Washington, the train from there to Hamlet was in fact only several through cars carried by the *Silver Comet* and *Tidewater* (a Washington-Jacksonville coach and Portsmouth-Jacksonville coach and sleeper). The northbound train did operate separately north of Hamlet, but had earlier replaced that segment of local No. 6. The *Silver Star* continued to move the Portsmouth cars northbound, except in winter when No. 16 did so. The *Sunland* started the decade as an all-year train only to Tampa, but its formerly winter-only Miami connecting train also became year-round after the FEC strike.

In December 1959 the *Sunland* acquired an unusual addition: a new winter-season sleeper line from Richmond to Jacksonville. The car may have been for Seaboard personnel traveling to and from the railroad's new Richmond general office; the *Silver Star* ran on a similar schedule and was available the rest of the year, but bypassed Jacksonville in the winter. The *Sunland* ran a little after the *Star* southbound and a little before it northbound, but still allowed travelers to have a full business day in either city in both directions. As with the Portsmouth sleeper, the Richmond-Jacksonville Pullman rode in the *Comet*

as far as Hamlet; likewise, the car went southbound only in the *Sunland* and went north on No. 16.

A 6 Sec-4 DB-6 Rmt sleeper (normally from the New Haven/Boston & Maine/Bangor & Aroostook group) was the first of several interesting cars to fill this line. The car changed in winter 1960-61 to a Union Pacific or Chicago & North Western 12 Rmt-4 DB. This configuration covered the service until replaced by a Pennsylvania *Cascade*-series 10 Rmt-5 DB in the winter of 1965-66 and a Rock Island 8 Rmt-6 DB in 1966-67. That season was the car's last appearance.

South of Jacksonville, Seaboard continued to transform the *Sunland* to a local that carried mostly mail and express. The *Sunland* may have run under the same name from Hamlet to Tampa and Miami, but it literally became a different train at Jacksonville. According to Seaboard consist memos, every car that came into Jacksonville from the north on No. 7

Seaboard printed this souvenir menu for a special Philadelphia-Miami train it ran in November 1960 for the Notre Dame-University of Miami football contest. The railroad often ran specials for sports events in the 1960s. (Larry Goolsby collection)

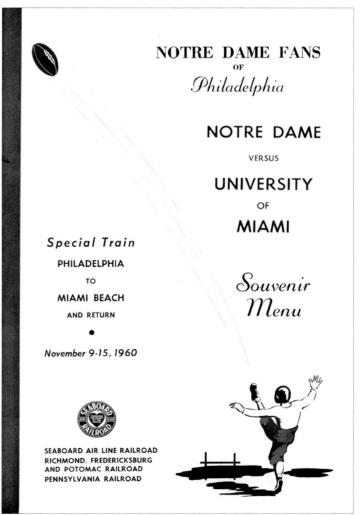

NOTRE DAME FANS
OF
Philadelphia

NOTRE DAME
VERSUS
UNIVERSITY
OF
MIAMI

Souvenir Menu

Special Train
PHILADELPHIA
TO
MIAMI BEACH
AND RETURN
•
November 9-15, 1960

SEABOARD AIR LINE RAILROAD
RICHMOND, FREDERICKSBURG
AND POTOMAC RAILROAD
PENNSYLVANIA RAILROAD

was removed, and an entirely new consist was substituted for the trek south. The Tampa train was made up of head-end cars except for one normally assigned full coach. Passengers riding the Wildwood-Miami train, Nos. 107-108, had to settle for a combine trailing along behind the head-end cars.

One E9 and 20 SDP35s

Although Seaboard upgraded its passenger car roster frequently in the 1950s, the railroad's passenger locomotive fleet remained essentially unchanged after the last new E8 in 1952. The engines did receive new colors starting at the end of 1954 as Seaboard replaced the attractive but labor-intensive citrus scheme with a light "mint green" body color accented by red striping and lettering and a dark green roof. One other change to the fleet came in 1963 when Seaboard ordered a single E9, No. 3060. The former EMD demonstrator unit replaced E6 3016, destroyed in a 1962 collision at Okeechobee, Florida. The railroad also occasionally pressed its freight units into service, particularly in summer when no steam heat was required; one unusual recorded example was a four-unit FT set on local No. 3 at Raleigh in 1960.

The locomotive status quo ended in 1964 when Seaboard bought 20 new freight-passenger SDP35 locomotives from EMD; SAL was the first railroad to purchase the model. The builder placed the 2,500-h.p., 89-m.p.h, dual-service units in its catalog specifically to appeal to railroads like Seaboard that needed to replace aging pre-war E units, yet – with further passenger service cuts clearly looming – did not want locomotives suited only for passenger trains. The SDP35s, essentially elongated SD35s with a steam generator added, allowed buyers to run them on passenger trains as long as the need lasted, then move them over to freights.

The units were delivered between July and November and were based out of Hamlet. They first went to work on several secondary and local passenger runs, starting with the Richmond-Miami *Palmland* and the Hamlet-Atlanta/Birmingham locals. Later assignments included the *Sunland*, winter-season Trains 15-16, and the Atlanta-Birmingham section of the *Silver Comet*. They eventually turned up on almost any train in the Seaboard lineup except for the *Silver Meteor* and *Silver Star*. True to their dual-purpose design, the SDP35s were also placed on piggyback trains or other fast freights where their moderately high speed could be put to good use. Seaboard in fact dressed the units in the railroad's Pullman green freight scheme, so they blended well with other freight locomotives but contrasted with the light green E units.

A single SDP35 could handle an average-size local run, but longer trains found them mixed with one or two E units. The *Palmland* often drew a back-to-back pair of the SDPs. One distinguishing feature of the SDP35s was their pleasant Hancock air whistles, something found also on a few SAL E units. Trade-ins for the SDP35s included Seaboard's remaining E4 and E6 units plus its three Baldwin DR6-4-1500s.

Passenger, Mail and Express

Although Seaboard had lost the last of its

branchline locals in late 1958, the railroad was still home to several long-distance Passenger, Mail and Express trains, dominated by the two pairs of trains from Richmond to Atlanta and Birmingham. No. 5 left Richmond after midnight, arrived at Birmingham the next evening, and boasted a through Washington-Birmingham coach. Continuing the pattern set in 1958, northbound counterpart No. 6 ended at Hamlet; timetables showed the northbound-only *Sunland*, No. 8, carrying No. 6's cars north to Richmond. That portion was listed as numbers "6-8", although No. 8 left some seven hours later. Any passenger wishing to travel north of Hamlet could quickly jump on the *Silver Meteor* if No. 6 was on time – the *Meteor* left a mere ten minutes after No. 6's scheduled arrival. For those who missed the *Meteor*, the *Silver Comet* came along about three hours later.

The other pair of locals was 3-4; No. 3 left Richmond about noon and went only to Atlanta, arriving in the Georgia capital early the next morning. No. 4 left Atlanta in the evening and got to Richmond the next afternoon. Neither train had through coaches, and passengers had to change cars at Hamlet. However, the layovers were tolerable in both directions – only about one hour southbound and two northbound. It appears that an entirely new train left for Atlanta, although perhaps with the same motive power. One Richmond-Monroe (N.C.) traveler, Bill Delmar, visited relatives in the late 1950s using No. 3 southbound and the *Silver Comet* northbound. He remembers the trips this way:

> Even though No. 3 was a "through" train, when it got to Hamlet it pulled in on one of the curved sidings on the north side of the station and all passengers had to get their stuff and get off (not many of us). Those continuing on towards Atlanta walked down the platform to the diamond, turned right, and boarded a coach or combine that was sitting beside the west side of the depot on a track parallel to the Monroe-Wilmington main. After about an hour this car (maybe two), a bunch of baggage-express cars, and an RPO pulled out towards Monroe and Atlanta. I never understood why I had to change cars and where the other cars went. I can remember that on at least one occasion the combine had a "Jim Crow" center partition.

While Nos. 3 and 4 were the very archetype of workaday mail trains, on at least a few occasions in the early 1960s the train's single coach was none other than one of the 6500-series coach-buffet-observations. Photographer David Salter snapped the car once and saw it on several other occasions. It is not clear what prompted this very odd assignment.

Seaboard also continued to run a local on the Jacksonville-Chattahoochee route, offering daytime service opposite the *Gulf Wind's* largely nocturnal schedule. Passenger, Mail and Express Nos. 36-37 normally

carried passengers in a lone baggage-coach combine, but the train's express and storage mail business was brisk. In the winter season of 1964-65, the train regularly carried cars west from Jacksonville to Tallahassee, Pensacola, Flomaton, New Orleans, and Dallas, and on occasion to other points such as Los Angeles. These "as-needed" destinations included Cottondale, Fla., Seaboard's junction with the Atlanta & St. Andrews Bay Railroad. Even at this late date, Seaboard still apparently had arrangements with the A&SAB to forward express to Panama City via that railroad's freight trains, or perhaps parcels were picked up at Cottondale by an REA truck route.

Finally, as discussed above, the *Palmland* and *Sunland* both served as locals on the southern ends of their routes, and by the time they terminated in Florida had essentially become mail and express runs with only minimal passenger accommodations.

Seaboard's locals, along with the southern portions of the *Palmland* and *Sunland*, all enjoyed substantial head-end business during most of the 1960s. Income from mail increased, although express income went downward during most of the early years of the decade. This pattern continued into the mid-1960s with some slight ups and downs. Even express earnings turned upward in 1964, rising 21.5 percent over 1963. Some of that jump came from a rate increase but other revenue was probably the result of express shipments that had formerly moved over the Florida East Coast. Mail and express together contributed more than a third of Seaboard's total passenger train revenue throughout the 1960s.

Revenue, millions of dollars:				
Year	Passenger	Mail	Express	Total
1961	13.8	7.0	1.9	22.7
1962	14.0	7.1	1.7	22.8
1963	14.7	8.0	1.6	24.3
1964	14.6	8.0	2.0	24.6
1965	14.8	7.5	2.1	24.4
1966	14.9	6.6	2.0	23.3

Seaboard's locals saw another revenue-enhancing change during this period, the addition of piggyback and auto rack cars. Following the introduction of intermodal cars on the *Tidewater* in 1960, piggyback flats became common on trains such as locals 5 and 6 and the *Sunland's* Jacksonville-Tampa leg. The *Sunland* was sometimes little more than an intermodal train with an express car and combine on the rear.

Seaboard added some passenger-equipped intermodal equipment of its own in 1962 and 1964 with orders for three Flexi-Van Mark III flatcars (Nos. 1-3) from Greenville Steel Car Company. The flats carried vans that could be lifted from their highway bogies and placed directly onto the cars, thus lowering overall height and saving substantial weight. A specially designed tractor slid the vans onto the flats and pivoted them into place; no overhead cranes or forklifts were required as with some versions of cargo containers. The Flexi-Vans were used on two routes: Jacksonville-Tampa on the *Palmland* and Atlanta-Birmingham on locals 5 and 6, then beyond to Memphis on Frisco's *Sunnyland* (later the *Southland*).

The Flexi-Van flatcars were painted silver-gray with red lettering when delivered, although repaints received black lettering. The vans resembled those in Seaboard's piggyback trailer fleet, in unpainted aluminum with the red stylized "Seaboard" logo. They also carried "U.S. Mail" signs. While several railroads like New York Central had large Flexi-Van fleets, Seaboard tried just three, and it appears they were not used in passenger service past the Seaboard Coast Line merger.

Despite some modestly encouraging mail and express numbers in the early 1960s, these trends would not last. Seaboard's 1965 annual report foretold the coming end of railroad mail business: on July 1, 1965, the Post Office initiated its new sectional center plan using trucks to connect new distribution centers. SAL said the plan would substantially lower mail revenues, especially in Florida. For 1966, Seaboard mail revenues fell by nearly $937,000, and in 1967 the combined drop for both predecessors of the new Seaboard Coast Line was 21.2 percent. It was the beginning of the end for the familiar Railway Post Office and long strings of head-end cars carrying the nation's letters, parcels, magazines, newspapers – the familiar elements that once kept thousands of railroad cars, employees, and stations busy across the country.

Unsurprisingly, the postal changes helped trigger two cuts in Seaboard passenger service in 1965 and 1966. On November 14, 1965, SAL discontinued the Wildwood-Tampa section of the *Palmland*, Nos. 11-12 (renumbered from 1-2 in 1964). The reason Seaboard gave would become an increasingly familiar one: "the diversion of mail traffic to truck routes." The train had declined to a shadow of its former self near the end; one memorable consist included only a freight C420 locomotive pulling an express car and a combine. On October 18, 1966, Jacksonville-Chattahoochee locals 36 and 37 succumbed to the same forces, exacerbated by the loss of the Louisville & Nashville connecting train that had forwarded cars from Chattahoochee to New Orleans.

Railroad express shipments were coming under similar pressure. The Railway Express Agency had been the railroads' exclusive contractor for express shipments since 1929, and for decades the company had made money as the premier carrier of high-value shipments. But REA increasingly moved packages by trucks and planes as railroad passenger service declined, and changed its formal name to REA Express in 1961. Some railroads, including the Southern Railway, even pulled out of the contract. The organization tried to stay afloat, but faced with accelerating contract cancellations and an outdated physical infrastructure, went out of business in 1975.

The Venice section of the Silver Meteor, *Nos. 257-258, was pulled by venerable rail motor car 2028 after about 1958 when the 1936-built unit was relieved of its last branchline local assignment. In this February 1961 view at Durant, Fla., No. 2028 still has many hallmarks of its earlier days including a large single-lens headlight and its Railway Post Office section. (David W. Salter photo)*

The Meteor's *Venice section often drew a boiler-equipped Alco road-switcher when rail car 2028 was in the shop. On New Year's Day 1966, RSC3 1533 stands at the Venice station with an express car, coach, and sleeper. (Robert A. Selle photo, Larry Goolsby collection)*

The Silver Fleet's Final Seasons

As Seaboard passed the mid-point of the 1960s, the railroad's passenger service was in overall good shape. The diesel fleet had been updated with the road's versatile new SDP35s, and the passenger car roster had received a fresh infusion of additional lightweight cars. Passenger volume was strong, particularly for summer vacations; Seaboard kept up its advertising campaign for Florida getaways, and offered special travel packages to the New York World's Fair in 1964 and 1965. By the summer of 1965, July and August had become the highest passenger months of the year, upending the traditional pattern in which winter travel dominated. The railroad enjoyed a particularly large surge in July and August 1966 because of a nationwide airline strike; passengers carried that year set a high for the decade, over 936,000 vs. 901,000 in 1960.

Seaboard had also pulled ahead of rival Atlantic Coast Line in some respects, particularly summer first-class travel between New York and Florida. Seaboard maintained two year-round separate trains from New York while ACL had begun consolidating its two *Champions* (east and west coast) north of Jacksonville in 1964 for parts of the summer and fall seasons. Seaboard also offered somewhat more summer Pullman space than did ACL; by summer 1967, the *East Coast Champion* carried just two regular sleepers to Miami while Seaboard operated three (including one with Pullman lounge space). ACL also began using "Budget Room Coaches," actually Pullmans that were all or mostly roomettes, which passengers could occupy for regular coach fare plus a modest space charge; Seaboard never introduced an economy sleeping car. Finally, the *Silver Meteor* remained distinguished by its unique Sun Lounge and

its year-round end-of-train observation car.

The Florida East Coast strike may have also hurt ACL's competitiveness. The ACL trains' post-strike rerouting away from much of the Florida coast robbed them of the traffic base they once enjoyed at stops between Jacksonville and West Palm Beach, including St. Augustine, Daytona, New Smyrna, and Ft. Pierce. The longer route was also slower than the former direct trip over the FEC. Finally, the summer ACL *East Coast Champion* schedules put the train into and out of Miami about an hour behind the *Meteor*, giving the impression to some passengers that it ranked behind the Seaboard train.

In the railroad's final winter season of 1966-67, the *Silver Meteor* ran with as many as 18 regularly assigned cars. The train left Washington with up to nine normally assigned sleepers, mostly 10-6s but also a Sun Lounge, an *Avon Park*-class 11 DB car, and one of the unusual *Boca Grande*-class 5 DB-2 Cpt-2 DR cars. A baggage-dormitory, coaches, two diners, and a coach-lounge filled out the train, capped by the 6600-series observation. By this date the train had become one of the last in the country that still regularly ran a properly positioned boat-tailed observation car, whose kin were only a few years earlier the common hallmark of U.S. streamliners. The *Meteor* continued its traditional schedule of afternoon departures from New York and morning departures from Miami, taking just under 26 hours southbound and about 25 ½ hours northbound.

The *Meteor's* connecting trains continued running as before, with cars for St. Petersburg and Venice splitting off at Wildwood as Trains 157-158. Counting the local heavyweight combine up front, the west

In a photo probably taken just before the merger, the 2028 has undergone some body and lettering style modifications, including a modern headlight and relocation of the road name along the bottom of the side. The train is at Venice with a Chesapeake & Ohio sleeper and two SAL coaches. (Bob's Photo collection)

coast train could carry as many as eight regularly assigned cars. A through coach and 10-6 sleeper were set out at Tampa for Nos. 257-258 to Bradenton, Sarasota, and Venice. Motor car 2028 continued to pull the Venice trains, which also included a heavy-weight baggage-express car except on Sundays.

The *Silver Star* remained the *Silver Meteor's* counterpart, with morning departures from New York and afternoon departures from Miami. The winter-season *Star*, which bypassed Jacksonville, posted the best New York-Miami timings in Seaboard's lineup (24 hours 50 minutes southbound). While it lacked the *Meteor's* best features, the Star remained a well-equipped train, featuring 10-6 sleepers, a *Mountain*-class 6 DB-lounge, two 4-1-5-4 sleepers, a mid-train tavern-lounge (normally one of the diaphragm-equipped 6600s), and a coach-lounge. A baggage-dorm and two diners rounded out the train, which could have as many as 17 regularly assigned cars south of Richmond. The *Star* also continued its winter-season-only practice of a west coast section to Tampa and St. Petersburg that included a coach, diner, 10-6 sleeper, and 4-1-5-4 sleeper.

The *Silver Comet* continued running much as it had in recent years, with only a coach and a 10-6 sleeper assigned all the way through from New York to Birmingham. However, for the last half of December 1966, the train's New York-Atlanta tavern-coach was extended to Birmingham. This peak holiday period also saw extra New York-Atlanta and Washington-Atlanta coaches added. One unusual photo from this period shows the Birmingham section with a 6500-series coach-lounge on the rear, correctly pointed, giv-

ing some semblance of a properly made-up streamliner even at this late date.

The *Comet* also carried a fairly substantial head-end consist, especially on the Atlanta-Birmingham segment. Effective with the winter season of 1966-67, the train was assigned a baggage-RPO and as many as three express cars south of Richmond; one each of the latter was set out at Hamlet and Columbia. South of Atlanta, the train carried up to four additional express cars for Midwest and California points, all of them handed off to the Frisco at Birmingham.

Adjustments for Seaboard's Other Trains

Although the Silver Fleet trains kept up their traditional services and passenger loadings, the *Tidewater* and *Gulf Wind* did not fare as well. The *Tidewater* suffered a substantial reduction in its services effective November 14, 1966, when it suddenly became coach-only. Gone were the Portsmouth-Atlanta sleeper, the Portsmouth-Jacksonville sleeper, and the dining car. The train ran with this shortened consist for the balance of Seaboard's separate existence.

Change also came to the *Gulf Wind* in fall 1966. On October 18, 1966, the Louisville & Nashville discontinued as a separate run the *Wind's* longtime eastbound connecting train, the *Piedmont Limited*. (L&N continued combining the westbound *Wind* with the *Pan American*.) The move caused L&N to take back its two *Royal* observation cars (which soon after appeared under lease on Atlantic Coast Line's winter-only *Florida Special*). The change also shifted the *Gulf Wind's* eastbound schedule several hours later, leaving New Orleans at 8:30 p.m. (Central time) and getting to Jacksonville at 1:10 in the afternoon.

Despite the loss of its observation car, the *Gulf Wind* underwent some minor expansions at the same time. The Seaboard dining car began running through to Chattahoochee rather than Tallahassee so it could serve breakfast eastbound on the revised schedule, and a weekend Jacksonville-Chattahoochee coach was added. The *Wind* also gained some head-end cars from locals 36 and 37, which had been discontinued at the same time; for the winter of 1966-67, the train carried three regularly assigned express and storage mail cars. The *Wind's* motive power also changed during the late Seaboard years, with SDP35s frequently replacing E units starting about 1965.

The *Palmland* and *Sunland* closed out their Seaboard careers with no significant additional changes. The *Palmland* still boasted New York-Miami and New York-Hamlet 10-6 Pullmans for the summer 1967 season, although the latter made its last trip on June 10. The train kept its Raleigh-Jacksonville food service along with a healthy complement of head-end cars. While a number of cars were dropped at Jacksonville, the train continued to Miami with its through coach and sleeper and even picked up a weekend Jacksonville-Miami coach.

The Hamlet-Florida *Sunland* still forwarded through coaches to Jacksonville from Washington (from the *Silver Comet*) and from Portsmouth (from the *Tidewater* and *Comet*). At Jacksonville, the train picked up an entirely new set of cars and proceeded to Wildwood, where it split and sent its Miami cars

south via connecting trains 107 and 108. Both sections carried only a regularly assigned combine to accommodate passengers. The Miami trains appeared to rarely run with more than three cars, and were put in charge of SDP35s at times.

Despite some cutbacks in mail revenue, Seaboard's two remaining Passenger, Mail and Express trains, Nos. 3-4 to Atlanta and 5-6 to Birmingham, continued running with reasonably healthy consists. But in what was perhaps another omen of the coming further reductions in mail and express, Seaboard's last employee timetables labeled the trains "Local Passenger" even though the PM&E designation remained in the public timetables.

The Seaboard Air Line's corporate existence came to an end on June 30, 1967; the next day it became part of the new Seaboard Coast Line Railroad. Seaboard brought to the new company a strong suit of well-known named trains and a substantial network of secondary and local trains. Many of these trains would not survive the short but turbulent SCL era, which would culminate in the most significant passenger service cuts in U.S. railroad history. Yet Seaboard's best streamliners would not only remain in place throughout these upheavals but would eventually become the sole standard-bearers of the long New York-Florida passenger tradition.

North of Wildwood, the Silver Meteor *attained its full length for the run to New York. E7 3035 leaves the SAL junction point with a long train for Jacksonville and north during April 1964. (David W. Salter photo)*

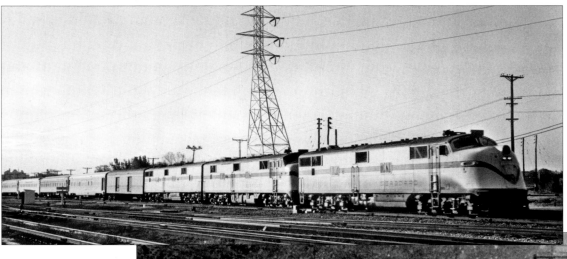

A typical Silver Star of the late 1950s-early 1960s period nears Richmond's Broad Street Station on November 8, 1959, behind an E4, E7, and B unit. Express cars were common on the train, which often carried several of the heavyweight cars on its southbound runs. (Gene Collora photo)

Seaboard E7 3026 and two more A-units lead the northbound Silver Star through a rare heavy snowfall at Raleigh, N.C., on the morning of March 6, 1962. The train features a heavyweight 180-series baggage-dorm up front, an ACL 10-6 County-series sleeper, and a modified 6600-series tavern-observation on the end. (Harvey W. George photo)

A moderate-size northbound Silver Star passes a Seaboard CTC signal at Belleview, Fla. (north of Wildwood), in April 1964. The train features E7 3032, and second E7A, a silver-gray baggage-RPO, and 10 or 11 lightweight cars. (David W. Salter photo)

The southbound Silver Comet, No. 33, is still making 60 m.p.h. just before slowing for Howells Yard as it slips under the Interstate 75 overpass in northwest Atlanta. This July 1965 scene shows E8 3049, two E7s, two head-end cars, and more than a dozen lightweight cars at 7:30 on this warm and humid morning. (David W. Salter photo)

By the 1960s, the Silver Comet's typical Birmingham section had become a mixture of through lightweight cars and local heavyweight head-end equipment. On an overcast April 1962 afternoon, Seaboard E4 3011 leads a motley collection out of Birmingham Terminal Station: an Illinois Central express car; a Seaboard silver-gray baggage-RPO and Budd coach; a Pennsylvania Tuscan red sleeper; and an SAL 225-class heavyweight diner and office car. The train was due out of Birmingham at 1:20 p.m. Central Time, and made the run to Atlanta in three hours 45 minutes. (Felix Brunot photo, Robert H. Hanson collection)

On an April 1965 day, members of the National Railway Historical Society's Atlanta Chapter took their ex-ACL 8 Sec-buffet-lounge Washington Club to Birmingham and back on the Silver Comet. Photographer David Salter took this photo of the westbound trip from heavyweight diner 227 at the south end of the CTC siding at mile 661.8 between Piedmont and Maxwellborn, Alabama. Ahead are RF&P 10-6 sleeper King George in Tuscan red, coach 6214, a baggage-RPO, two express cars, and finally SDP35 1108. (David W. Salter photo)

A long Birmingham section of the Silver Comet leaves Atlanta behind a single SDP35 on this July 1966 morning. New Haven City Point and a second NH 14 Rmt-4 DB sleeper bring up the rear; the 14-4s normally covered the Portsmouth-Atlanta sleeper line but have been pressed into extra service to Birmingham today, probably because of the airline strike that has swelled passenger trains nationwide. Other equipment includes four express cars, four coaches (including an RF&P heavyweight and a Seaboard American Flyer car), and an ex-FEC diner. The train has just backed north from Terminal Station to the east end of Howells Yard, and has now turned onto the Birmingham main to resume its run to the Alabama industrial center. (David W. Salter photo)

This view of No. 33's Birmingham section confirms that this part of Seaboard's route is far away from Florida's sand and surf. With the Alabama hills in the background, SDP35 1116 leads an 11-car consist (four head-end cars and seven lightweights, swollen by the airline strike) at Borden Springs on the morning of July 23, 1966. (David W. Salter photo)

On rare occasions, the Silver Comet got to Atlanta too late to allow time at Birmingham to clean, service, and turn the train on schedule. When that happened, those tasks were performed on the main consist in Atlanta and Seaboard operated a separate "make-up" train to Birmingham. The example pictured here in August 1963 had GP7 1778, two express cars, an RPO-baggage, and two lightweight coaches. The photo was taken at the west (timetable south) end of Howells Yard. (David W. Salter photo)

The Tidewater's schedule was closely aligned with the Silver Comet, which forwarded a Tidewater coach and sleeper to Atlanta. E7 3030, which was often the Tidewater's power in the mid-1960s, stands at Raleigh after the train had made its evening southbound evening rendezvous with the Comet. The Tidewater was scheduled to get to Raleigh at 8:30 p.m., and the Comet left at 9:10. (Harvey W. George photo)

This going-away view of the Tidewater at Suffolk, Va., in April 1966 reveals a Seaboard (ex-C&O) coach from the 6242-6251 series on the rear. Next are a New Haven 14-4 sleeper; a lightweight coach and sleeper; an SAL heavyweight diner; and a baggage-RPO behind the E7. (William H. Todd collection)

Seaboard's rarely photographed No. 16 played the dual role of a winter-season mail and express train between Jacksonville and Hamlet as well as transportation for the Tidewater's northbound through cars. The train's 6:15 p.m. departure from Jacksonville provided just enough light for this April 1965 view at the Trout River bridge showing an E7, two express cars, a heavyweight combine, and three lightweight cars. (Wayne Johnson photo, William H. Todd collection)

Right and Below: The Gulf Wind got one of Seaboard's SDP35s from time to time in the mid-1960s, as with No. 1106 on this occasion in August 1965. The train is making its evening departure from Jacksonville and has the Wind's typical combination of heavyweight and lightweight cars. Behind the 2,500-h.p. locomotive are three express cars, two Seaboard coaches, and a Seaboard diner, all heavyweight. The final two cars are L&N lightweights, a blue Pine-series sleeper and one of the Royal 5 DB-observation cars. (David W. Salter photos)

These two views of the Gulf Wind at Tallahassee about 1967 show a typical consist of the train's last months under the Seaboard banner. Behind E7 3020 are express cars from the Georgia Railroad, Railway Express Agency, Pennsylvania, and Louisville & Nashville. The passenger-carrying equipment includes Seaboard coaches 853 and 815 in Pullman green and silver-gray, respectively; L&N 6-4-6 sleeper Dixiana Pine; and SAL heavyweight diner 1009. (Randy Young photos)

Upholding its role as workhorse of the east coast route during the later 1950s and the 1960s, this southbound edition of the Palmland in December 1962 has no fewer than four E units and 25 cars, starting with a large group of heavyweight Pullmans up front. The cars could be carrying servicemen to Ft. Jackson outside Columbia. E8 3055 leads the train as it sweeps around a curve at Wise, N.C., at 11:55 a.m. – more than five hours late. (Curtis C. Tillotson Jr. photo)

In a coming-and-going scene showing the Palmland in its mid-1960s prime, Seaboard 1102 and a sister SDP35 carry northbound No. 10 through peach orchards north of Columbia, S.C., in June 1966. Following a half-dozen express cars and an RPO are two silver-gray heavy-weight coaches; a Chesapeake & Ohio 10-6 protecting the New York-Miami sleeper line; one of Seaboard's heavyweight grill cars (probably No. 849 today); and full diner 6102. Although normally assigned only between Raleigh and Hamlet, the full diner sometimes ran farther south if passenger loadings required. (David W. Salter photos)

The latter-day Palmland not only made numerous local stops for passengers but also had several pickups and setouts of express cars along the way. One such point was Columbia, S.C., where the train added or dropped express cars operating between there and several northeastern cities. The first photo in this August 1966 set shows northbound No. 10 with Railway Express Agency 8290 bringing up the rear the train. The former troop sleeper trails a mix of SAL and RF&P coaches, the Jacksonville-New York 10-6 sleeper (apparently a Seaboard Atlanta-class car), and the train's normal heavyweight grill car. The second photo shows a long southbound Palmland with numerous passenger cars followed by an express car and about five auto racks on the rear. (Chris Allen photos)

Seaboard No. 7, the southbound Sunland, blasts through Kingsland, Ga., early on the morning of April 23, 1966. By the 1960s, the Sunland had evolved into two different trains; the Hamlet-Jacksonville segment shown here was a respectable passenger train with a Washington-Jacksonville coach, a winter-season Richmond-Jacksonville sleeper, and a through coach and sleeper from Portsmouth. But south of Jacksonville, the Sunland became a local that often trailed intermodal cars behind a combine and coach. (J.E. Parker photo, David W. Salter collection)

In the winter, and year-round after October 1963, Seaboard operated a Miami section of the Sunland (No. 107) south of Wildwood. At 12:20 p.m. on April 16, 1964, a typical five-car Tampa section (No. 7) has just passed the Miami line junction at Coleman behind frequently assigned Baldwin 2702. Coleman was just south of Wildwood, and double track extended between the two points. Five minutes later, No. 107 veers off on the "X" line to Winter Haven, West Palm Beach, and Miami. Two E4s, 3010 and 3004, have a far longer train than the day's Tampa side. The only passenger accommodation is a Wildwood-Miami combine on the rear; the ACL lightweight sleeper up front is deadheading to Miami. ACL passenger equipment was unusual on Seaboard trains, but Coast Line's sleepers and head-end cars appeared from time to time. (David W. Salter photos)

The Sunland's Tampa section frequently added loaded auto rack cars and piggyback flats behind its passenger equipment. This photo north of Plant City shows the southbound Sunland with four head-end cars, a combine, and a coach plus about seven intermodal cars in November 1961. Photographer Salter noted that the last two racks were loaded with new 1962 Thunderbirds. (David W. Salter photos)

No. 3 could draw varied locomotive consists depending on whether it needed more horsepower or had been enlisted to transfer freight units between terminals. In these two scenes at Norlina, N.C., on August 16, 1960, E7 3030 leads GP9 1924 and an FT set as well as a lengthy train of head-end cars. (Felix Brunot photos, Robert H. Hanson collection)

This September 10, 1966, edition of No. 4 has four deadheading Pullmans right behind SDP35 1118, ACL Cumberland County and three others. The train is making 60 m.p.h. at 9:40 in the morning as it moves north through Sandhills country at the Hoffman, N.C., siding. An RF&P heavyweight coach brings up the rear. (David W. Salter photo)

Passenger, Mail and Express No. 4 is arriving at the Hamlet station after its overnight run from Atlanta early on September 10, 1966. Behind SDP35 1119 and GP7 1768 is a motley consist of instruction car 75000, express cars, a baggage-coach combine, and several piggyback cars. The train is entering one of the tracks used by Atlanta-line passenger trains directly behind (north of) the station; the track at right is the connection track used by freight trains moving from the Monroe/Atlanta line to the Richmond main. (David W. Salter photo)

Nos. 3 and 4 drew early assignments of the SDP35s, with one of the units usually sufficing even for long trains. A good example is this December 1964 view of No. 1106 bringing northbound Train 4 around the curve at Raleigh Tower, a favorite location of local photographers. The Norfolk Southern crosses at an angle behind the tower, and the Southern mainline extends to the left; this was the north end of SR-SAL paired track between here and Cary. (Warren Calloway photo)

A 16-car No. 5 makes its early morning entrance at Hamlet on September 10, 1966. Trains 5-6 were listed in the timetable as running between Richmond and Birmingham, but no cars went all the way through. Passengers riding in the single silver-gray coach behind all the box and refrigerator cars had to change at Hamlet to continue beyond the Seaboard crossroads town. E7 3023 and SDP35 1115 provide the horsepower today. (David W. Salter photo)

Local No. 6 was a frequent subject of David Salter's camera. Locals 5 and 6 ran on the schedule of the old Cotton Blossom and served Birmingham as well as Atlanta, and appeared in daylight south of Hamlet. This portrait from November 1963 shows GP7 1811, E7 3029, and a second E7 at Mina, Ga. (just east of Atlanta), with four regular passenger cars followed by five piggybacks and a rider combine added at Howells Yard. (David W. Salter photo)

On November 4, 1965, SDP35 1107 takes a 10-car edition of No. 6 over Pumpkinvine Creek west of Dallas, Ga., with express cars, baggage-RPO, coach, and a Flexi-Van flat on the rear. The Flexi-Vans ran for several years in the mid-1960s carrying storage mail between Atlanta and Memphis. (David W. Salter photo)

E7 3048 has paused with seldom-photographed local No. 37 at Tallahassee, Fla., on its westward (timetable south) daily trek between Jacksonville and Flomaton, Alabama. The train often had Louisville & Nashville head-end cars that ran through, including an usual example of an interline baggage-RPO. Two L&N cars lead the consist on this day in mid-1966, followed by a box express car, a Seaboard American Flyer combine, and a Seaboard silver-gray coach. (W.E. Mims photo)

Seaboard purchased three Flexi-Van flatcars for storage mail service on its local passenger trains. These views at Howells Yard in Atlanta about July 1966 show the loaded cars and the special truck tractor used to slide the vans off their bogies and onto the flatcars, which were in Atlanta-Birmingham-Memphis service. (Richard Stewart photos)

This mid-April 1965 photo, taken late in Seaboard's winter season (between the mid-December and late-April timetable changes), shows a 22-car northbound Silver Star just south of Norlina, N.C., in double-track territory. Both the Star and the Meteor often exceeded 20 cars in peak travel times during the mid-1960s. Three E units led by E7 3018 keep the train moving at track speed. (Curtis C. Tillotson Jr. photo)

The Seaboard Coast Line merger is less than two weeks away in this view from June 17, 1967, as the southbound Silver Meteor leaves Jacksonville Terminal Station under the Myrtle Avenue bridge. The Meteor would remain a hallmark of the new SCL's passenger service as well. (W.E. Mims photo)

Passenger, Mail and Express ... and Hamlet

Seaboard's iconic Hamlet passenger station has rightly been celebrated as the symbolic hub of the system, with five mainlines radiating from the crossing diamonds on the station's southern corner. Passengers by the thousands used its modest waiting room and café over the years, some quickly changing trains and others staying overnight at the nearby Seaboard Hotel. But the L-shaped station was also the epicenter of the brisk mail and express commerce brought to town by the *Palmland, Sunland,* and locals. The railroad express activity and local truck routes were overseen from the Railway Express Agency's building just behind the passenger station.

A fleet of baggage and express floats lined the station's platforms whenever a Passenger, Mail and Express or secondary train rolled in. The Richmond-Columbia line passed by the station from northeast to southwest; crossing it at right angles from northwest to southeast was the Monroe/Atlanta-Wilmington main. Curving behind the station on its north side were several connec-tion tracks between the two mains, starting with a passenger connection track close to the station and, farthest away, the freight connection. Other sidings were used for unloading express and car storage. Spurs on the southwest side of the station (parallel to the Monroe line) were also used for storage or to make up locals for Atlanta and Birmingham. Finally, there was another set of storage tracks south of and parallel to the Richmond main.

In later years, passenger diesels were another element of the busy station scene. Refueling racks were located on the Richmond-Columbia line on both sides of the crossing and along the connection tracks to the Monroe/Atlanta line behind the station. Road units were also set out or picked up if they needed servicing or inspection at the Hamlet shops. Meanwhile, a station switcher, often an EMD 1400-series engine, stayed busy taking cars on and off trains or making up trains that originated/terminated at Hamlet, like the latter-day *Sunland* and locals 3 and 4.

This daily memo of extra and bad-order equipment on hand at Hamlet for August 9, 1962, gives a snapshot of the great amount of passenger car activity there. Most of these cars were probably in the storage tracks at the station, with others at the shops for light repairs. The cars are all heavyweights except for Pennsylvania 10-6 Allegheny Rapids, which like several other cars is bad-ordered (B/O). Other items of interest include the many 1200-series sleeping cars converted to coach use and the lineups of mail and express cars to be placed on Trains 4, 5, 8, and 9. The memo also lists six E units either ready for service or awaiting inspection. (Larry Goolsby collection)

Hamlet, N.C., August 9, 1962

Mr. C. H. Crumpler – Richmond
Mr. R. C. Jones – Raleigh
Mr. J. A. Odom

Passenger equipment on hand Hamlet:

Allegheny Rapids B/O   REX 4071-6839-Rfgrs. Prr 6950-9643-6946-REX 7198-7728-5189 Wash DH.
Sal 1201
Sal 1202
Sal 1233   No.8   No.5   No.9   No.4
Sal 1254
Sal 1258   ACL 1605 SM   Sal 173   N&W 1338   Sal 334   DH Rich
Sal 1270   Sal 824   Sal 103   RFP 518   "   "
Sal 1271   L&N 1475 DH   Sal 849   RFP 521   "   "
Sal 810   Sal 811 DH Jax   Sal 96
Sal 813   Sal 586 "   "   Sal 279
Sal 819   MOTORS HERE   Sal 852
Sal 831
Sal 853   3028 in shop OK 10th.
Prr 1721-1763   3038 in shop OK 10th.
Sal 275-342 B/O 3054 in shop for insp
Sal 707-746 B/O 3059 in shop for trip insp.
Sal 97-82   B/O 3053 to 8
                 3058 in shop for insp.

                              W. F. Robbins

The southbound Palmland *and northbound local No. 4 stand at the Hamlet station early on the morning of March 24, 1967. This view looks southwest along the Raleigh-Columbia main, and includes diesel fuel racks in the foreground and a loaded auto rack car on the right, perhaps just set out by No. 4. Floats full of mail and express fill the platform between the two trains. (Bill Ingram photo)*

The station's News Stand, shown at left in this afternoon scene facing northeast, was an essential stop for Hamlet passengers, especially those changing trains and wanting a quick lunch or snack. In the center of the scene is the entrance to the subway that went under the two main tracks, and at right is the northbound Palmland. *(Bill Ingram photo)*

Two March 24, 1967, photos show some of the many extra passenger cars kept at the Hamlet station. The first photo shows the west side of the station and looks northwest along the Monroe-Charlotte line; spur tracks on both sides of the main hold strings of extra heavyweight coaches and Pullmans. The spur at right was where locals Nos. 13-14 once waited for their connections on their daily runs between Wilmington and Rutherfordton. The second view shows more extra coaches on a curved siding that parallels the freight connecting track between the Raleigh and Monroe/Charlotte lines; the location is north of the station and looks west. (Bill Ingram photos)

menu

Patrons of the Silver Meteor enjoyed selecting their meals from this October 1962 menu. Dinners could range from just over $2 to $4.95 for the sirloin steak. Many a la carte items and desserts were also available. (Michael W. Savchak collection)

Silver Meteor

Dinner Suggestions

(Please order by letter and write on meal check each item desired)

E—$2.10

Golden Brown Western Omelet
French Fried Potatoes
Whole Wheat or White Toast
Apple Tapioca Pudding
Coffee   Tea   Milk

F—$2.25

Grilled Chopped 8 oz. Sirloin Steak
on Toast
French Fried Potatoes
Slice Raw Onion   Pickle Strips
Apple Tapioca Pudding
Coffee   Tea   Milk

G—$2.50

Baked Meat Loaf, Spanish Sauce
Whipped Potatoes
Assorted Bread
Apple Tapioca Pudding
Coffee   Tea   Milk

(Please order entree by number and write on meal check each item desired, as waiters are not permitted to accept or serve oral orders)

Table d'Hote Dinners

(Price after entree includes the complete meal)

Choice

Half Chilled Grapefruit   Chilled Apple Juice
Old Fashioned Bean Soup   Consomme, Hot or Jellied

1. Fried Haddock Fillet, Tartar Sauce _____ $2.50
2. Chicken a la King on Hot Corn Bread _____ $2.65
3. Roast Fresh Ham, Apple Sauce _____ $2.85
4. Oven Broiled Calf's Liver with Bacon _____ $2.85
5. Charcoal Broiled 8 oz. Steak with Mushrooms ___ $2.95

Choice of Two

Fluffy Whipped Potatoes   Baked Hubbard Squash
Candied Sweet Potatoes   Mashed White Turnips

Dinner Rolls   Assorted Bread

Choice

Ice Cream with Wafers   Pumpkin Pie with Whipped Cream
Banana Shortcake   Apple Tapioca Pudding
Your Favorite Cheese, Saltines

Coffee   Tea   Milk

10/15/62

CIGARETTES

Popular Brands 35¢

CIGARS

Various Prices as Indicated
on Individual Box

ALE AND BEER

An Assortment of
National Brands 45¢

NECTAROSE
Vin Rosé d'Anjou

This delightful Rosé is an outstanding wine imported from the historic Loire Valley in France. Light, gay, and graceful, it harmonizes perfectly with fish, fowl, or meats, served chilled.

**The Half-Bottle
$1.00**

A la Carte

SOUPS AND JUICES	Chilled Fruit or Vegetable Juices, Large Glass _____	40
	Chicken Soup (Cup) _____	40
	Cream of Tomato Soup (Cup) _____	40
	Consomme, Hot or Jellied (Cup) _____	40
	Turtle Soup with Sherry (Cup) _____	40
SALAD	Tossed Green Salad, French Dressing _____	50
	Hearts of Lettuce, French Dressing _____	50
GRILLED	Grilled Ham or Bacon (5 Strips) with Eggs _____	1.75
	(Toast, Rolls or Assorted Bread with Butter served with above)	
SEAFOOD	Broiled or Fried Filet of Fresh Fish _____	1.50
SANDWICHES	"Double Decker" Sandwiches—	
	(served with Pickle Strips and Potato Chips)	
	Baked Ham _____ 90 Chicken _____	1.00
	American Cheese _____ 75 Club _____	1.50
	Bacon, Lettuce and Tomato _____ 90 Sardine _____	1.25
DESSERTS	Ice Cream with Wafers _____	35
	Bartlett Pears _____	45
	Baked Apple with Cream _____	45
	Prunes with Cream _____	45
	Chilled Florida Grapefruit _____	45
	Preserved Figs with Cream _____	60
	Sliced Pineapple _____	45
	Your Favorite Cheese with Saltines _____	45
	Apple Pie with Cheese _____	45
	Apple Tapioca Pudding _____	40
BEVERAGES	Coffee, Pot _____ 35 Tea, Pot, Hot or Iced _____	35
	Cocoa, Pot _____ 35 Milk, Individual _____	25
	Buttermilk _____ 25	

For Members of our Armed Services holding Government Meal Orders we offer a special dinner. Please consult Dining Car Steward.

An extra charge of 35¢ per person will be made for meals served outside of Dining Car. This service is subject to delay during meal periods.

Prices shown subject to change.

**SIRLOIN STEAK DINNER
$4.95**

Appetizer
Charcoal Broiled Sirloin Steak
French Fried Potatoes or Crisped Onion Rings
Tossed Green Salad, French Dressing
Bread and Butter
Choice of Dessert

Coffee   Tea   Milk

On July 1, 1967, the Seaboard Air Line and Atlantic Coast Line merged to form the Seaboard Coast Line Railroad. SAL president John W. Smith and ACL president W. Thomas Rice had begun merger talks in 1958, and the union finally became effective when opponents exhausted their legal efforts. Both railroads had strong passenger train traditions that carried over into the new company. SCL ads announcing "The New Railroad is Here" led with photographs of passenger E units, and roadside billboards featured streamliners as often as freight trains. Rice, who became SCL president, said the new company would run passenger trains as long as the public patronized them. SCL emerged as one of the relatively few railroads in the late 1960s that still had a "pro-passenger" attitude.

The first SCL passenger timetable, issued on the merger date, was simply a combination of both partners' existing services and schedules. The new timetable adopted the dark orange cover used by Seaboard, complete with SAL's traditional drawing of the *Silver Meteor's* observation on the cover – although an SCL emblem replaced the *Meteor's* tail sign.

The first SCL annual report's passenger train statistics were less encouraging than Seaboard's last years: the combined report showed a significant 24 percent decrease in passenger revenue compared to the two companies' 1966 figures. SCL explained that 1966's numbers had been inflated due to that year's airline strike, and that 1967's normally lucrative summer travel had been hurt by a four-day railroad strike in July. Mail and express revenue also declined; mail alone dropped 21 percent below the 1966 totals. As a result, SCL said it was being forced to seek discontinuance of "lightly patronized passenger trains which had depended upon mail as their principal source of revenue." These pressures, plus steady increases in automobile and air travel, would soon begin showing their effects on former Seaboard passenger trains.

Modest Changes – At First

SCL's second passenger timetable, issued December 15, 1967, carried most of the same trains and basic services as before. One visible exception was in the *Silver Star's* consist: a "Budget Room Coach" replaced the *Star's* earlier *Mountain*-series 6 DB-lounge. Using the same cars ACL had operated under this label starting in 1966, the *Star* employed leased Baltimore & Ohio 16 duplex roomette-4 double bedroom sleepers named for birds, such as *Gull* and *Oriole*. The cars offered passengers a room for regular coach fare plus a room charge. The bedrooms were identical to regular first-class bedrooms, while the duplex roomettes were slightly smaller than a regular roomette and were on two levels. The *Star* otherwise was similar to its traditional makeup, with a number of 10-6s and an 11 DB sleeper from New York plus a 4 Rmt-1 Cpt-5 DB-4 Sec car from Richmond. The train added a west coast section for the winter as it had before the merger.

Another noticeable December change came in ex-ACL service as the *Champion* lost its east coast section and began operating only to Tampa and St. Pe-

Merger Day – July 1, 1967 – finds the Silver Meteor *proudly leaving Jacksonville Terminal Station with nothing changed except the name of its owner. The now ex-Seaboard flagship train has a typical lineup of the railroad's finest motive power and cars, with E8 3049 leading two more sisters elephant-style and a long string of matched stainless steel equipment. The train would endure throughout the SCL years with only minimal changes. (W.E. Mims photo)*

Seven months into the SCL merger, the northbound Silver Meteor rolls out over the Trout River bridge in the late afternoon of February 25, 1968. The train shows a few changes, including the two trailing E7s in black paint and lead E7 550 (ex-SAL 3023) in the so-called "split image" scheme – SCL lettering but still in Seaboard colors. The train's Sun Lounge is seventh back. (W.E. Mims photo)

tersburg, ending that train's traditional main route to Miami dating back to 1939. The shift left the *Silver Star* and *Silver Meteor* as the only all-year streamliners to Miami and appeared to ratify the relative weakness the *East Coast Champion* had exhibited before the merger. However, the ex-ACL *Florida Special* continued to operate to Miami each winter with a premium consist, including Louisville & Nashville and Pennsylvania observations on the rear during winter 1967-68.

One other change in former Seaboard service was the elimination of winter-season No. 16 and its role in taking the *Sunland's* through Jacksonville cars back north. Instead, SCL adjusted the schedules of the *Sunland* and *Tidewater* enough to let the northbound *Sunland* do the job. Little remained for the former No. 16 to do anyway; the *Tidewater* had only a through Jacksonville coach left, and the winter-only Richmond-Jacksonville sleeper had also been discontinued.

By late 1967, SCL had also relettered and renumbered many lightweight cars. The old road names were buffed off and the new italic-style "Seaboard Coast Line" name applied along with SCL heralds on the sides. Car names and SCL 5000-series numbers were stenciled in ACL's traditional block Gothic font. Seaboard's sleeper names were retained with two interesting exceptions. The three Sun Lounges, *Hollywood Beach*, *Miami Beach*, and *Palm Beach*, were renamed *Sun Ray*, *Sun View*, and *Sun Beam* respectively. Then, the old *Beach* names were applied to the former *Mountain*-series 6 DB-lounges to group them

with six former ACL *Beach* cars of similar configuration; *Kennesaw Mountain*, *Red Mountain*, and *Stone Mountain* became the "new" *Hollywood Beach*, *Palm Beach*, and *Miami Beach*. The change put an official stamp on the cars' Florida service after carrying *Silver Comet* route names since their delivery.

Seaboard's conventional cars were also renumbered when fully repainted, although the majority of standard cars never received fresh paint; many, especially head-end cars, were either scrapped or converted to maintenance-of-way equipment. SCL repainted its heavyweights in Pullman green with dulux lettering in the same lettering styles used on lightweight cars.

The first SCL winter season also witnessed a fairly thorough mixing of former ACL and Seaboard equipment, particularly coaches and on the conventional trains. However, the *Silver Meteor* and *Silver Star* avoided wholesale changes, and the *Meteor* normally kept its Sun Lounge and round-end observations. Former ACL 251-series blunt-end observations sometimes appeared at the end of the *Meteor*, and also regularly served as the *Star's* lounge car. Other changes included ex-ACL heavyweight café-lounge cars sometimes substituting for the full diner on the *Gulf Wind*.

Breaks with Tradition

By the issuance of SCL's third timetable, in April 1968, adjustments in former Seaboard trains were many and noticeable – including several significant breaks with Seaboard tradition. The *Silver Meteor's* west coast section was dropped and the train began running only to Miami for the first time in its existence. And while the *Silver Star* kept running sections to both Florida coasts, the west coast *Star* moved over from the former SAL route to Tampa (via Wildwood, Dade City, and Plant City) and instead traveled as a separate train south of Jacksonville down the ex-ACL through Sanford and Orlando. The change ended former Seaboard-route passenger service between Wildwood and the west coast.

Despite the *Meteor's* sudden absence from Tampa and St. Petersburg, Seaboard Coast Line still provided a number of trains to the west coast, starting with the *Star's* new summertime west coast section. The revised *Champion* also served both west coast cities, and finally SCL operated a connecting train for the alternating ex-ACL Chicago streamliners from Jacksonville directly to St. Petersburg over the ACL route. SCL also continued the *Meteor's* through 10-6 sleeper and coach for Venice by moving the cars over to the *Champion*. However, ex-SAL motor car 2028, now numbered 4900 and repainted in SCL locomotive black, was reassigned to the former ACL Lakeland-Naples connecting train, leaving the Venice train in the hands of E units.

Other Seaboard trains beyond the Silver Fleet also suffered cutbacks. The *Tidewater* was the first SAL named train to disappear from the timetables, making its last run in February 1968. The coach-only train carried its through cars for Atlanta and Jacksonville to the end, but passenger demand along the route was not strong enough to sustain it. Finally, former Seaboard local service took a hit; the *Sunland* was cut back to Jacksonville, ending the train's local service south of that city, and Richmond-Atlanta locals Nos. 3-4 were discontinued. However, the daytime locals to Atlanta and Birmingham (renumbered 15-16) stayed on.

The December 1968 timetable repeated what would become a common theme: the *Silver Meteor* and *Silver Star* largely remained intact after the initial SCL changes, but other ex-SAL service continued to suffer cuts. Gone were the remaining segment of the *Sunland* plus Nos. 15-16; the Atlanta-line locals were the last of the ex-Seaboard Passenger, Mail and Express trains.

Change also came for the first time to the *Palmland*, which began operating only as far south as Columbia. However, the train did retain a 10-6 sleeper from New York and now offered food service between Richmond and Hamlet – even though no longer from the ex-SAL grill coaches. Those cars were moved to the Jacksonville-St. Petersburg connecting trains for the Chicago streamliners, and the *Palmland* now often carried former ACL café-lounge *Augusta*, renumbered SCL 4221. The *Palmland* still served many small towns on its Richmond-Columbia run, and two ex-ACL trains, the *Gulf Coast Special* and the *Everglades*, still offered local service along the ex-ACL east coast mainline.

The *Gulf Wind*, which had thus far remained a well-equipped if short train, had also lost its sleeper by this time. The *Wind* did keep its Jacksonville-Chattahoochee diner and regularly ran with all-lightweight cars.

The third member of the Silver Fleet, the *Silver Comet*, also came under the knife. Already the poor cousin in the former SAL lightweight trio, the train now faced fresh pressure from declining passenger demand in its market and from strong Southern Railway competition between its end cities. Reflecting the train's long-standing weakness at the extremes of its route, the *Comet* was shortened at both ends: its New York cars were cut back to Washington effective at the end of 1968, and the Atlanta-Birmingham section was discontinued on January 18, 1969.

Even the *Meteor* and *Star* had a brush with cost-cutting efforts. A short-lived food service trial was implemented for the winter 1968-69 season in which one of the two diners on each train was relabeled a

SCL continued running the Sun Lounges on the Silver Meteor *but with new names. Sun View, formerly SAL Miami Beach, is in Amtrak service at Sunnyside Yard outside New York City on March 25, 1972. "Hamburg" on the letterboard ends refers to the company that took over SCL sleeping cars in 1969. (J.W. Swanberg photo, ACL & SAL Historical Society collection)*

An occasional sight after the merger was assignment of the ex-SAL SDP35s to the west coast portion of the *Silver Star*. In this December 1969 scene SCL 603, formerly Seaboard 1102, is moving south (but timetable north) with the west coast *Star* just northeast of Tampa on the ex-SAL St. Petersburg line. The first car is a silver-gray heavyweight combine, standard equipment on the west coast sections of the *Meteor* and *Star*. (Joseph L. Oates photo)

"budget meal car." The car offered a limited, low-cost menu with smaller portions and some pre-prepared reheated items, apparently aimed at budget-conscious coach passengers. The former full dining service for both cars was reinstated on both trains later in 1969.

Exit Pullman, Enter Hamburg

Another significant change came in mid-1969 when the Pullman Company, an institution synonymous with railroad sleeping car travel for over a century, exited the business. Each railroad that formerly leased its sleepers to Pullman for operation and maintenance had to make other arrangements. SCL chose to sell its sleepers to Hamburg Industries, a freight car repair company in North Augusta, S.C., and Hamburg then leased them back to SCL. "Hamburg" replaced "Pullman" at the ends of the sleeping cars' letterboards, and SCL added a 6000-series number to the cars.

Hamburg also soon purchased, then leased to SCL, a number of cars that SCL itself had been leasing for its flagship trains. These included three ex-Baltimore & Ohio 5 Rmt-3 Cpt-1 SB domes; eight ex-B&O 16 Rmt-4 DB "bird" cars; and five ex-Chesapeake & Ohio 11 DB cars. SCL also leased a number of Union Pacific 11 DB cars primarily for the seasonal *Florida Special*. The former B&O domes first ran on the *Florida Special*, then moved to the *Silver Star* during the summer 1969 season. The cars ran only south of Richmond due to clearance restrictions on the northeast corridor. The domes went back to the *Special* in December 1969 but were not regularly assigned to any other trains afterward.

Finis for the *Comet* and RPOs

Although SCL strongly supported its east coast streamliners, the *Silver Comet* faced a grim future as 1969 began. Even the train's shortened Washington-Atlanta version could not attract enough passengers to meet costs. An early signal of the train's fate came on May 8, when the RF&P dropped its portion from Richmond to Washington. Left with a Richmond-Atlanta train cut off from long-haul service to the northeast, the *Comet's* losses mounted even further; SCL said the train was expected to lose $924,000 in 1969. The railroad soon received permission to discontinue the train altogether, and the *Comet* made its last run on October 15, 1969 – bringing an end to passenger service on what had once been Seaboard's premier passenger route.

At the end, the *Comet* was down to just a Richmond-Atlanta 10-6, an ex-SAL 6500-series coach-tavern-observation, and a couple of coaches – often with a healthy string of auto racks on the rear. Dining service had been supplanted by sandwiches and other light fare served in the tavern-lounge. Ironically, the *Palmland* and *Gulf Wind* outlived this once-proud member of the Silver Fleet. Those two trains, plus the *Meteor* and *Star*, were now the only remaining former SAL trains in SCL's timetables.

Another long-time fixture rapidly disappearing from all railroads was the Railway Post Office. The Post Office Department (renamed the U.S. Postal Service in 1971) had accelerated its move to sectional centers and trucks in the late 1960s, and on-board mail sorting vanished from all but a handful of long-distance routes. By 1969, one of the last SCL RPOs was the Raleigh & Jacksonville RPO route via the *Silver Star*.

One more loss in the Seaboard column came for the *Palmland*, which carried a sleeping car for the last time in the winter 1969-70 season. This car, a New York-Columbia 4 Rmt-1 Cpt-5 DB-4 Sec, provided the final sleeping car service on a former Seaboard conventional train. It ended a tradition on SAL's heavyweight trains stretching back to the railroad's earliest days.

SCL's Final Passenger Service

Seaboard Coast Line issued its 1970-71 winter timetable on December 11, 1970, covering what would prove to be its last season of privately owned operation. The four remaining ex-Seaboard trains – the *Silver Meteor*, *Silver Star*, *Gulf Wind*, and *Palmland* – took their places beside the former ACL *Florida Special*, *Champion*, the alternating *City of Miami* and *South Wind*, *Gulf Coast Special*, and *Everglades*. The *Meteor* continued to be the premier former Seaboard train, with most of its traditional cars intact except for the addition of the 16 Rmt-4 DB budget room car. However, the train's regularly assigned consist was down to just 12 cars: a baggage-dorm, six sleepers, one diner, three coaches, and observation.

The *Silver Star* had a similar consist, with 11 regular through cars capped by the Richmond-Miami 6 DB-lounge on the rear. The train added a baggage car and café-lounge to the west coast section, whose through cars included a New York-St. Petersburg coach and a Washington-St. Petersburg 10-6. Of course, both *Silver* trains often carried extra cars as passenger demand required. The now coach-only *Palmland* retained a bit of its former status by still offering a through New York-Columbia coach plus café-lounge service between Richmond and Hamlet.

The timetable reflected a surprising change in the *Gulf Wind* that had occurred on October 18. The train had been coach-only since 1968 and had lost its dining service earlier in 1970, but on that date regained both amenities – although at the expense of going to a tri-weekly schedule. The rare restoration of sleeping car and food service was made to coordinate with an equally unusual change, the re-establishment of a coast-to-coast sleeping car line for the first time since 1956. The car ran from Los Angeles to New York via New Orleans in Southern Pacific's *Sunset Limited* and Southern Railway's *Crescent*. The Interstate Commerce Commission allowed tri-weekly service for the SP train if SP restored sleeping and dining service. Seaboard Coast Line evidently sought, and received, permission to make equivalent changes in the *Gulf Wind*.

The *Gulf Wind* left eastbound from New Orleans on Sundays, Tuesdays, and Thursdays, and westbound from Jacksonville on the same days, and connected with the *Sunset*. Passengers had to spend the night laying over in New Orleans both ways, but that circumstance was advertised as an appealing opportunity to enjoy a night in the city. The changes occasioned another adjustment in the *Wind's* schedule, with a 10:00 a.m. arrival in Jacksonville and a 7:45 p.m. departure.

The *Gulf Wind's* restored sleeping service was normally protected by a 4-1-5-4, of which SCL had several from both the SAL and ACL rosters; however, consists show other sleeper types were used at

The *Silver Comet is shown in its waning days as it waits to depart Atlanta's Terminal Station in June 1969. The train was down to two E7s, an ex-ACL RPO-baggage, one express car, and a lightweight coach, diner, and 10-6 sleeper. The* Comet *ran only between Atlanta and Richmond by this date, and routinely coupled intermodal cars onto its rear when it reached Howells Yard. It disappeared from the timetables four months later. (A.M. Langley Jr. photo)*

times, such as 10-6s and an ex-Seaboard 11 DB car. The train's food service during this period was normally provided by the unique ex- SAL, ex-FEC tavern lounge, now renumbered as SCL 5837. SCL or L&N lightweight coaches rounded out the passenger-carrying consist together with an express car most days.

Amtrak: New York-Florida Only

Although Seaboard Coast Line clearly supported its better passenger trains, the mounting costs and competition bearing down on all passenger railroads spared no carrier from a bleak long-term outlook. The railroads' growing passenger losses had turned the problem into a national policy crisis by 1970. Congress and the Nixon Administration agreed to a solution: the quasi-governmental National Railroad Passenger Corporation, first called "Railpax" but soon renamed Amtrak. The Amtrak law relieved any participating railroad from further passenger responsibilities in return for operating the trains under contract and letting Amtrak purchase the passenger locomotives and cars of its choice. Seaboard Coast Line and nearly all other intercity train operators joined. The takeover occurred May 1, 1971; SCL had run passenger trains for only three years and ten months.

The new corporation's most consequential impact was that it could drop any trains it deemed unnecessary for a coordinated "core" national system. Well-patronized long-distance trains survived, but two-thirds of U.S. runs were immediately discontinued. SCL's New York-Florida streamliners remained, including the mainline runs of the *Silver Meteor* and *Silver Star*. But Amtrak kept no other former Seaboard trains; neither the *Palmland*, the *Gulf Wind*, nor the Tampa-Venice connecting service survived. The *Meteor* and *Star* were joined by the other two SCL survivors, the ex-ACL *Champion* and the Chicago-Florida *South Wind* (changed to a daily run and shortly renamed the *Floridian*).

As had been the case under Seaboard Coast Line, the *Champion* served Tampa and St. Petersburg. Likewise, the Chicago-Florida *Floridian* served both coasts as had its predecessors, the alternating *City of Miami* and *South Wind*. In all, the four trains and their east/west coast sections provided three daily arrivals to both Miami and Tampa/St. Petersburg.

The *Silver Meteor* and *Silver Star* at first adhered to the former Seaboard Coast Line operating pattern. The *Meteor* served Miami via the SAL route through Wildwood; the *Star* served both coasts via the ex-ACL to Tampa, then over former Seaboard rails to St. Petersburg, plus a separate section that ran from Auburndale to Miami. But by 1972 Amtrak had moved the *Meteor* over to the former ACL "A Line" through the Carolinas, and often ran the *Meteor* combined with the *Champion* during summers in the mid-1970s.

Amtrak purchased the best cars and locomotives from member railroads, including most of the former ACL and Seaboard lightweight cars and E8/9s. Amtrak also leased four ex-Seaboard E7s for sever-

Early in the SCL merger, the Gulf Wind *was often still a fairly long train. On March 8, 1968, the inbound* Wind *swings around Honeymoon Wye near Jacksonville Terminal Station's Beaver Street Tower before backing into the station tracks. E8 594 (formerly Seaboard 3055) has three express cars, a Seaboard coach, an L&N sleeper, an SAL ex-FEC diner, and an ACL coach on the rear. (W.E. Mims photo)*

al years (SCL 549, 554, 557, and 558, formerly SAL 3022, 3028, 3031, and 3032). The Amtrak car consists were similar to those used by SCL at the transition, including the *Meteor's* budget room car, but there were some noticeable changes. The Sun Lounge cars were placed on the *Florida Special* during the train's only season under Amtrak, winter 1971-72. Perhaps most jarring to any Seaboard partisan was the use of the ex-SAL 6600 observations on the *Champion* at times. Amtrak eventually began buying new locomotives and cars in the mid-1970s, and much of the former ACL and SAL equipment was later retired or dispersed to other routes.

Smaller Stations and Abandoned Routes

Another very visible change was Amtrak's abandonment of many historic but now oversized downtown stations. Once the urban hallmarks of rail trans-portation, these buildings cost far more in taxes and maintenance than Amtrak could justify for the relatively few passenger trains they now served. An early example was Jacksonville Terminal, which Amtrak vacated in 1974 for a small new building on the ex-ACL northwest of downtown. Jacksonville counted more than a hundred separate daily movements in the 1940s; when Amtrak pulled out, there were 12. Other changes included Richmond's Broad Street Station, which Amtrak left in favor of a new station on the RF&P, and Miami, where Amtrak began terminating at Hialeah. The Jacksonville and Richmond buildings survive as a convention center and science museum, but the Miami station was torn down.

The new Jacksonville location caused additional route changes for former Seaboard trains. Because the station was now on the former ACL main, the

These attractive mid-1968 portraits show the Gulf Wind *near Tallahassee, Fla., with a short but classy train behind E7 573: a Louisville & Nashville rebuilt heavyweight coach; a Tuscan red RF&P 10-6 sleeper, probably* King & Queen; *and SAL dining car 6119, formerly FEC* Fort Ribault. *(Randy Young photos)*

Meteor and *Star* took the ACL route between Jacksonville and Callahan, Florida. Here a new passenger connection track allowed them to move east to Gross, Fla., and regain the ex-SAL main to Savannah, enabling service to continue at Thalmann, Georgia. But this hybrid ACL-SAL route lasted only until late 1979, when all trains were moved over to the A-Line for the entire Savannah-Jacksonville run. The middle portion of the former Seaboard Savannah-Jacksonville line was pulled up in the mid-1980s.

Political and financial support for Amtrak was always ambiguous, and many policymakers assumed the corporation would last only a few years. Even though Amtrak had enough champions in Congress to keep it going year by year, its budgets were always slim at best. Amtrak encountered the first of many serious budget crises in 1979 and was forced to cut a number of trains, including some of the original core routes. On the Seaboard Coast Line, the venerable *Champion* fell, leaving only the *Silver Meteor* and *Silver Star* on the New York-Florida run. The *Floridian* was also discontinued, together with its east and west Florida coast sections. However, Amtrak did restore a Tampa/St. Petersburg section for the *Meteor*, returning that train's traditional service to both coasts. The net result of the cuts left two daily arrivals at Miami and St. Petersburg.

With the 1979 cuts behind it, Amtrak moved forward again with several improvements and additions in former SCL service. In late 1981, the corporation announced that the *Silver Meteor* had been re-equipped with refurbished "Heritage Fleet" equipment – cars rebuilt to accept Head-End Power electrical cooling and heating rather than the time-honored steam heat in winter and various mechanical systems for air conditioning. The re-equipped trains no longer required locomotives with steam generators and could use Amtrak's latest F40PH locomotives. In addition Amtrak had equipped the *Silver Star* with new long-distance-type, 59-seat Amfleet II coaches.

Cross Florida Service Returns (Temporarily)

In late 1982, Amtrak added a new Florida train to its timetables, the *Silver Palm*, a near-reincarnation of the SAL "Cross Florida Service" that last ran from Tampa via West Lake Wales to Miami in the winter of 1957-58. The *Palm* left Miami in the morning and traveled to Auburndale, then "turned left" onto the ex-ACL and arrived at Tampa in the early afternoon. The train returned to Miami that evening. Alas, the *Palm* depended on support from the state of Florida, and funding ran out in early 1986. Although *Silver Palm* was not a "silver astronomy" name, it was still

an interesting combination of Seaboard's *Silver* label and the "Palm" portion of the old *Palmland*.

While a bit of the old Seaboard's service came back with the *Silver Palm*, the year 1986 saw more of the railroad quite literally disappear. Starting in the early 1980s, SCL successor Seaboard System had begun significant abandonments on routes it deemed redundant or unproductive. In addition to the S-Line between Savannah and Jacksonville, SBD also axed the former SAL main between Petersburg, Va. (Collier Yard), and Norlina, N.C.; as a result, the *Silver Star* was rerouted in October 1986 from Raleigh to Selma, N.C., via the Southern Railway, then north over the former ACL.

The Raleigh rerouting occasioned another move out of a former Seaboard station. Since trains now used the ex-Southern mainline in Raleigh and no longer passed by the ex-SAL station, Amtrak moved into the ex-Southern building on the south side of the city. Another ex-SAL station vacated about this time was Columbia, which Amtrak left when the city moved all rail lines out of the downtown area. Both buildings survive.

Amtrak made other changes in the late 1980s and the 1990s to trim services and costs. The company stopped service to St. Petersburg in 1984, ending over a century of rail passenger service to the retirement haven. Trains terminated at Tampa and buses carried St. Pete passengers to their final destination. The change eliminated the 1-hour, 40-minute run via the ex-Seaboard route in favor of a half-hour bus trip over the highway bridge across Tampa Bay.

Amtrak did make a number of upgrades to its rolling stock roster. Amtrak's Heritage coach fleet had already been largely displaced by Amfleet equipment, but the Heritage sleeping cars (including some ex-SAL sleepers) lasted much longer. In the mid-1990s Amtrak finally began gradually replacing its sleeping cars with new Viewliner cars; the last Heritage sleeper was retired in 2001. A few Heritage diners and baggage cars still work for Amtrak today.

More Florida Expansions and Contractions

Amtrak was not done with adjusting its service to Florida's west coast; in 1997, it dropped the west coast sections of the *Silver Meteor* and *Silver Star*, making both trains New York-Miami. However, Amtrak began a new train that kept Tampa service in place – the "new" *Silver Palm*, running this time all the way from New York to Miami and thus placing a third New York-Florida train in the timetable for the first time since 1979. The train, actually a lengthened and renamed *Palmetto*, reached Tampa by traveling the S-Line from Jacksonville through Wildwood, then over a combination of former ACL and Seaboard trackage to Lakeland, then via the ex-ACL into Tampa. From Tampa, like the 1980s *Silver Palm* "cross Florida" service, the train backtracked to Lakeland, continued to Auburndale, and there turned south on the former SAL to Miami. Amtrak itself labeled the schedule as "Cross Florida Service."

Another 1990s Florida expansion came in early 1993 when Amtrak extended the tri-weekly Los Angeles-New Orleans *Sunset Limited* to Jacksonville and Miami. The train continued east using the *Gulf Wind's* old route, including the former Seaboard through Tallahassee to Jacksonville – returning passenger service to the Tallahassee line after an absence of 22 years. While the change once again brought back a through coast-to-coast sleeper (although to Florida rather than New York or Washington), the extended *Sunset* became the first true transcontinental train in U.S. railroad history.

Unfortunately, the extended *Sunset* ran into problems almost from the start, notably poor timekeeping caused by freight congestion on the western portion of its route. Getting the train to Miami and turning it around on time became so difficult that the train was cut back to Orlando in 1997. The final setback came when Hurricane Katrina devastated the Gulf Coast in late August 2005, ending service east of New Orleans. Although CSX soon repaired the ex-Louisville & Nashville trackage between New Orleans and Mobile, Amtrak has so far not reinstated the *Sunset Limited's* New Orleans-Florida run.

Change has continued for Amtrak's former Seaboard trains in recent years. The *Silver Palm* became

the *Palmetto* again in 2002 and lost its sleeping cars, and in 2004 the train was cut back to Savannah – the *Palmetto's* original end point. Again, service to Tampa was preserved when the *Silver Star* took over the *Palmetto's* former service to the city. However, the *Star* remained on the former ACL between Jacksonville and Tampa; the new arrangement meant Amtrak no longer ran on the S-Line via Wildwood and left that city plus Waldo, Gainesville, Ocala, and Dade City without passenger service for the first time (although Amtrak does provide connecting bus service to these points). The *Palmetto's* retrenchment also once again left Miami with only two daily passenger train arrivals.

The Seaboard Legacy

Despite Amtrak's vicissitudes, Seaboard's presence remains strong today. While significant portions of the old SAL mainline have been lost or no longer see passenger service, the *Silver Star* travels over a long stretch of the S-Line in the Carolinas and all trains run over the former Seaboard between Auburndale and Miami. Both the *Meteor* and *Star* still offer long-distance sleeping car and dining service, and the *Meteor's* New York-Miami schedule remains a reasonably respectable 27 ½ hours – certainly longer than in Seaboard days, but not greatly so. However, the *Star's* lengthier route has stretched its New York-Miami time to over 31 hours. Freight train congestion and track maintenance often conspire to make the trips even longer. But the two trains remain part of Amtrak's busiest long-distance corridor, and space is frequently sold out.

While no former Seaboard locomotives or cars run today in revenue service, a few ex-SAL cars operate for private owners and a number have been restored

Capping the southbound Silver Star *on July 5, 1969, are two distinctive cars assigned to the train in the summer 1969 season, the New York-Miami 16 Rmt-4 DB "Budget Room Coach" and the Richmond-Miami 5 Rmt-3 Cpt-1 SB dome, both leased from B&O. The domes ran on the* Star *for just this one season and were otherwise found on the winter-only* Florida Special. *The train is racing past at an estimated 75 m.p.h. near Kittrell, N.C., at 7:07 p.m. (Curtis C. Tillotson Jr. photo)*

by various museums. The Gold Coast Museum in Miami owns several SAL cars, including "Jim Crow" combine 259, lightweight coach-tavern 6300, and Florida East Coast lightweight coach *Belle Glade*, which Seaboard owned as No. 6262. Some other examples include tavern-observation 6601 displayed at the Naples (Fla.) depot museum; ex-FEC observation 6607 in service on the SAM Shortline tourist train at Cordele, Ga.; and privately owned Sun Lounge *Hollywood Beach*, which is Amtrak-compliant. One passenger locomotive, SDP35 1114, is on display at Hamlet, and former ACF motor car 2026 operates in regular California Western Railroad excursion service.

One portion of the ex-Seaboard passenger route has not merely endured but prospers: the 71 miles between West Palm Beach and Miami, now owned by the Florida Department of Transportation and operated by the Tri-Rail commuter system. Tri-Rail purchased the line from CSX in 1989, and steady passenger growth soon required double-tracking (completed in 2007) to relieve train congestion and avoid delays. Tri-Rail has also renovated and modernized a number of former Seaboard stations along the route, leaving them looking better than they had been in decades and restoring many to their SAL coral pink colors. Amtrak trains continue to use the trackage and stations, and CSX – now the tenant line – runs a few freights at night.

Another stretch of former Seaboard track may someday rival Tri-Rail's highly developed corridor, but for now lies beneath pine trees and overgrowth. That is the segment between Petersburg, Va., and Norlina, N.C., abandoned in 1986 but still owned by CSX. The route has been designated part of the proposed Southeast High-Speed Rail Corridor between Washington and Atlanta, and is now under study for 110-m.p.h. passenger train operation combined with freight train use. The proposal for the 71-mile line envisions a completely grade-separated right-of-way with five-mile sidings every ten miles.

One factor in the SEHSR's favor is North Carolina's aggressive support of passenger rail service. NC DOT currently supports a Charlotte-Raleigh train plus a second over that same route, which then continues to Rocky Mount and New York. North Carolina has on its drawing boards additional intrastate routes, including possible restoration of service over the former Seaboard between Pembroke and Wilmington as part of a Raleigh-Wilmington route.

A proposed high-speed rail project is also moving forward for central and south Florida between Tampa and Orlando and between Orlando and Miami. The route again roughly replicates Seaboard's Cross Florida service, although with a northward "bump" to Orlando. Planners propose a dedicated right-of-way and 150-m.p.h. trains.

Few would argue that the present-day incarnations of Seaboard's fine trains do justice to their long, fast, well-maintained, and heavily patronized predecessors of four decades past. But considering Amtrak's many travails, it may be satisfaction enough that they are still with us – and still let travelers leave the cold northeast, travel safely and smoothly over shining rails, and a day later enjoy the beaches of south Florida.

Although SCL usually kept the Silver Meteor's *Sun Lounge and round-end observation on the train per Seaboard tradition, there were exceptions. ACL flat-end observations sometimes appeared on the rear, or as in this photo, one of the ex-SAL pre-war 6400-series cars. The diaphragm-equipped cars had normally run only on the* Silver Star *in SAL days. The scene shows a long northbound* Meteor *leaving Jacksonville Terminal Station on January 4, 1971. (A.M. Langley Jr. photo)*

Sharp declines in mail and express revenue in the late 1960s meant the ex-Seaboard local trains were living on borrowed time. This photo of No. 4 near Henderson, N.C., not long after the merger shows how many of Passenger, Mail & Express runs looked in their last days. The short Atlanta-Richmond train and its southbound counterpart, No. 3, were dropped in April 1968. (Warren Calloway photo)

SCL 5837 began life in 1950 as FEC diner-lounge South Bay for the New Royal Palm and was converted by FEC in 1956 to a tavern-lounge. The car became Seaboard 6620 and was the only car on the roster with this design. The car often ran on the Gulf Wind late in the SCL era. (Paul Coe photo)

Shortly after the merger, the southbound west coast section of the Sunland rolls through Valrico, Fla., with an E7, a box express car, and combine 277. The Sunland was changed to terminate at Jacksonville effective with the April 1968 timetable. (Joseph L. Oates photo)

Amtrak trains clearly bore the new owner's stamp by 1974. This March 23 view of the northbound Silver Star at Old Wake Forest Road north of Raleigh shows three E units in the company's platinum mist scheme and most of the passenger cars with Amtrak striping. (Larry Goolsby photo)

Mid-1974 witnessed Amtrak's first significant purchase of new equipment – SDP40F locomotives from EMD. No. 611, part of the second group purchased that year, wears its unmistakable red nose on the northbound Silver Star at Raleigh in July. The units were later linked to derailments at speed and were replaced by the four-axle F40PH model within a few years. (John Sullivan photo)

Silver Fleet trains 1940s-50s

SAL 31, southbound west coast *Silver Meteor*, Columbia, S.C., Oct. 30, 1945
3 engines, 12 cars, all cars heavyweight except as noted

Road	Number or Name	Type	Car Route
SAL	3015	E6A locomotive	
SAL	3000	E4A locomotive	
SAL	6003	Baggage-dorm-coach (LW)	NY-St. Pete
Pullman	Mount Gretna	10 Sec-1 DR-2 Cpt sleeper	NY-Venice
Pullman	Poplar Vale	6 Sec-6 DB sleeper	NY-St. Pete
Pullman	Chimes Tower	8 Sec-3 DB-1 DR sleeper	NY-St. Pete
Pullman	Weeper's Tower	8 Sec-3 DB-1 DR sleeper	NY-St. Pete
SAL	231	Diner	NY-St. Pete
PRR	4024	Coach (LW)	NY-St. Pete
SAL	835	Coach	NY-St. Pete
SAL	588	Coach	NY-St. Pete
SAL	6209	Coach (LW)	NY-St. Pete
SAL	6210	Coach (LW)	NY-St. Pete
SAL	6500	Coach-buffet-lounge (LW)	NY-St. Pete

PRR 113, southbound *Silver Meteor*, Penn Station, New York, N.Y., Oct. 28, 1950
1 engine, 17 cars, all cars lightweight except as noted

Road	Number or Name	Type	Car Route
PRR	4848	GG1 locomotive	
SAL	6051	Baggage-dorm	NY-Miami
SAL	6219	Coach	NY-Miami
SAL	Sarasota	10-6 sleeper	NY-Miami
SAL	Raleigh	10-6 sleeper	NY-Miami
SAL	Kennesaw Mountain	6 DB-lounge sleeper	NY-Miami
PRR	Clinton	10-6 sleeper	NY-Venice
Pullman	Independence Square	6 Cpt-3 DR sleeper (HW)	NY-St. Pete
SAL	Atlanta	10-6 sleeper	NY-St. Pete
SAL	Richmond	10-6 sleeper	NY-St. Pete
SAL	6103	Diner	NY-St. Pete
RF&P	852	Coach	NY-St. Pete
SAL	6224	Coach	NY-St. Pete
SAL	6232	Coach lounge	NY-St. Pete
SAL	6105	Diner	NY-Miami
SAL	6221	Coach	NY-Miami
SAL	6222	Coach	NY-Miami
SAL	6216	Coach	NY-Miami
SAL	6300	Tavern-coach	NY-Miami

Note: Tavern-coach 6300 was substituting for 6600-series tavern observation, which was being shopped.

SAL 58, northbound *Silver Meteor*, Columbia, S.C., July 10, 1952
3 engines, 18 cars, all cars lightweight

Road	Number or Name	Type	Car Route
SAL	3005	E4A locomotive	St. Pete-Richmond
SAL	3016	E6A locomotive	Miami-Richmond
SAL	3101	E4B locomotive	Miami-Richmond
SAL	6051	Baggage-dorm	Miami-NY
PRR	4014	Coach ("colored")	Miami-NY
SAL	Lake Wales	10-6 sleeper	Miami-NY
SAL	Sarasota	10-6 sleeper	Miami-NY

SAL	Red Mountain	6 DB-lounge sleeper	Miami-NY
SAL	Birmingham	10-6 sleeper	St. Pete-NY
RF&P	Chesterfield	10-6 sleeper	Venice-NY
PRR	Elberton	11 DB sleeper	St. Pete-NY
SAL	6109	Diner	St. Pete-NY
PRR	4057	Coach	St. Pete-NY
RF&P	855	Coach	St. Pete-NY
SAL	6218	Coach	St. Pete-NY
SAL	6113	Diner	Miami-NY
SAL	6222	Coach	Miami-NY
SAL	6233	Coach lounge	Miami-NY
RF&P	857	Coach	Miami-NY
SAL	6206	Coach	Miami-NY
SAL	6605	Tavern-observation	Miami-NY

Note: Consist recorded by Arthur M. Waldrop. Train had space for 122 Pullman passengers and 416 coach passengers.

PRR 114, northbound *Silver Meteor*, New York, N.Y., August 7, 1954
1 engine, 18 cars, all cars lightweight

Road	Number or Name	Type	Car Route
PRR	4936	GG1 locomotive	
SAL	6050	Baggage-dorm	Miami-NY
PRR	4056	Coach	Washington-NY (?)
RF&P	841	Coach (Old Dominion blue scheme)	Washington-NY (?)
PRR	Clinton	10-6 sleeper	Miami-NY
SAL	Kennesaw Mountain	6 DB-lounge sleeper	Miami-NY
SAL	Jacksonville	10-6 sleeper	Venice-NY
SAL	Miami	10-6 sleeper	St. Pete-NY
SAL	6101	Diner	St. Pete-NY
RF&P	852	Coach	St. Pete-NY
PRR	4065	Coach	St. Pete-NY
SAL	6232	Coach lounge	St. Pete-NY
SAL	6206	Coach	St. Pete-NY
SAL	6103	Diner	Miami-NY
SAL	6219	Coach	Miami-NY
RF&P	855	Coach	Miami-NY
PRR	4014	Coach	Miami-NY
SAL	6225	Coach	Miami-NY
SAL	6604	Tavern-observation	Miami-NY

Note: Consist recorded by Sam Appleby Jr.; car routes not recorded, but interpolated from timetable consist information

SAL 21, southbound *Silver Star*, Columbia, S.C., Nov. 25, 1950
3 engines, 15 cars, all cars lightweight except as noted

Road	Number or Name	Type	Car Route
SAL	3051	E8 locomotive	
SAL	3107	E7B locomotive	
SAL	3004	E4 locomotive	
PRR	9554	Box express	Washington-Jax
PRR	2649	Refrigerator express	Washington-Jax
PRR	2305	Box express	Washington-Jax
REX	1634	Refrigerator express	Washington-Jax
SAL	6005	Baggage-dorm-coach	Washington-Miami
RFP	854	Coach	NY-Miami
PRR	4061	Coach	NY-Miami
SAL	6204	Coach	NY-Miami
SAL	6500	Buffet-lounge-coach	Washington-Miami
SAL	6109	Diner	Washington-Miami

Road	Number or Name	Type	Car Route
SAL	Tampa	10-6 sleeper	Washington-Miami
SAL	Lake Wales	10-6 sleeper	Washington-Miami
SAL	Columbia Basin	10 Sec-lounge sleeper (HW)	NY-Miami
Pullman	Franklin Square	6 Cpt-3 DR sleeper (HW)	NY-Miami
Pullman	Glen Springs	6 Cpt-3 DR sleeper (HW)	NY-Miami

SAL 22, northbound *Silver Star*, New York, N.Y., January 1955 (exact date not recorded)
1 engine, 18 cars, all cars lightweight except as noted

Road	Number or Name	Type	Car Route
PRR	4933	GG1 locomotive	
SAL	180	Baggage-dorm (HW)	Miami-NY
Pullman	Fir Woods	6 Sec-4 Rmt-4 DB sleeper (HW)	Miami-Washington
PRR	Elberton	10-6 sleeper	Miami-NY
Pullman	Ibsen	6 Cpt-3 DR sleeper (HW)	Miami-NY
Pullman	Romney	6 Cpt-3 DR sleeper (HW)	Miami-NY
Pullman	Palm Lane	3 Cpt-1 DR-buffet-lounge (HW)	Miami-NY
Pullman	Glen Ashdale	6 Cpt-3 DR sleeper (HW)	Port Boca Grande-NY
SAL	Poplar City	6 Sec-6 DB sleeper (HW)	St. Pete-NY
SAL	6107	Diner	St. Pete-NY
Pullman	Elm Lawn	12 Rmt-2 SB-3 DB sleeper (HW)	St. Pete-NY
SAL	6201	Coach	St. Pete-NY
SAL	6215	Coach	St. Pete-NY
SAL	6101	Diner	Miami-NY
SAL	6208	Coach	Miami-NY
RF&P	852	Coach	Miami-NY
PRR	4018	Coach	Miami-NY
RF&P	854	Coach	Miami-NY
SAL	6603	Tavern-observation	Miami-NY

Note: Consist recorded by Sam Appleby Jr.

Silver Fleet trains 1960s

PRR 114, northbound *Silver Meteor*, Washington, D.C., Feb. 12, 1962
1 engine, 17 cars, all cars lightweight

Road	Number or Name	Type	Car Route
PRR	4876	GG1 locomotive	
SAL	6052	Baggage-dorm	Miami-NY
PRR	Magic Brook	12 SB-5 DB sleeper	Miami-NY
RF&P	Essex	10-6 sleeper	Miami-NY
SAL	Norfolk	10-6 sleeper	Miami-NY
SAL	Ft. Lauderdale	5 DB-2 Cpt-2 DR sleeper	Miami-NY
SAL	Petersburg	10-6 sleeper	Miami-NY
SAL	Palm Beach	5 DB-lounge	Miami-NY
SAL	Sebring	11 DB sleeper	St. Pete-NY
SAL	6102	Diner	St. Pete-NY
RF&P	Lancaster	10-6 sleeper	St. Pete-NY
SAL	Charlotte	10-6 sleeper	Venice-NY
SAL	6240	Coach lounge	Venice-NY
SAL	6209	Coach	St. Pete-NY
SAL	6106	Diner	Miami-NY
SAL	6217	Coach	Miami-NY
SAL	6201	Coach	Miami-NY
SAL	6601	Tavern-observation	Miami-NY

SAL 57, southbound _Silver Meteor_, Savannah, Ga., Dec. 3, 1964
3 engines, 19 cars, all cars lightweight

Road	Number or Name	Type	Car Route
SAL	3050	E8 locomotive	
SAL	3020	E7 locomotive	
SAL	3051	E8 locomotive	
SAL	6052	Baggage-dorm	NY-Miami
SAL	Jacksonville	10-6 sleeper	NY-Miami
PRR	Mineral Brook	12 SB-5 DB sleeper	NY-Miami
SAL	Columbia	10-6 sleeper	NY-Miami
SAL	Ft. Lauderdale	5 DB-2 Cpt-2 DR sleeper	NY-Miami
SAL	Orlando	10-6 sleeper	NY-Miami
PRR	Catalpa Falls	6 DB-lounge sleeper	NY-Miami
SAL	Tallahassee	11 DBR sleeper	NY-St. Pete
FEC	Fort Matanzas	Diner	NY-Miami
SAL	Winter Haven	10-6 sleeper	NY-Venice
SAL	Tampa	10-6 sleeper	NY-St. Pete
SAL	6235	Coach lounge	NY-St. Pete
FEC	Cocoa-Rockledge	Coach	NY-St. Pete
RF&P	862	Coach lounge	NY-Venice
SAL	6103	Diner	NY-Miami
SAL	6209	Coach	NY-Miami
RF&P	850	Coach	NY-Miami
SAL	6223	Coach	NY-Miami
SAL	6601	Tavern-observation	NY-Miami

SAL 58, northbound _Silver Meteor_, Jacksonville, Fla., May 29, 1967
3 engines, 13 cars, all cars lightweight

Road	Number or Name	Type	Car Route
SAL	3047	E7 locomotive	
SAL	3058	E8 locomotive	
SAL	3057	E8 locomotive	
SAL	6052	Baggage-dorm	Miami-NY
SAL	Boca Grande	5 DB-2 Cpt-2 DR sleeper	Miami-NY
SAL	Petersburg	10-6 sleeper	Miami-NY
SAL	Red Mountain	6 DB-lounge sleeper	Miami-NY
SAL	6103	Diner	St. Pete-NY
SAL	Lake Wales	10-6 sleeper	Venice-NY
SAL	Richmond	10-6 sleeper	St. Pete-NY
RF&P	850	Coach	St. Pete-NY
SAL	6241	Coach lounge	Venice-NY
SAL	6108	Diner	Miami-NY
SAL	6224	Coach	Miami-NY
RF&P	853	Coach	Miami-NY
SAL	6601	Tavern-observation	Miami-NY

SAL 21, southbound *Silver Star*, Raleigh, N.C., March 18, 1966
4 engines, 24 cars, all cars lightweight

Road	Number or Name	Type	Car Route
SAL	3021	E7 locomotive	
SAL	3029	E7 locomotive	
SAL	3049	E8 locomotive	
SAL	3050	E8 locomotive	
PRR	5512	Box express	
PRR	2102	Box express	
PRR	9574	Box express	
PRR	9630	Box express	
SAL	6054	Baggage-dorm	
SAL	6604	Tavern-observation	
PRR	4058	Coach	
SAL	6215	Coach	
SAL	6243	Coach	
PRR	4067	Coach	
SAL	6220	Coach	
SAL	6109	Diner	
PRR	Greenwood	10-6 sleeper	
RF&P	Essex	10-6 sleeper	
SAL	6108	Diner	
PRR	Athens	10-6 sleeper	
SAL	Stone Mountain	6 DB-lounge	
SAL	Hialeah	11 DB sleeper	
SAL	Orlando	10-6 sleeper	
PRR	Birch River	10-6 sleeper	
SAL	Pinehurst	4-1-5-4 sleeper	
C&O	City of Maysville	10-6 sleeper	
PRR	Cambria County	13 DB sleeper	

Note: Car routes not recorded

SAL 21, southbound *Silver Star*, Savannah, Ga., August 4, 1966
4 engines, 19 cars, all cars lightweight

Road	Number or Name	Type	Car Route
SAL	3021	E7 locomotive	
SAL	3053	E8 locomotive	
SAL	3023	E7 locomotive	
SAL	3034	E7 locomotive	
PRR	5243	Box express	-Jax (Storage mail)
PRR	6843	Box express	-Jax (Storage mail)
PRR	9556	Box express	-Jax (Storage mail)
PRR	1865	Box express	-Jax (Storage mail)
ACL	545	Express	-Jax
SAL	6058	Baggage-dorm	-Miami
SAL	6258	Coach	-Miami
PRR	4058	Coach	-Miami
SAL	6273	Coach	-Miami
SAL	6238	Coach lounge	-Miami
SAL	6229	Coach	-Miami
SAL	6105	Diner	-Miami
RF&P	853	Coach	-Miami
SAL	6214	Coach	-Miami
SAL	6620	Tavern-lounge	-Miami
SAL	6115	Diner	-Miami
SAL	Columbia	10-6 sleeper	-Miami

| PRR | Imperial Range | 4 Cpt-4 DB-2 DR sleeper | -Miami |
| SAL | West Palm Beach | 10-6 sleeper | -Miami |

Note: Unit 3034 to be cut off at Jacksonville and hold for use on SAL 7, southbound Sunland.

SAL 22, northbound *Silver Star*, Savannah, Ga., May 4, 1963
3 engines, 20 cars, all cars lightweight

Road	Number or Name	Type	Car Route
SAL	3058	E8 locomotive	
SAL	3005	E4 locomotive	
SAL	3015	E4 locomotive	
?	?	Express	Jax-Boston
SAL	6055	Baggage-dorm	Jax-Washington
SAL	6400	Coach-observation	Miami-Washington
SAL	6246	Coach	Miami-Washington
SAL	6220	Coach	Miami-Washington
SAL	6222	Coach	Miami-Washington
PRR	4060	Coach	Miami-Washington
RF&P	855	Coach	Miami-Washington
RF&P	853	Coach	Miami-NY
SAL	6224	Coach	Miami-NY
SAL	6225	Coach	Miami-NY
SAL	6600	Tavern-observation	Miami-Washington
SAL	6112	Diner	Miami-Washington
SAL	6101	Diner	Miami-Washington
SAL	Charlotte	10-6 sleeper	Miami-Washington
SAL	Sebring	11 DB sleeper	Miami-NY
ACL	Chatham County	10-6 sleeper	Miami-NY
PRR	Athens	10-6 sleeper	Miami-Richmond
B&M	Dartmouth College	6 Rmt-4 DB-6 Sec sleeper	Jax-Portsmouth
SAL	6234	Coach lounge	Jax-Portsmouth

Notes:

Jax-Boston express car marked through, car name and number not recorded; may not have ever been placed on train.

B&M owned both a Dartmouth College I and Dartmouth College II; the consist did not indicate which one.

PRR 121, carrying through *Silver Comet* cars, New York, N.Y., Jan. 1, 1962
All cars lightweight unless noted; other cars omitted

Road	Number or Name	Type	Car Route
PRR	4883	GG1 locomotive	NY-Washington
PRR	4029	Coach	NY-Atlanta
SAL	810	Coach (HW)	NY-Atlanta
SAL	6300	Tavern-coach	NY-Birmingham
SAL	6231	Coach	NY-Birmingham
RF&P	705	Coach (HW)	NY-Birmingham
L&N	Green River	10-6 sleeper	NY-Birmingham

SAL 33, southbound *Silver Comet*, Atlanta, Ga., Feb. 5, 1966
2 engine, 9 cars, all passenger cars lightweight unless noted

Road	Number or Name	Type	Car Route
SAL	3018	E7 locomotive	
SAL	3056	E8 locomotive	
SAL	107	Baggage-RPO	Richmond-Atlanta
SAL	6055	Baggage-dorm	NY-Atlanta
SAL	6501	Buffet-lounge-coach	NY-Atlanta
SAL	6203	Coach	NY-Birmingham
PRR	Coldwater Creek	12 SB-4 DB sleeper	NY-Birmingham
SAL	6103	Diner	NY-Birmingham

Road	Number or Name	Type	Car Route
PRR	Huron Rapids	10-6 sleeper	NY-Atlanta
SR	Cashier's Valley	14 Rmt-4 DB sleeper	Portsmouth-Atlanta
SAL	6232	Coach-lounge	Portsmouth-Atlanta

SAL 33, southbound *Silver Comet*, Raleigh, N.C., March 18, 1966
3 engines, 16 cars, all passenger cars lightweight unless noted

Road	Number or Name	Type	Car Route
SAL	3046	E8 locomotive	
SAL	3035	E8 locomotive	
SAL	1113	SDP35 locomotive	
SR	517	Express	
REX	6322	Refrigerator express	
SAL	107	Baggage-RPO	Richmond-Atlanta
SAL	6005	Baggage-dorm-coach	Washington-Atlanta
SAL	6300	Coach-lounge	NY-Atlanta
SAL	6207	Coach	NY-Bham
C&O	City of Montgomery	10-6 sleeper	NY-Bham
SAL	6101	Diner	Washington-Bham
SAL	6255	Coach	Washington-Bham
SAL	820	Coach (HW)	Washington-Bham
EL	Pride of Youngstown	10-6 sleeper	Richmond-Atlanta
C&O	City of Ashland	10-6 sleeper	Richmond-Atlanta
Sou	Piedmont Valley	14 Rmt-4 DB sleeper	Portsmouth-Atlanta
SAL	6232	Coach lounge	Portsmouth-Atlanta
SAL	6265	Coach	Portsmouth-Atlanta
NH	Monument Beach	6 Rmt-4 DB-6 Sec sleeper	Portsmouth-Atlanta

Note: Last four cars added at Raleigh from Tidewater.

Other named trains 1940s-50s

SAL 107, southbound *Sun Queen*, Columbia, S.C., Oct. 30, 1945
3 engines, 16 cars, all cars heavyweight

Road	Number or Name	Type	Car Route
SAL	3029	E7A locomotive	
SAL	3004	E4A locomotive	
SAL	3020	E7A locomotive	
SAL	109	Baggage-RPO	-Jax
NH	5368	Baggage	-St. Pete
PRR	918	Coach	-St. Pete
PRR	4353	Coach	-St. Pete
PRR	4397	Coach	-Miami
RF&P	532	Coach	-Jax
PRR	4326	Coach	-Miami
RF&P	561	Coach	-Jax
SAL	228	Diner	-Miami
Pullman	North Berne	10 Sec-1 DR-2 Cpt sleeper	-Miami
Pullman	Columbia Lake	10 Sec-lounge sleeper	-Miami
Pullman	Judson	12 Sec-1 DR sleeper	-St. Pete
Pullman	Carnforth	12 Sec-1 DR sleeper	-Miami
VGN	200	Coach	-Starke
C&O	683	Coach	-Starke
SAL	2 – Southland	Office	-Sarasota

Note: Last 2 coaches are MAIN (Military Assigned Identification Number) 41346 for Camp Blanding at Starke, Florida.

SAL 108, northbound *Sun Queen*, Wildwood, Fla., Oct. 28, 1945
3 engines, 16 cars, all cars heavyweight

Road	Number or Name	Type	Car Route
SAL	3015	E6A locomotive	
SAL	3018	E7A locomotive	
SAL	3000	E4A locomotive	
SAL	391	Express	-Jax
SAL	85	Baggage-RPO	-Jax
PRR	9267	Baggage	-NY
PRR	1052	Coach	-NY
PRR	3546	Coach	-NY
PRR	7663	Coach	-NY
PRR	3473	Coach	-NY
SAL	815	Coach	-NY
SAL	1009	Diner	-Wash.
Pullman	Columbia County	10 Sec-lounge sleeper	-NY
Pullman	Lake Geneva	10 Sec-1 DR-2 Cpt sleeper	-NY
Pullman	New Portage	10 Sec-1 DR-2 Cpt sleeper	-NY
Pullman	Lake Poygan	10 Sec-1 DR-2 Cpt sleeper	-NY
Pullman	Carnforth	12 Sec-1 DR sleeper	-Portsmouth
Pullman	McClish	12 Sec-1 DR sleeper	-Jax
SAL	4 – Jacksonville	Office	-NY

SAL 10, northbound *Palmland*, Wildwood, Fla., Nov. 2, 1950
2 engines, 13 cars, all cars heavyweight

Road	Number or Name	Type	Car Route
SAL	3026	E7 locomotive	
SAL	3053	E8 locomotive	
PRR	5852	Baggage-horse-express	-Richmond (deadhead)
SAL	173	Baggage-RPO	-Jax
SAL	346	Express	-Jax
SAL	394	Express	-Jax
SAL	384	Express	-Jax
SAL	107	Baggage-RPO	-Jax
SAL	277	Baggage-coach	-Jax
SAL	818	Coach	-NY
RF&P	189	Express	-Washington
SAL	831	Coach	-NY
SAL	816	Coach	-NY
Pullman	Weeper's Tower	8 Sec-1 DR-3 DB sleeper	Miami-NY
Pullman	Lake Belanona	10 Sec-1 DR-2 Cpt sleeper	St. Pete-Cleveland

SAL 39, westbound *Gulf Wind*, Jacksonville, Fla., summer 1949 (exact date not recorded)
1 engine, 6 cars, all cars heavyweight

Road	Number or Name	Type	Car Route
SAL	3041	E7 locomotive	Jax-Chattahoochee
SAL	1310	Express	Jax-? (mail)
SAL	286	Baggage-coach	Jax-Flomaton
L&N	2550	Coach	Jax-New Orleans
SAL	Poplar Springs	6 Sec-6 DB sleeper	Jax-New Orleans
L&N	Mt. Olympus	10 Sec-lounge sleeper	Jax-New Orleans
SAL	232 - Lake Tulane	Diner	Jax-Tallahassee

Other named trains 1960s

SAL 10, northbound *Palmland*, Wildwood, Fla., Dec. 23, 1964
4 engines, 35 cars, all cars heavyweight unless noted

Road	Number or Name	Type	Car Route
SAL	3056	E8 locomotive	
SAL	1114	SDP35 locomotive	
SAL	1104	SDP35 locomotive	
SAL	1102	SDP35 locomotive	
REX	7020	Refrigerator express	-Jax (mail)
PRR	6823	Box express	-Jax (mail)
REX	7521	Refrigerator express	-Atlanta (mail)
PRR	1887	Box express	-Jax (mail)
SOU	123	Express	-Jax
SAL	155	RPO	-Jax
PRR	9369	Baggage	-Jax
NYC	8807	Baggage	-NY
PRR	4871	Express	-Jax
REX	7279	Refrigerator express	-Jax (mail)
REX	7256	Refrigerator express	-NY (mail)
SOU	454	Express	-Jax
ACL	1607	Express	-Jax
WofA	222	Express	-Jax (mail)
L&N	1425	Mail and baggage	-Jax
Pullman	Prairie Lawn	14 Sec sleeper	-Jax (deadhead)
SAL	6203	Coach (LW)	-Jax (deadhead)
SAL	6400	Coach-observation (LW)	-Jax (deadhead)
FEC	Dania	Coach (LW)	-Jax (deadhead)
SAL	708	Box express	-Jax
PRR	9703	Box express	-Jax
FEC	621	Box express	-Jax (storage mail)
PRR	9518	Box express	-Jax (storage mail)
SAL	3	Flexi-Van	Tampa-Jax (storage mail)
FEC	322	RPO	-Jax
IC	566	Express	-Jax (mail)
SAL	280	Baggage-coach	-Jax
SOU	510	Baggage	-Jax
SAL	832	Coach	Miami-Jax
SAL	851	Coach	Miami-Jax
SAL	845	Coach	Miami-NY
UP	Western Scene	12 Rmt-4 BR sleeper (LW)	Miami-NY
PRR	Morning Brook	12 SB-5 DB sleeper (LW)	Miami-Richmond (deadhead)
SAL	6249	Coach (LW)	Miami-Jax (deadhead)
SAL	6222	Coach (LW)	Miami-Jax (deadhead)

Note: This consist is the longest known SAL passenger train (excluding trains with intermodal cars attached). Two factors, holiday mail and deadheading cars, made the train about triple the length of a typical Palmland of the period.

SAL 9, southbound *Palmland*, March 23/24, 1967
All cars heavyweight unless noted

Note: The following consist shows the *Palmland* between Philadelphia and Miami, with the various locomotive and car changes made en route. Only three cars, SAL coaches 857 and 834 and SP sleeper 9047, ran all the way through from the train's New York origin to Miami. (The train operating over the Philadelphia-Washington segment was PRR 155, the *Embassy*, which included the *Palmland's* through cars.) The information was recorded by Bill Ingram, who rode the train from Philadelphia to Miami.

Road	Number or Name	Type	Car Route
PRR	4913	GG1 locomotive	**Phila-Washington**
PRR	7135 Leonard Calvert	Parlor (LW)	
PRR	Colonial Lanterns	3 DB-1 DR-lounge (LW)	
PRR	4525	Diner	
PRR	1546	Coach	
PRR	1584	Coach	
PRR	1533	Coach	
PRR	1538	Coach	
PRR	1531	Coach	
PRR	3928	Coach	
NH	7200	Coach	
NH	8616	Coach	
NH	8608	Coach	
SAL	817	Coach	
SAL	857	Coach	
SAL	834	Coach	
SP	9047	10-6 sleeper (LW)	
L&N	Pearl River	10-6 sleeper (LW)	
RF&P	1005	E8 locomotive	**Washington-Richmond**
RF&P	1001	E8 locomotive	
PRR	1884	Box express	
PRR	6902	Box express	
SR	137	Express	
NH	8616	Coach	
NH	8608	Coach	
SAL	817	Coach	
SAL	857	Coach	
SAL	834	Coach	
SP	9047	10-6 sleeper (LW)	
L&N	Pearl River	10-6 sleeper (LW)	
RF&P	ONE	Office	
SAL	1104	SDP35 locomotive	**Richmond-Hamlet**
SAL	1103	SDP35 locomotive	
PRR	1884	Box express	
PRR	6902	Box express	
SR	137	Express	
NH	8616	Coach	
NH	8608	Coach	
SAL	817	Coach	
SAL	857	Coach	
SAL	834	Coach	
SP	9047	10-6 sleeper (LW)	
L&N	Pearl River	10-6 sleeper (LW)	
SAL	6106	Diner (LW)	(added at Raleigh)
SAL	1104	SDP35 locomotive	**Hamlet-Jax**
SAL	1103	SDP35 locomotive	
PRR	6902	Box express	
PRR	2162	Box express	
L&N	1404	Express	
SAL	100	Baggage-RPO	
SR	137	Express	

NH	8616	Coach	
SAL	817	Coach	
SAL	857	Coach	
SAL	834	Coach	
SP	9047	10-6 sleeper (LW)	
SAL	849	Coach-grill	
SAL	281	Combine	(dropped at Columbia)
TTX	902293	Auto rack	(dropped at Columbia)
PRR	1884	Box express	(dropped at Columbia)
SAL	1104	SDP35 locomotive	**Jax-Miami**
SAL	1103	SDP35 locomotive	
SAL	1300	Express	
SAL	857	Coach	
SAL	834	Coach	
SP	9047	10-6 sleeper (LW)	
SAL	769	Box express	
			(29 piggyback cars added at West Jacksonville yard)

SAL 15, southbound mail and express, Savannah, Ga., Dec. 17, 1964
1 engine, 5 cars, all cars heavyweight

Road	Number or Name	Type	Car Route
SAL	1109	SDP35 locomotive	Hamlet-Jax
REX	6402	Refrigerator-express	Hamlet-Jax
PRR	9365	Box-express	Hamlet-Jax
PRR	9674	Box-express	Hamlet-Jax
SAL	287	Combine	Hamlet-Jax
SAL	1235	Coach	Hamlet-Jax (crew and deadheads)

Note: All express cars were carrying storage mail

SAL 16, northbound mail and express and *Tidewater* connection, Jacksonville, Fla., Feb. 7, 1967
1 engine, 3 cars, all cars lightweight except as noted

Road	Number or Name	Type	Car Route
SAL	3017	E7 locomotive	
SAL	287	Combine (HW)	Jax-Hamlet
CRI&P	Golden Journey	8 Rmt-6 DB	Jax-Richmond
SAL	6232	Coach lounge	Jax-Portsmouth

Local and connecting trains 1940s-50s

SAL 38, eastbound mail and express, Tallahassee, Fla., Oct. 30, 1945
1 engine, 15 cars, all cars heavyweight

Road	Number or Name	Type	Car Route
SAL	217	M1 4-8-2 locomotive	
NRC	470	Refrigerator express	-St. Pete (via SAL 1, Palmland)
SAL	339	Express	-Jax
L&N	1214	Baggage-RPO	-Jax
SAL	392	Express	-Jax
SAL	596	Coach	-Jax
L&N	1841	Coach	-Jax
SAL	684	Coach	-Jax
Pullman	Orange Dale	12 Sec-1 DR sleeper	New Orleans-Jax
Pullman	Orange Town	12 Sec-1 DR sleeper	New Orleans-Jax
Pullman	7356	13 Sec sleeper	-Starke
SAL	354	Express	-Jax (deadhead)
Pullman	Herrick	12 Sec-1 DR sleeper	-Jax (deadhead)

Pullman	Flambeau	10 Sec-1 DR-1 Cpt sleeper	-Jax (deadhead)
Pullman	1437	13 Sec sleeper	-Jax (deadhead)
Pullman	Ibsen	6 Cpt-3 DR sleeper	-Jax (deadhead)

Note: Pullman 7356 had troops for Camp Blanding at Starke, Florida

SAL 11, westbound Savannah-Montgomery local, Cordele, Ga., May 30, 1948
1 power unit, 2 cars, all cars heavyweight

Road	Number or Name	Type	Car Route
SAL	2027	Motor car	
SAL	2056	Trailer coach	Savannah-Montgomery
SAL	2053	Trailer coach	Savannah-Montgomery

SAL 26, northbound Charleston-Hamlet local, Andrews, S.C., 1955 (exact date not recorded)
1 power unit, 2 cars, all cars heavyweight

Road	Number or Name	Type	Car Route
SAL	2028	Motor car	
SAL	433	Express	Charleston-Hamlet
SAL	585	Coach	Charleston-Hamlet

Local and connecting trains 1960s

SAL 3, southbound Washington-Atlanta local, Atlanta, Ga., Feb. 5, 1966
1 engine, 8 cars, all cars heavyweight

Road	Number or Name	Type	Car Route
SAL	1114	SDP35 locomotive	
REX	6485	Refrigerator express	NY-New Orleans
REX	6545	Refrigerator express	Trenton-Atlanta
SAL	352	Express	Philadelphia-Atlanta
PRR	5508	Box express	Washington-Atlanta
SAL	108	Baggage-RPO	Hamlet-Atlanta
SAL	272	Baggage-coach	Hamlet-Atlanta
SAL	1235	Coach (laborers)	-Atlanta
PRR	5221	Box express	-New Orleans

SAL 5, southbound Washington-Birmingham local, Atlanta, Ga., April 30, 1966
1 engine, 9 cars, all cars heavyweight except as noted

Road	Number or Name	Type	Car Route
SAL	1110	SDP35 locomotive	
SAL	6257	Coach (LW)	(deadhead)
NH	?	Box express	
REX	?	Express refrigerator	
?	?	Box express	
?	?	Box express	
?	?	Box express	
SAL	100	Baggage-RPO	
SAL	392	Express	
SAL	820	Coach	

Note: Car routes not recorded.

SAL 11, southbound *Palmland*, Tampa section, Wildwood, Fla., July 10, 1965
1 engine, 13 cars, all passenger cars heavyweight

Road	Number or Name	Type	Car Route
SAL	1105	SDP35 locomotive	-Tampa
SAL	279	Baggage-coach	-Tampa
SAL	156	RPO	-Tampa
(11 loaded TTX auto racks on rear, Jax-Tampa)			

Painting and Lettering

Heavyweight Pullmans

Seaboard's heavyweight Pullmans were painted in five known schemes:

Pullman green – It appears that most Seaboard standard sleepers were painted in the Pullman Company's standard Pullman green scheme when SAL purchased its allotment in 1948. Lettering was always in the streamliner font.

Two-tone gray scheme – Some Pullmans in the 1948 purchase may have been painted in Pullman's two-tone gray scheme, consisting of dark gray except for a lighter gray window band with silver-gray lettering and stripes. The two-tone gray scheme was applied at least by the mid-1950s to a number of SAL sleepers, particularly all-room cars.

***Orange Blossom Special* scheme** – The sleepers assigned to the *Blossom's* last two seasons (winter 1951-52 and 1952-53) were Chinese red, including the roof and ends and lettering, except the letterboard band and area below the windows, which were light gray. Seaboard-owned Pullmans repainted in the scheme included 6 Sec-6 DB cars *Poplar Brook*, *Poplar Castle*, *Poplar City*, and *Poplar Creek* and 8 Sec-1 DRm-3 DB cars *Bartlett Tower*, *Giotto's Tower*, *Siebers Tower*, and *Weeper's Tower*. Several Pullman-owned cars assigned to the train also wore the colors.

Shadowlining scheme – The shadowlining colors consisted of solid aluminum (including roof) with black lettering and shadowlining. The scheme was used on the *Columbia*-series 10 Sec-lounges and at least five other sleepers: 6 Sec-6 DB *Poplar Run* and 10 Sec-1 DR-2 Cpt *Hollywood Beach* (1st), *Mount Gretna*, *Mount Joy*, and *Norlina*. The *Columbia* cars were painted for *Silver Comet* and *Silver Star* service in 1947 (while still under Pullman ownership) and appear to have remained in that scheme until converted to coaches in 1959. The other cars were likely shadowlined about 1953 and repainted into the two-tone gray scheme about 1955.

L&N colors for *Gulf Wind* cars – From the *Gulf Wind's* inaugural in 1949 to about 1957, cars assigned to the train were kept in L&N's scheme of dark blue body, gray roof, and dulux yellow lettering and stripe. Seaboard's contributions to the consist were painted in these colors as well; known SAL sleepers in the scheme included 6 Sec-6 DB cars *Poplar Road* and *Poplar Springs*.

Other Heavyweight Cars

SAL's other heavyweight cars had the following schemes:

Standard Pullman green – Seaboard's standard colors for heavyweight cars were Pullman green sides, ends, and roof with black underbody. Lettering was the extended Roman font similar to that used by many other railroads, applied in imitation gold originally and changed to a dulux yellow after World War II. Lettering was changed to the railroad's "streamliner" font effective with cars repainted after February 10, 1956. Some cars repainted just before the merger were given a black roof.

Box express cars – Lettering for these cars normally remained in the Roman font through the SAL era. However, there was at least one known exception, No. 744, which received the streamliner font.

Aluminum and silver-gray schemes – Certain coaches, baggage-coaches, baggage-dorms, and baggage-RPOs assigned to lightweight trains were painted an aluminum body color before WWII and a more subdued silver-gray after the war. Roofs were also aluminum through the early postwar years but later were black. Lettering was black and always in the streamliner font.

***Orange Blossom Special* scheme** – In addition to certain Pullmans, selected 180-series baggage-dorms and 225-series dining cars were also painted in the special *Orange Blossom Special* scheme of Chinese red and light gray.

L&N colors for *Gulf Wind* cars – Aside from sleepers, Seaboard contributed at least one blue-painted American Flyer combine to the *Wind's* early consists. One recorded consist shows car 286 on the train, which may have been the normally assigned blue car. A few heavyweight coaches were probably also painted blue.

Lightweight cars

Seaboard's lightweight fleet was maintained in unpainted stainless steel with black lettering. Pullman-Standard cars with flat side panels above the windows had these areas painted in silver-gray. Seaboard also painted truck sideframes silver through at least 1950, but the practice was dropped soon after. Seaboard also applied silver paint to the full-width diaphragms used on its earlier lightweight equipment.

Car roofs were also left unpainted except that Seaboard applied black roof paint to the former C&O 6242-6251 group; these cars were built by Pullman-Standard with flat roof panels. In addition, the majority of the ex-FEC cars came to SAL with painted black roofs (including a number of Budd cars), and the roofs were left this way while in Seaboard service.

The one known lightweight exception was flat-sided coach 6269, formerly FEC *Lantana*, which came

from FEC in Illinois Central chocolate brown and orange. Seaboard retained the car's colors and substituted its road name in dulux yellow and the new car number in black.

Car lettering used the same "streamliner font" introduced on the E4 diesel locomotives of 1938. The letter S in this font resembled a "backward Z" on cars through the 1947 deliveries but was revised with more rounded contours effective with later purchases and relettering.

General notes:

With a few exceptions, this roster is limited to those series with cars on the SAL revenue roster after World War II. The "Off Roster" column indicates the last year any cars in the series were on the SAL revenue car roster. A blank entry indicates that one or more cars in the series conveyed to SCL with the 1967 merger.

The SCL series column shows the new SCL number (or name) applied if and when the car was repainted or relettered. Lightweight equipment was rapidly relettered after the merger, but relatively few heavyweight cars ever received SCL paint and lettering; office cars were an exception and were quickly repainted. The number in parentheses following the SCL series shows the quantity of cars that conveyed to SCL.

Key to builders' abbreviations:

ACF – American Car & Foundry
B&S – Barney & Smith
GAC – General American Car Company
P-S – Pullman-Standard
PSC – Pressed Steel Car Company

Heavyweight cars

1. All cars steel unless noted.
2. All passenger-type cars have six-wheel trucks unless noted; all motor cars and trailers have four-wheel trucks.
3. All coaches and coach-combination cars built with partitions.
4. All combines and coaches air-conditioned by circa 1950 unless noted.

Numbers	RR class	Qty.	SCL series	Builder, date	Outside length	Off roster	Notes
Express							
300	EX2	1	4400 (1)	SAL, 1912	74-0		
301-303	EX1	3	4401-4403 (3)	Pullman, 1911	74-0		
304-305	EX2	2	4404-4405 (2)	Pullman, 1912	74-0		
307-311	EX3	5	4406-4410 (5)	Pullman, 1914	74-0		
312-320	EX4	9	4411-4418 (8)	PSC, 1915	74-0		
321-335	EX5	15	4419-4432 (14)	PSC, 1916	74-0		
336-341	EX6	6	4433-4438 (6)	ACF, 1924	74-0		
342-347		6	4439-4442 (4)	Pullman, 1913	78-1		Converted 1932 from diners 994-999.
349		1		Pullman, 1913	82-5	1966	Converted 1932 from diner 993.
350		1	4443 (1)	Pullman, 1925			Converted 1953 from diner 235.
352 (1st)		1		Pullman, 1911		1951	Converted by SAL in 1916; composite construction.
352 (2nd)		1	4444 (1)	PSC, 1912	80-4		Converted 1953 from coach 599.
353		1	4445 (1)	PSC, 1915	79-10		Converted 1953 from combine 261.
354-355 (2nd)		2	4446-4447 (2)	PSC, 1915 and 1913	73-3		Converted 1962 from baggage-RPO 83 and 88 respectively.
356			4448 (1)				Converted 1964 from baggage-RPO 84.
358		1		B&S, 1909		1953	Wood construction; 4-wheel trucks.
360-391		32	4449-4479 (31)	Pullman, 1926	68-4		4-wheel trucks.
392		1	4480 (1)	Pullman, 1917	82-5		Converted 1942 from diner 1003.
393-395		3	4481-4483 (3)	PSC, 1924	74-2		

| 400-404 | | 5 | 4484-4488 (5) | See notes | See notes | | Converted 1966 from baggage-RPOs 90, 97, 103, 110, and 172 respectively. |
| 432-433 | | 2 | 4489-4490 (2) | Bethlehem, 1926 | 66-4 | | Former GF&A 92-93; 4-wheel trucks. |

Horse express

| 1300-1314 | EX8 | 15 | 4880-4890 (11) | ACF, 1926 | 77-8 | | Horse stalls and related equipment removable; some equipment may have been permanently removed by the 1960s to facilitate regular express service. Cars originally also had names of famous race horses as follows; names probably removed by the early postwar years or sooner: 1300 *Display*, 1301 *Paul Jones*, 1302 *Fair Star*, 1303 *Bubbling Over*, 1304 *Zev*, 1305 *Scara Flow*, 1306 *Man o' War*, 1307 *Bagenbaggage*, 1308 *Nurmi*, 1309 *Crusader*, 1310 *Boon Companion*, 1311 *Sir Barton*, 1312 *Exterminator*, 1313 *Broomstick*, 1314 *Duettiste*. |

Box express

16000-16999 series [See notes]	B5	?		Richmond Car Works, 1930	42-8	[See notes]	Several converted from this series by late 1930s; total quantity unknown; 16257 was one. At least one car remained in service as late as 1949.
700-754		55	4800-4851 (52)	P-S, 1937	44-0		Converted 1943-45 from 18000-series boxcars (700-729 1943, 730-735 1944, 736-754 1945). Equipped with Allied Full Cushion trucks at conversion; Buckeye C-R trucks substituted in 1950-51.
755		1	4852 (1)	GAC, 1930	53-3		Converted 1962 from refrigerator-express 3626; insulated.
756-770		15	4853-4867 (15)	P-S, 1937	44-0		Converted 1963 from 18000-series boxcars; trucks have roller bearings.

Refrigerator express

| 3600-3641 | | 42 | 4749-4755 (7) | GAC, 1930 | 50-1 | | Built with wood bodies. Rebuilt with steel bodies beginning in the mid-1950s; all remaining cars in series (13) steel by 1959. Capacity was 2383 cu.ft. |

Baggage-RPO

80-84	MB7	5	4330-4332 (3)	PSC, 1915	73-3		30' mail compartment; 83-84 converted 1956 to storage mail car.
85-91	MB8	7	4333-4335 (3)	PSC, 1913	73-3		30' mail compartment; 85 converted 1956 to storage mail car; 87 converted 1961 to full RPO.
96-97	MB8	2	4336 (1, 96)	PSC, 1924	74-2		30' mail compartment.
98-99	MB8	2		PSC, 1924	74-2	1967	15' mail compartment.
100-111	MB8	12	4337-4345 (9)	ACF, 1924-25	74-2		30' mail compartment. In 1949 102, 103, 105, and 106 received electro-pneumatic brakes and telephone train line, evidently for streamliner service.
112-113	MB8	2		ACF, 1925	74-2	1967	15' mail compartment.
171-173		3	4346 (1, 173)	Bethlehem, 1926	69-5		Former GF&A 94-96; 4-wheel trucks; 30' mail compartment. Originally coach-RPOs with seating capacity of 34 (171) and 36 (172-173); converted to baggage-RPO, 1948. 172 converted to express car 404, 1966.

RPO

| 150-156 | AP4 | 7 | 4313-4318 (6) | PSC, 1915 | 64-0 | | 60' mail compartment; all with roller bearings except 156. |
| 157 | | 1 | 4319 (1) | PSC, 1913 | 73-3 | | 60' mail compartment; converted from baggage-RPO 87, 1961; with roller bearings. |

RPO-coach

| 171-173 | | 3 | | Bethlehem, 1926 | 69-5 | 1966 | 34 seats (171), 36 seats (172-173). Former GF&A 94-96; 4-wheel trucks; 30' mail compartment. Converted to baggage-RPO in 1948. |

Baggage-dormitory

| 180-187 | | 8 | 4272-4273, 4275-4276 (4) | Pullman, 1926-30 | 83-8* | | 20 crew bunks; converted 1946 from Pullman baggage-club cars *Old Colony*, *Sandy Hook*, *Jekyl Island*, *Hanging Rock*, *Barren Hill*, *Van Twiller*, *Van Winkle*, and *Van Rensselaer* respectively. Car 185 apparently assigned SCL number 4274 but did not actually convey at the merger. *Cars 185-187, length 84-8. |

Baggage-coach

254-259	PB5	6		PSC, 1913	76-11	1959	36 seats except 259, 42 seats. No A/C. 259 preserved at Gold Coast Museum in Miami, restored to 1950s appearance.
261-269	PB6	9	4240 (1, 265)	PSC, 1915	79-10		42 seats, except 265 has 36 deluxe seats.
270	ODD	1		PSC, 1912	77-9	1954	52 seats.
271-282	PB7	12	4241-4252 (12)	ACF, 1924 and 1926	79-8		36 deluxe seats. 271-276 built 1924, 277-282 built 1926.
283		1		PSC, 1925	76-4	1966	40 seats. Originally Bessemer & Lake Erie 21, purchased 1944; 4-wheel trucks. No A/C.
285-288	PB8	4	4253-4256 (4)	P-S, 1937	84-7		46 or 48 deluxe seats. Semi-lightweight "American Flyer" design; 4-wheel trucks.

Coach

| 571-580 | PC6 | 10 | | PSC, 1913 | 78-2 | 1966 | 66 seats. |

Numbers		Qty.	SCL series	Builder, date	Outside length	Off roster	Notes
581-590	PC7	10	4131 (1, 586)	PSC, 1914	81-0		68 seats except 585, 82 seats (does not have reclining seats), and 583 and 586, 64 seats.
591-598	PC8	8	4132 (1, 594)	PSC, 1915	81-0		68 seats (82 seats before rebuilding).
599	ODD	1		PSC, 1915	80-4	1953	68 seats.
604		1		ACF, 1923	80-3	1955	86 seats. Former Bessemer & Lake Erie 204 (ex-Pittsburgh & Lake Erie); does not have reclining seats; 4-wheel trucks. No A/C.
682-684		3		Bethlehem, 1926	72-6	1958	72 seats. Former GF&A 97-99; non-reclining seats; 4-wheel trucks. No A/C.
801-804	PC8	4		PSC, 1915	81-0	1958	90 seats; not reclining. No A/C.
807-826	PC9	20	4025-4034 (10) and 4133-4142 (10)	ACF, 1926	81-1		Nos. 808, 810, 812-814, 816, 819 had interior and exterior modernization in 1953-54 with 48 seats, no partitions, large restrooms, new AC, wide windows, and roller bearings. Nos. 807, 815, 817 modernized 1953-54 as above except partitions retained and with 68 seats; all 10 painted silver-gray. Other cars had between 60 and 74 seats
830-835	PC10	6	4143-4148 (6)	P-S, 1936	84-7		76 seats, except 831 has 74 seats and two sets of toilets (apparently for blacks and whites). Semi-lightweight "American Flyer" design; 4-wheel trucks.
840-859		20	4149-4166 (18); 4200-4201 (2, 849 and 858)	Pullman, 1930	79-3		Between 45 and 64 seats. 840-841 had no partitions and had 54 seats. 849, 858 converted in 1953 to coach-grill, 18 seats. Purchased from C&O in 1949-50, ex-C&O 728, 730, 731, 743, 745, 746, 748, 749, 750, 751, 726, 729, 732, 738, 739, 741, 742, 747, 753, 754 respectively.
1001, 1002		2		Pullman, 1917	82-5	1958	88 seats, not reclining. Converted 1942 from diner, same number.
1051		1		Pullman, 1917	81-10	1958	88 seats, not reclining. Converted 1942 from parlor-diner, same number. Former Western Maryland café-parlor car 406.

Buffet-coach

990, 992	DC3	2		Pullman, 1913	82-5	1958	48 seats. Converted 1942 from diners, same numbers.

Coach-diner

1000	DC3	1		Pullman, 1913	82-5	1954	36 seats, 22 in coach section, 12 in dining section. Converted by SAL in 1934.

Parlor-diner

1021	DC5	1		Pullman, 1916	83-3	1955	36 seats, 12 in parlor section, 24 in dining section. Converted by SAL in 1934.
1050	DC10	1		Pullman, 1917	81-10	1961	30 seats, 12 in parlor section, 18 in dining section. Purchased 1926 from Western Maryland as WM café-parlor car 405; converted 1932.

Diner

225-236	DC8	12	4210-4211 (2)	Pullman, 1925	82-1		36 seats. Cars also originally carried names, removed about 1950: 225 *Lake Istokpoga*, 226 *Lake Okeechobee*, 227 *Lake Wales*, 228 *Mountain Lake*, 229 *Lake Apopka*, 230 *Lake Worth*, 231 *Lake Lotela*, 232 *Lake Tulane*, 233 *Lake Julianna*, 234 *Lake Ariana*, 235 *Lake Altura*, and 236 *Lake Myakka*.
237-243	DC9	7	4212-4213 (2)	Pullman, 1926	82-1		36 seats except cars 237 and 242, 48 seats. Cars also originally carried names, removed about 1950: 237 *Lake Lochloosa*, 238 *Lake Panasofkee*, 239 *Lake Dora*, 240 *Lake Lafayette*, 241 *Lake Eloise*, 242 *Lake Agnes*, and 243 *Lake Magdalene*.
1007	DC6	1	4214 (1)	Pullman, 1922	81-5		36 seats. Car also originally carried name *Silver Springs*, removed about 1950.
1008-1009	DC7	2		Pullman, 1924	81-5		36 seats.

Mark III Flexi-Van flatcars

1-2		2	4910-4911 (2)	Greenville Steel Car Co., 1962	86-9		Carried two Flexi-Vans. 1 converted by SCL to truck transport flat 772980.
3		1	4912 (1)	Greenville Steel Car Co., 1964	86-9		Carried two Flexi-Vans. 3 converted by SCL to truck transport flat 772981.

Motor cars and trailers

Numbers	Qty.	SCL series	Builder, date	Outside length	Off roster	Notes
Motor cars						
2002-2003	2		St. Louis Car, 1926	73-4	1943	34 seats plus baggage compartment. 2002 to Sperry 133, 1943; 2003 to Sperry 132, 1942.
2013-2014	2		Brill, 1927	75-1	1947	Baggage compartment and 15' RPO compartment.
2015-2021	7		Brill, 1927	75-1	1951	Baggage compartment; 2017, 2018, and perhaps others originally had 15' RPO compartment. 2017 rebuilt as express 2045 in 1943. 2018 leased by Macon, Dublin & Savannah for a time around 1940.
2022-2023	2		St. Louis Car, 1928	74-3	1945	Baggage compartment. 2022 to Sperry 134, 2023 to Sperry 135, 1945. Sperry 135 to Danbury (Ct.) Railway Museum, 2004.

Number	Qty	SCL series	Builder, date built/rebuilt	Outside length	Off roster	Notes
2024-2026	3		ACF, 1935	64-1	1944	57 seats (38 white, 19 "colored"). 2024, 2025 sold to Norfolk Southern Ry. (NS 105, 106) 1942. 2026 sold to Aberdeen & Rockfish 1944; later to Salt Lake, Garfield & Western; later to California Western as M-300, currently in "Skunk Train" service.
2027-2028	2	4900 (1, 2028)	St. Louis Car, 1936	75-1		Baggage compartment and 15′ RPO compartment. 2027 retired 1957; 2028 to SCL 4900, retired 1971.
Trailer express						
2041	1		Brill, 1927	62-1	1953	
2045	1		Brill, 1927	74-10	1958	Rebuilt 1943 from motor car 2017.
Trailer coach						
2051-2059	9		ACF (Kuhlman Car Co.), 1927	75-7	1953	96 seats.
2060-2061	2		St. Louis Car, 1928	75-2	1948	96 seats.
2062	1		Brill, 1926	60-1	1947	74 seats. Former Lehigh Valley T-52. Retired 1945.
2063-2065	3		Brill, 1926	60-1	1948	76 seats. Former Lehigh Valley T-62, T-66, T-67.

Heavyweight sleeping cars

Names	No.	Qty.	SCL series	Builder, date built/rebuilt	Outside length	Off roster	Notes
8 section-5 double bedroom							
Clover Harvest	1200	3		Pullman, 1914/1940	82-6	1967	
Clover Nest	1201			Pullman, 1914/1940	82-6		Transferred to coach service by 1963; name removed.
Clover Pond	1202			Pullman, 1913/1936	84-6		Transferred to coach service by 1963; name removed.
6 section-6 double bedroom							
Poplar Brook	1210	7		Pullman, 1923/1937	82-6		Transferred to coach service by 1963; name removed.
Poplar Castle	1211			Pullman, 1921/1937	82-6		Transferred to coach service by 1964; name removed.
Poplar City	1212		Poplar City	Pullman, 1923/1937	82-6		
Poplar Creek	1213		Poplar Creek	Pullman, 1917/1937	82-6		
Poplar Road	1214		Poplar Road	Pullman, 1925/1939	83-6		
Poplar Run	1215			Pullman, 1925/1939	83-6		Transferred to coach service by 1965; name removed.
Poplar Springs	1216		Poplar Springs	Pullman, 1925/1939	83-6		
8 section-1 drawing room-3 double bedroom							
Bartlett Tower	1231	6		Pullman, 1925	83-6	1966	Transferred to coach service by 1965; name removed.
Chimes Tower	1232			Pullman, 1925	83-6		
Giotto's Tower*	1233			Pullman, 1925	83-6		Transferred to coach service by 1963; name removed.
Pinnacle Tower	1230			Pullman, 1927	83-6		Transferred to coach service by 1965; name removed.
Siebers Tower	1234			Pullman, 1925	83-6		
Weeper's Tower*	1235			Pullman, 1925	83-6		Transferred to coach service by 1965; name removed.

* SAL rosters did not use an apostrophe but Pullman's did; photos show the apostrophe version stenciled on the car.

Names	No.	Qty.	SCL series	Builder, date built/rebuilt	Outside length	Off roster	Notes
10 section-1 drawing room-2 compartment							
Hollywood Beach (1st)	1253	11		Pullman, 1923	82-5		Renamed Norlina in 1955. Transferred to coach service by 1963; name removed.
Lake Alexander	1251			Pullman, 1924	82-5		Transferred to coach service by 1963; name removed.
Lake Borgne	1250			Pullman, 1926	82-5		Transferred to coach service by 1965; name removed.
Lake Chicot	1252			Pullman, 1923	82-5		
Mackay	1260			Pullman, 1917	82-5		Transferred to coach service in 1958; name removed.
Mount Gretna	1254			Pullman, 1923	82-5		Transferred to coach service by 1963; name removed.
Mount Joy	1255			Pullman, 1923	82-5		Transferred to coach service by 1963; name removed.
New Lyme	1256			Pullman, 1923	82-5		Transferred to coach service in 1958; name removed.
New Portage	1257		New Portage	Pullman, 1923	82-5		
New Waterford	1258			Pullman, 1923	82-5		Transferred to coach service in 1958; name removed.
Norlina	1253			Pullman, 1923	82-5		Formerly Hollywood Beach (1st); renamed in 1955. Transferred to coach service in 1958; name removed.
North Berne	1259			Pullman, 1923	82-5		Transferred to coach service in 1958; name removed.
10 section-observation-lounge							
Columbia Basin	1271	4		Pullman, 1915	82-7	1963	Transferred to coach service in 1959; name removed.
Columbia Bluffs	1272			Pullman, 1914	82-7		Transferred to coach service in 1959; name removed.
Columbia Bridge	1270			Pullman, 1914	82-7		Transferred to coach service in 1959; name removed.
Columbia Lake	1273			Pullman, 1911	82-7		Transferred to coach service in 1959; name removed.

Official cars

1. It appears that all older official cars were of composite construction when new.
2. Most cars were rebuilt one or more times over the years.
3. Cars had other former names at times; the former names listed below include only those that could be reasonably well documented using available records.
4. All cars originally had numbers; those shown are as of 1947. Numbers were removed about 1948 except for Virginia (No. 1), which carried its number until 1957.
5. All were all-steel or steel-sheathed by the late 1940s.

6. Cars retained the same name under Seaboard Coast Line except as noted.

Name	Qty.	SCL name	Builder, date	Outside length	Off Roster	Notes
Birmingham	1	Birmingham	Pullman, 1914	82-7		Originally SAL office car Baltimore (1st); renamed Southland (1st), No. 2, in 1927; renamed Birmingham (2nd) 1953.
Jacksonville	1	Jacksonville	PSC, 1927	84-1		No. 4. Purchased from Pullman 1944; originally Pullman Pioneer.
Miami	1	Miami	Pullman, 1930	83-11		Purchased 1964 from West India Fruit & Steamship Co. as Sea Level.
Norfolk	1	Norfolk	SAL, 1910	84-0		No. 3. Built by SAL as office car 100; renamed several times, was Norfolk by 1920. Rebuilt 1944.
Raleigh	1		Pullman, 1902	81-2	1965	No. 7. Earlier named Portsmouth at some point before late 1940s. Purchased from Pullman 1918.
Richmond	1	Richmond	Pullman, 1911	82-0		Purchased from Pullman 1917; originally Pullman Winchester. Renamed Portsmouth, then renamed Richmond, No. 5, 1920.
Savannah	1	Savannah	Pullman, 1911	78-0		Rebuilt by SAL in 1915 from coach 564, named Savannah, No. 8.
Southland	1	Southland	AT&SF, 1914	83-5		Originally AT&SF parlor car, purchased 1948 and rebuilt as Birmingham (1st); renamed Southland (2nd) 1953.
Tampa	1		1891	72-6	1965	No. 6. Rebuilt by SAL in 1905; modernized 1949 with steel sheathing.
Virginia	1	Virginia	Pullman, 1924	83-5		Originally SAL office car Baltimore (2nd); renamed Carolina 1928; renamed Virginia, No. 1, 1933. Under SCL, renamed Alabama in 1970; under CSX, renamed Baltimore in 1986 and remains in active service.

Lightweight cars

1. All have 4-wheel trucks.
2. No lightweight equipment had railroad class designations.
3. All cars have outside length of 85-0 except as noted.
4. The "Amtrak series" column shows the number of cars, in parentheses, that Amtrak purchased from the SCL series. If no entry, Amtrak purchased no SCL cars in the series.

Numbers	Qty.	SCL series	Amtrak series	Builder, date	Notes
Baggage-dormitory-coach					
6000-6002	3			Budd, 1939	18 seats; bunks for 15 crew members (6000, 12 crew members). 6000, 6001 rebuilt 1957 as baggage-dorms 6054, 6055 respectively. 6002 wrecked 1946, rebuilt 1947 as baggage-dorm 6053.
6003-6005	3	5031-5032 (2)	1591-1592 (2)	Budd, 1940	18 seats; bunks for 15 crew members. 6003 converted to baggage-dorm 6056 in 1957.
6006	1	5030 (1)	1590 (1)	Budd, 1939	22 seats; bunks for 12 crew members. Purchased 1965 from FEC, ex-FEC Indian River.
Baggage-dormitory					
6050-6052	3	5022-5024 (3)	1522-1524 (3)	Budd, 1947	24 crew bunks.
6053	1	5025 (1)	1525 (1)	Budd, 1939	24 crew bunks. Rebuilt by Budd from 6002 in 1947.
6054-6055	2	5011-5012 (2)	1511-1512 (2)	Budd, 1939	6054, 20 crew bunks; 6055, 23 crew bunks. Converted from 6000, 6001 respectively in 1957.
6056	1	5017 (1)	1517 (1)	Budd, 1940	23 crew bunks. Converted from 6003 in 1957.
6057	1	5013 (1)	1513 (1)	Budd, 1939	24 crew bunks. Purchased 1965 from FEC, formerly Halifax River.
6058	1	5021 (1)	1521 (1)	Budd, 1946	24 crew bunks. Purchased 1965 from FEC, formerly St. Johns River.
Baggage-express					
6070	1	5001 (1)		ACF, 1950	Purchased 1965 from FEC, formerly 501.
Diner					
6100-6103	4	5900-5903 (4)	8000-8003 (4)	Budd, 1939	48 seats. 6103 delivered as diner-lounge (24 dining seats, 18 lounge seats); rebuilt as full diner about 1945.
6104-6105	2	5909-5910 (2)	8009-8010 (2)	Budd, 1940	48 seats.
6106-6114	9	5911-5919 (9)	8011-8019 (9)	Budd, 1947	48 seats.
6115	1	5904 (1)	8004 (1)	Budd, 1939	48 seats. Purchased 1965 from FEC, formerly Fort Lauderdale.
6116-6118	3	5920-5922 (3)	8020-8022 (3)	Budd, 1946	48 seats. Purchased 1965 from FEC, formerly Fort Dallas, Fort Matanzas, Fort San Marco.
6119-6120	2	5959-5960 (2)	8089-8090 (2)	P-S, 1950	36 seats. Purchased 1965 from FEC, formerly Fort Ribault, Fort Drum.
Coach					
6200-6207	8	5604-5611 (8)	5604-5611 (8)	Budd, 1939	60 seats.
6208-6214	7	5616-5622 (7)	5616-5622 (7)	Budd, 1940	56 seats.
6215-6226	12	5200-5211 (12)	5200-5211 (12)	Budd, 1947	52 seats.
6227-6231	5	5130-5134 (5)	5000-5004 (5)	Budd, 1948	50 seats. Original center lounges removed by SAL, converted to 50-seat full coach. Purchased 1950 from C&O, formerly 1504, 1505, 1510, 1601, 1604 respectively.
6232-6234	3	5106-5108 (3)	4406-4408 (3)	Budd, 1948	44 seats. Original center lounges retained; 36 seats in coach sections, 8 seats in center lounge. Purchased 1950 from C&O, formerly 1606, 1607, 1608, respectively.
6235-6241	7	5265-5271 (7)	5265-5271 (7)	P-S, 1955	52 coach seats, 10 seats in center lounge.
6242-6251	10	5254-5263 (10)	5254-5263 (10)	P-S, 1950	52 seats. Purchased 1958 from C&O, formerly 1656-1663, 1667, 1668. Decorative partial partition mid-car.

6252-6257	6	5122, 5612-5613, 5123, 5614-5615 (6)	4802, 5612-5613, 4803, 5614-5615 (6)	Budd, 1939	60 seats; cars 6252, 6255 had 52 seats. Purchased 1965 from FEC, formerly *Delray Beach, New Smyrna Beach, Melbourne, Vero Beach, Pompano, Boca Raton*.
6258-6264	7	5623-5626, 5417, 5627-5628 (7)	5623-5626, 5417, 5627-5628 (7)	Budd, 1946	56 seats; 6262 had 54 seats. Purchased 1965 from FEC, formerly *Dania, Eau Gallie, Ormond, Wabasso, Belle Glade, Jacksonville, Stuart*.
6265	1	5212 (1)	5212 (1)	Budd, 1949	56 seats. Purchased 1965 from FEC, formerly *Pahokee*.
6266-6270	5	5470-5473, 5264 (5)	5470-5473, 5264 (5)	P-S, 1950	56 seats; 6270 had 54 seats. Purchased 1965 from FEC, formerly *Sebastian, Canal Point, Salerno, Lantana, Hypoluxo*. FEC purchased *Sebastian* and *Canal Point*, and later modified *Lantana*, for *City of Miami* service; cars had smooth sides and IC colors. FEC purchased *Lantana* as a stainless steel-sheathed car for ACL service but later rebuilt it as a smooth-side car for *City of Miami* service. SAL 6266 (presumed) and 6269 (confirmed) were relettered but retained the IC scheme. It appears that SAL added fluting to the lower half of 6267 and repainted the upper half in silver-gray.
6271-6274	4	5474-5477 (4)	5474-5477 (4)	P-S, 1954	56 seats. Purchased 1965 from FEC, formerly *St. Augustine, Miami, Hollywood, Cocoa-Rockledge*.

Coach-tavern

6300-6302	3	5810-5812 (3)	3810-3812 (3)	Budd, 1939	60 seats, 30 in each section. 6300, outside length 84-8.

Coach-observation

6400-6402	3	5820-5822 (3)		Budd, 1939	48 seats, 24 in each section. 6400 wrecked in 1942, rebuilt in 1943 to flat-end configuration; 20 seats in observation section. Diaphragms added to ends of 6401-6402 about 1955. 6400, outside length 84-10.

Coach-buffet-observation

6500-6502	3	5800-5802 (3)	3800-3802 (3)	Budd, 1940	30 seats, 24 in lounge section. Flat-end configuration.

Tavern-observation

6600-6605	6	5840-5845 (6)	3340-3345 (6)	Budd, 1947	34 seats in tavern section, 24 in observation section. 6600, 6603, and 6604 modified about 1955 with diaphragms added to observation end.
6606-6607	2	5850-5851 (2)	3338-3339 (2)	Budd, 1939	36 seats in tavern section, 21 in observation section. Purchased 1965 from FEC, formerly *Lake Worth, Bay Biscayne*. Round-end configuration; SAL added diaphragms after purchase.

Tavern-lounge

6620	1	5837 (1)		ACF, 1950	55 seats. Purchased 1965 from FEC, formerly *South Bay*. Built for *New Royal Palm* as diner-lounge; converted to tavern-lounge by FEC in 1956.

Lightweight sleeping cars

1. SCL 6000-series numbers were added in 1969.

2. Amtrak numbers are those assigned at the original Amtrak takeover in 1971. Amtrak retained most SCL car names.

Names	No.	Qty.	SCL names	SCL No.	Amtrak numbers	Builder, date	Notes
6 double bedroom-lounge-buffet							
Kennesaw Mountain	17	3	Hollywood Beach	6600	3220	ACF, 1949	Cars named for points on the *Silver Comet* route but were assigned to the *Silver Meteor* and *Silver Star*. Renamed by SCL to conform to ex-ACL *Beach*-series cars of the same configuration.
Red Mountain	15		Palm Beach	6602	3222		
Stone Mountain	16		Miami Beach	6601	3221		
5 double bedroom-bar-lounge ("Sun Lounge")							
Hollywood Beach (2nd)	20	3	Sun Ray	6500	3231	P-S, 1956	
Miami Beach	18		Sun View	6501	3232		
Palm Beach	19		Sun Beam	6502	3230		
10 roomette-6 double bedroom							
Atlanta	36	19	Atlanta	6610	2770	P-S, 1949	
Birmingham	37		Birmingham	6611	2769		
Charlotte	35		Charlotte	6612	2771		
Columbia	30		Columbia	6613	2772		
Jacksonville	32		Jacksonville	6614	2767		
Lake Wales	41		Lake Wales	6615	2700		
Miami	43		Miami	6616	2701		
Norfolk	27		Norfolk	6617	2773		
Orlando	33		Orlando	6618	2764		
Petersburg	26		Petersburg	6619	2765		
Portsmouth	28		Portsmouth	6620	2768		
Raleigh	29		Raleigh	6621			*Raleigh* wrecked in 1970.
Richmond	25		Richmond	6622	2774		
St. Petersburg	38		St. Petersburg	6623	2702		
Sarasota	29		Sarasota	6624	2703		
Savannah	31		Savannah	6625	2766		
Tampa	34		Tampa	6626	2775		
West Palm Beach	42		West Palm Beach	6627	2704		
Winter Haven	40		Winter Haven	6628	2705		

4 roomette-1 compartment-5 double bedroom-4 section							
Bay Pines	50	6	Bay Pines	6402		Budd, 1955	
Camden	53		Camden	6403			
Cedartown	55		Cedartown	6404			
Henderson	54		Henderson	6405	2105		
Pinehurst	52		Pinehurst	6406			Named for Pinehurst, N.C., which was not on the SAL but was about 6 miles west of Southern Pines.
Southern Pines	51		Southern Pines	6407			

5 double bedroom-2 compartment-2 drawing room							
Boca Grande	60	3	Boca Grande	6520	2310	P-S, 1956	
Clearwater	62		Clearwater	6521	2311		
Ft. Lauderdale	61		Ft. Lauderdale	6522	2312		

11 double bedroom							
Avon Park	74	6	Avon Park	6100	2230	P-S, 1956	
Hialeah	72		Hialeah	6101	2231		
Ocala	70		Ocala	6102	2232		
Sebring	73		Sebring	6103	2233		
Tallahassee	74		Tallahassee	6104	2234		Tallahassee was the only car named for a city on the Gulf Wind route.
Venice	71		Venice	6105	2235		

Express

Express car 322 was photographed on the New Haven at New London, Conn., on December 22, 1957. The car wears Seaboard's Roman-style lettering; the star within a circle indicates the car has facilities for an express messenger. (Bob's Photo collection)

Seaboard express car 352 was rebuilt from coach 599 in 1953, and its ancestry shows clearly in the car's 80-foot length and vestibule space that remains at right. The car was standing by for service at Atlanta on February 19, 1966. (Larry Goolsby photo)

Seaboard 395 was one of three 74-foot express cars purchased from Pressed Steel Car in 1924. (Paul Faulk collection)

Seaboard's horse express carried names of famous horses when new; No. 1310, shown here set aside for retirement at Tampa about 1967, was originally named Boon Companion. Some cars were later used for ordinary express service. (William J. Lenoir photo)

Seaboard converted box express 16257 from a class B-5 boxcar of the same number by making changes such as the end doors. The car was photographed in service on the Atlantic Coast Line at Mt. Olive, N.C., on July 16, 1939. (F.M. Seiffert photo, Frank Moore collection)

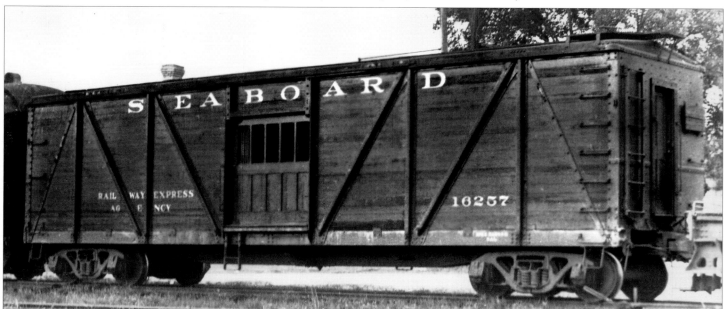

SAL's first steel box express cars came during World War II when the railroad rebuilt 55 cars selected from 18000-series boxcars and numbered them 700-754. Example No. 702 was photographed at Hamlet, N.C., on October 6, 1951. (Bob's Photo collection)

Seaboard went back to the 18000-series boxcars in 1963 for 15 more box express car conversions, 756-770, and this group received roller bearing trucks. No. 756 is shown at Jacksonville in May 1967. (W.E. Mims photo)

Refrigerator express 3602 was spotted at Hamlet on July 30, 1952. The wood-bodied car was one of an original series of 42 built by General American Car in 1930. The remaining cars in the group had been rebuilt with steel sides by 1960. (Bob's Photo collection)

Baggage-RPO 81 had a 30-foot Railway Post Office compartment at right; the half-length postal section was the most common arrangement on Seaboard's roster. It was photographed in Raleigh, N.C., in 1965. (Harvey W. George photo)

Seaboard selected several baggage-RPOs to run on its streamliners and painted them silver-gray with black lettering so they would blend with lightweight cars. They were also upgraded with electro-pneumatic brakes and telephone train lines. One was No. 102, shown resting between runs at Hamlet on July 30, 1952. (Bob's Photo collection)

Baggage-RPO 111 was one of 12 such cars Seaboard purchased from ACF in 1924-25. This photo at Hamlet on August 3, 1952, shows the car much as it looked when new. (Bob's Photo collection)

Seaboard rostered seven full (60-foot) RPOs built by Pressed Steel Car in 1915. No. 153 is at Columbia, S.C., on May 14, 1942. (George Votava photo, ACL & SAL HS collection)

In 1961, Seaboard converted baggage-RPO 87 into a full RPO at its Portsmouth shops. The unusual result was a car with the Post Office's regulation 60-foot mail compartment plus a nine-foot "excess compartment" for storage at one end. The interior photo reveals the car's compact yet efficient layout for sorting mail en route. Seaboard converted a number of other baggage-RPO cars to full express cars in the 1960s. (SAL photos, TLC Collection)

Baggage-RPO 172 began life as a rare coach-RPO for the Georgia, Florida & Alabama. SAL converted the cars to baggage-RPOs in 1948. In 1966 No. 172 was further rebuilt as full express car 404. The photo was taken at Hamlet on November 17, 1958. (Bob's Photo collection)

GF&A coach-RPO 96 poses for its builder's photo at Bethlehem Shipbuilding's Harlan Plant at Wilmington, Del., in June 1926. The cars, which seated 36 passengers and contained a 30-foot RPO compartment, later became baggage-RPOs. (SAL photo, Ron Dettmer collection)

Flexi-Van Flat

Seaboard bought three Flexi-Van flats for storage mail service. No. 1 stands with a single van at Tampa in the early 1960s; the cars ran for several years on the Palmland between Jacksonville and Tampa. (Stanley Jackowski photo, Kevin Pytlak collection)

Combination

Pullman-Standard delivered four baggage-coach combines of the "American Flyer" semi-streamlined design in 1937. No. 285 was assigned to the west coast Silver Meteor for several years when that train was new and wore special aluminum paint and black lettering to blend with SAL's new Budd lightweight cars. This view is probably at St. Petersburg about 1940. (Interstate Commerce Commission collection)

American Flyer combine 287 is at Tampa Union Station in August 1966. The car and its three sisters were usually found in Florida on the Palmland's and Sunland's east and west coast sections in the 1960s. (Larry Goolsby photo)

Combine 277 was typical of the 271-282 series; they were regulars on secondary trains. In addition several were painted silver-gray for the west coast sections of the Silver Meteor and Silver Star. The car was photographed at Jacksonville in May 1967. (W.E. Mims photo)

SAL 187 was former Pullman Van Rensselaer, *one of eight baggage-club cars Seaboard purchased in 1946 and converted to baggage-dormitory cars for the Orange Blossom Special. No. 187 is serving as the crew dorm on a football special in this 1967 view at Tallahassee, Florida. Some of the cars received silver-gray paint to blend with the railroad's streamliners. (Randy Young photo)*

Coach

Coach 583 was built in 1914 but was rebuilt by Seaboard after the war. It emerged from the Portsmouth shops with a streamlined-style roof profile, one of the few SAL cars to have this appearance. The car is in local service at Atlanta on April 16, 1966. (Larry Goolsby photo)

No. 808 was typical of the 20 long-distance coaches in series 807-826. A number received streamlined-style wide windows and other improvements in the early 1950s. This photo was taken at Columbia, S.C., on May 3, 1942. (George Votava photo, Larry Goolsby collection)

Coach 809 shows the rebuilt appearance of the 807-826 series. While a number received silver-gray paint, No. 809 was among those less extensively rebuilt and that retained Seaboard's standard Pullman green. The car is at Atlanta on April 2, 1967. (Oscar W. Kimsey Jr. photo)

Seaboard 851, one of 20 former C&O deluxe coaches, held 58 passengers in comfortable "Sleepy Hollow" seats and was often found on the Palmland and other conventional trains. The photograph was taken at Hamlet, N.C., on November 17, 1958. (Bob's Photo collection)

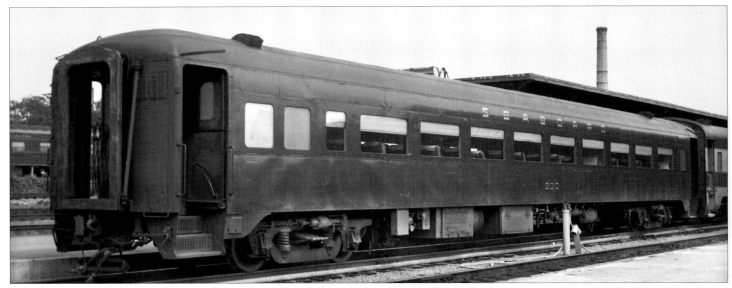

SAL's six "American Flyer" coaches were purchased in 1936 for the west coast section of the Orange Blossom Special, but were soon found in other trains from streamliners to locals. No. 830 is at Richmond on May 26, 1969. (R.S. Short photo, J. Michael Gruber collection)

SAL 682 was among three shorter coaches that came from the Georgia, Florida & Alabama. Ex-GF&A 97 is shown here on lease to the New York, Ontario & Western for summer excursion service at Middletown, N.Y., on June 28, 1949. The car could often be found behind Seaboard motor cars when on home rails. (George Votava photo, ACL & SAL HS collection)

Seaboard converted some of it sleepers for coach service; they were taken out of Pullman lease status and their sleeping equipment was removed. No. 1231, formerly 8 Sec-1 DR-3 DB Bartlett Tower, is at Atlanta on April 30, 1966. (Larry Goolsby photo)

Seaboard coach 1260 is former 10 Sec-1 DR-2 Cpt sleeper Mackay. The car is shown shortly after its November 1958 conversion (at Hamlet on May 15, 1959) and is dressed in silver-gray paint for overflow assignment on lightweight trains. (Bob's Photo collection)

Coach-Grill

Coach-grill 858 gleams in fresh Pullman green paint in the fall of 1966. The car was a regular on the Palmland, where it served light but tasty meals between Hamlet and Jacksonville. (Richard Stewart photo)

Dining

Dining car 1009 shows the typical rebuilt appearance of this series and the 225 series. The 1924 Pullman product was one of three (1007-1009) that frequented the Gulf Wind, the train it is serving here at Tallahassee about 1967. (W.E. Mims photo, Ron Dettmer collection)

Sleeper

Lake Alexander, *a 10 Sec-1 DR-2 Cpt sleeper built by Pullman in 1924 and dressed in standard Pullman green, saw frequent service on Seaboard trains in the immediate postwar years. Deliveries of lightweight sleepers eventually relegated the car to the railroad's secondary trains. (Jay Williams collection, courtesy A.B. Dean)*

Seaboard Pullmans with double bedrooms were among those that received the two-tone gray scheme with silver-gray lettering and striping. Weeper's Tower, shown in the early 1960s, was an 8 Sec-1 DR-3 DB car built in 1925. (Jay Williams collection, courtesy A.B. Dean)

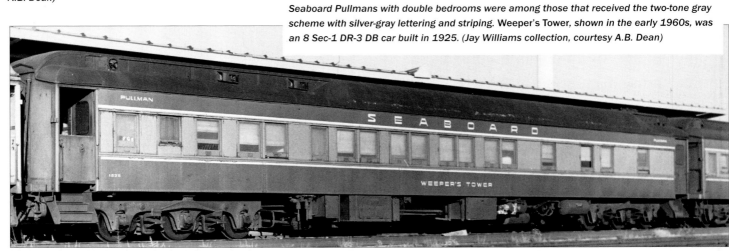

New Portage, a 10 Sec-1 DR-2 Cpt car from 1923, brings up the rear of a train on Pennsylvania rails around the late 1950s or early 1960s. Its two-tone gray scheme includes the small SAL car number at lower left, 1257. (Bob's Photo collection)

The most colorful Seaboard heavyweight Pullman scheme was the one used for the Orange Blossom Special's last seasons. *Poplar Creek, a 6 Sec-6 DB rebuilt in 1937, stands in the Chinese red and gray scheme at Tampa in the early 1950s. (Larry Goolsby collection)*

Some SAL heavyweight sleepers had black lettering and shadowlining applied over aluminum paint, which let them blend with lightweight consists. Columbia Lake, a 10 section-observation-lounge, is at Hamlet about 1960 in coach service after its name had been removed. A close look at the letterboard reveals its pre-1948 PULLMAN lettering emerging behind the fading Seaboard name. (Bob's Photo collection)

Office

Like many of Seaboard's office cars, Jacksonville began life as a Pullman car – in this case, the Pioneer *in 1927. This view shows the car in SCL dress at Augusta, Ga., in April 1971, where the car was in town for the Masters Golf Tournament. (A.M. Langley Jr. photo)*

Seaboard built the Norfolk at its Portsmouth shops in 1910 as office car 100. The car was 56 years young when this photo was taken at Savannah in August 1966, having benefitted from several rebuildings and upgrades. (Richard Stewart photo)

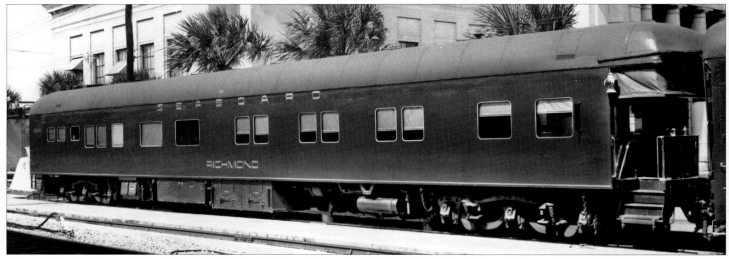

Office car Richmond projects understated, modern elegance as it basks in the Jacksonville sun on October 2, 1967. The car included three staterooms, dining and observation space, a shower, and kitchen facilities. (George Votava photo, ACL & SAL HS collection)

The Savannah started life as a wood, arch-window coach in 1911, and like most office cars has clearly been extensively rebuilt. The car is at Waynesboro, Ga., in 1972 after being sold to a private individual. Some cars repainted for Seaboard Coast Line retained the SAL-style name lettering shown here while others used the SCL italic font. (Oscar W. Kimsey Jr. photo, Robert H. Hanson collection)

The Southland *is at Augusta in April 1967 for the Masters, an event that still brings office cars to town every spring. Like most other Seaboard office cars, the* Southland *earlier had other SAL names; it was originally the first* Birmingham. *(A.M. Langley Jr. photo)*

Lightweight Baggage-Dormitory

Passenger-baggage-dormitory car 6004 was built in 1940 for the Silver Meteor's expanded consist. The car is shown here at Atlanta on September 22, 1968, on the Silver Comet, its regular assignment during that the 1960s. (Larry Goolsby photo)

Baggage-dormitory 6050 is outside the Budd factory in 1947. SAL lightweight cars were still being delivered with full-width diaphragms at the time, but only the dormitory end has one. (SAL photo, Larry Goolsby collection)

SAL 6057 came with the FEC purchase in 1965; the 1939 Budd product was Halifax River on that railroad. Most former FEC cars were easily identified by their long letterboards. The car is at Miami in May 1968. (R.S. Short photo, J. Michael Gruber collection)

Lightweight Coach

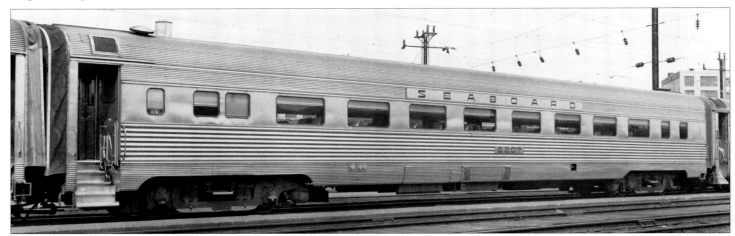

Budd-built coach 6207 is from Seaboard's original order for the February 1939 Silver Meteor. Still looking much as it did when delivered (including full-width diaphragms), the 60-seat car is at New York City's Sunnyside Yard on August 24, 1953. (Bob's Photo collection)

Coach 6220 is from the 1947 postwar group and is similar to Seaboard's prewar cars except for larger restroom lounges and more legroom, resulting in a seating capacity of only 52. The car was at North Philadelphia, Pa., on October 12, 1947. (Bob's Photo collection)

Coach-lounge 6234 was a regular on the two Florida Silver trains. The car was purchased from the C&O in 1950, and seated 36 in its coach area and eight in a center lounge. The car's stainless steel fluting was a good match for Seaboard's existing fleet. (Richard Stewart photo)

The seven coaches delivered by Pullman-Standard in 1955, including No. 6238, were easily spotted by their wider fluting and flat roofs. SAL had dropped full-width diaphragms by this date but still specified skirting – an attractive touch that most of its non-sleeping cars retained throughout the Seaboard years. (SAL photo, Larry Goolsby collection)

SCL 5255 is ex-SAL 6243, ex-C&O 1657, and is at Atlanta on September 1, 1968, on the Silver Comet. The cars featured a decorative partial partition to break up the "tunnel" effect. They had outside fluting only on the lower half with silver-gray panels on the upper half, and flat roofs painted black – an unusual feature on SAL cars. (Larry Goolsby photo)

One of the more unusual cars in the FEC group was 6267, ex-Canal Point. Available records indicate that the 1950 Pullman-Standard product was delivered with smooth sides for City of Miami service and that SAL added fluting to the car's lower half after purchase and repainted the upper half in silver-gray. The result appears here at Jacksonville on August 28, 1969. (Conniff Railroadiana Collection)

SAL 6272, formerly FEC Miami, was in Amtrak service at Boston on June 4, 1972. The 56-seat car, one of four such Pullman-Standard coaches built for FEC in 1954, had a flat black-painted roof. (Robert H. Hanson collection)

Opposite top: No. 6257 (ex-FEC Boca Raton) was one of six such cars built by Budd in 1939. The car, which is at Atlanta on April 30, 1966, blended well with SAL's existing Budd fleet except for its black-painted roof. (Larry Goolsby photo)

Opposite Center: Postwar Budd coaches were also in the FEC purchase, such as 1946-built No. 6263 (ex-Jacksonville). The car has been pressed into service shortly after the purchase with no road name yet applied, just its new number, at Raleigh on December 11, 1965. (Harvey W. George photo)

Opposite Bottom: Another distinctive ex-FEC coach was No. 6269, painted for City of Miami service in Illinois Central colors; SAL kept the car's paint scheme. The 56-seat car was in Silver Comet service at Atlanta on April 30, 1966. (Larry Goolsby photo)

Lightweight Diner

Seaboard 6102, from Seaboard's original Silver Meteor consist, was typical of the railroad's 15 Budd 48-seat dining cars delivered between 1939 and 1947. The car was at Hamlet, N.C., on April 5, 1959. (Bob's Photo collection)

Diner 6120, formerly FEC Fort Drum, is on the Silver Comet at Atlanta September 1, 1968. The 36-seat car and sister 6119 became SAL's only Pullman-Standard diners. (Larry Goolsby photo)

Lightweight Sleeper

Stone Mountain was one of three 6 double bedroom-lounge cars built in 1949 by American Car & Foundry. They were intended for the Silver Comet and thus bore names of Georgia and Alabama mountains, but were placed immediately on the Silver Meteor instead. After 1956 they were shifted over to the Silver Star. (Bill Folsom collection)

With its lounge shades down against the strong morning light, Sun Lounge Palm Beach *leaves Jacksonville with the Silver Meteor on June 17, 1967. The car and its two sisters distinguished the Meteor throughout the Seaboard and SCL years. (W.E. Mims photo)*

Clearwater *was one of three 5 DB-2 Cpt-2 DR cars built for the Silver Meteor. The car stands in front of Pullman-Standard's Chicago works on a cold January 25, 1956. (Pullman-Standard photo, Ron Dettmer collection)*

Ocala *was part of a group of six 11 double bedroom cars assigned to the Silver Meteor. The car was completed by Pullman-Standard in late December 1955. (Pullman-Standard photo, Ron Dettmer collection)*

Lightweight Tavern-Lounge-Observations

Coach-observation 6400 was part of the original 1939 Meteor consist. The car was rebuilt to this flat-end configuration in 1943 and offered a total of 48 seats, 24 in each section. (Bob's Photo collection)

SAL 6501, one of three coach-buffet-observation cars built in 1940 for the expanded Silver Meteor. This April 16, 1967, photo in Atlanta shows the car assigned to the Silver Comet as its mid-train coach-lounge. (A.M. Langley Jr. photo)

Opposite Top: In this May 1948 scene, tavern-observation 6603 gleams at Sunnyside Yard in New York. Three of the striking cars were assigned to the Silver Comet, as confirmed by 6603's tail sign; the other three in the 1947 Budd order went to the Meteor. (George Votava photo, ACL & SAL HS collection)

Opposite Center: The Silver Comet's three 6600-series observations were reassigned to the Silver Star in 1954. They were soon modified with end diaphragms to allow use within the train's consist. The modified cars were 6600, 6603, and 6604; No. 6604 is at Miami on August 18, 1968. (J. Michael Gruber collection)

Opposite Bottom: SAL 6607 was one of two ex-FEC round-end observations; Seaboard added diaphragms to the observation ends. The car was Bay Biscayne on the FEC and arrived in 1939 for the original ACL-FEC Champion. It still operates today in excursion service. (Larry Goolsby collection)

Bibliography

This list does not include such commonly available sources as the *Official Guide* or a variety of materials published by the Seaboard, particularly its public and employee timetables and annual reports.

Books

Bramson, Seth H., *Speedway to Sunshine*, second edition. Boston Mills Press, 2003.

Calloway, Warren L. and Paul K. Withers, *Seaboard Motive Power*. Withers Publishing, 1988.

Clemons, Marvin, and Lyle Key, *Birmingham Rails: The Last Golden Era*. Red Mountain Press, 2007.

Faulk, Paul, *Seaboard Air Line Color Guide to Freight and Passenger Equipment*. Morning Sun Books, 1998.

-----, *Seaboard Air Line in Color, Volume 1: Motive Power and Memories*. Morning Sun Books, 2009.

Goolsby, Larry, *Atlantic Coast Line Passenger Service*. TLC Publishing, 1999.

Griffin, William E., Jr., *All Lines North of Raleigh*. Published by the author, 1991.

-----, *Richmond, Fredericksburg & Potomac Railroad Passenger Service 1935-1975*. TLC Publishing, 2000.

-----, *Seaboard – The Route of Courteous Service*. TLC Publishing, 1999.

Johnson, Robert Wayne, *Through the Heart of the South*. Boston Mills Press, 1995.

Key, R. Lyle, Jr., *Midwest Florida Sunliners*. RPC Publications, 1979.

Langley, Albert M., Jr., W. Forrest Beckum, Jr., and C. Ronnie Tidwell, *Seaboard Air Line Railway Album*. Union Station Publishing, 1988.

Prince, Richard E., *Seaboard Air Line Railway Steam Boats, Locomotives, and History*. Published by the author, 1969.

Massengill, Stephen E. and C. Vernon Vallance, *Richmond County and the Seaboard Air Line Railway*. Arcadia Publishing, 2005.

Randall, W. David, *The Official Pullman-Standard Library: Vol. 7, Southeast Railroads*. Railway Production Classics, 1989.

Roseman, V.S., *Railway Express: An Overview*. Rocky Mountain Publishing, 1992.

Rubin, Louis D., Jr., *A Memory of Trains*. University of South Carolina Press, 2001.

Shrady, Theodore, *The Sleeping Car: A General Guide*. ACL & SAL Historical Society, 2004.

-----, and Arthur M. Waldrop, *Orange Blossom Special*, second edition. ACL & SAL Historical Society, 2000.

Turner, Gregg M., *A Journey into Florida Railroad History*. University Press of Florida, 2008.

-----, *Railroads of Southwest Florida*. Arcadia Publishing, 1999.

Welsh, Joseph M., *By Streamliner: New York to Florida*. Andover Junction Publications, 1994.

-----, and William F. Howes, Jr., *Travel by Pullman: A Century of Service*. MBI Publishing Company, 2004

Zimmerman, Karl R., *Burlington's Zephyrs*. MBI Publishing Company, 2004.

Periodicals

Appleby, Sam, Jr., "Through the Heart of the South," *Trains*, February 1949.

Bundy, Harry, "Seaboard's Specialty," *Lines South*, 19:3, Third Quarter 2002.

Golden, John, and Buddy Hill, "The E.C.," parts 1 and 2, *Lines South*, 19:4 and 20:1, Fourth Quarter 2002 and First Quarter 2003.

Goolsby, Larry, "Seaboard's 'American Flyer' Passenger Equipment," *Lines South*, 16:3, Third Quarter 1999.

-----, "Stations 2, Tech 0" *Lines South*, 21:2, Second Quarter 2004.

-----, "The Well-Traveled 2028 (and 2027)," *Lines South*, 19:1, First Quarter 2002.

Griffin, William E., Jr., "The Seaboard Air Line in Richmond," *Lines South*, 24:2, Second Quarter 2007.

Morgan, David P., "Who Shot the Passenger Train?" *Trains*, April 1959.

Rubin, Louis D., Jr., "Where the Boll Weevil Went," *Lines South*, 18:2, Second Quarter 2001.

Salter, David W., "Railfanning the Seaboard in Atlanta," *Lines South*, 21:2, Second Quarter 2004.

Savchak, Michael W., "Chesapeake & Ohio and Nickel Plate Passenger Cars Purchased by the ACL, SAL, and SCL," *Lines South*, 21:3, Third Quarter 2004.

-----, "Observation Cars South," *Lines South*, 17:3, Third Quarter 2000.

-----, "Riding the Secondary Trains: A 1960s 'Sentimental Journey,'" *Lines South*, 19:2, Second Quarter 2002.

-----, "Stopping for the Red Block," *Lines South*, 19:4, Fourth Quarter 2002.

Shrady, Theodore, and William F. Howes, Jr., "Seaboard's Inconspicuous Gulf Wind," *Lines South*, 19:2, Second Quarter 2002.

Turner, Gregg M., "Seaboard's Fort Myers-Naples Extension," *Lines South*, 18:3, Third Quarter 2001.

Turner, Jack, "Silver Star: From Seaboard to Amtrak," *Passenger Train Journal*, April 1993.

Welsh, Joseph M., "The Silver Meteor," *Passenger Train Journal*, October 1989.